Making It Happen

Fred Goodwin, RBS and the Men Who Blew up the British Economy

IAIN MARTIN

**SIMON &
SCHUSTER**

London · New York · Sydney · Toronto · New Delhi

A CBS COMPANY

Firs~~t~~ published in Great Britain by Simon & Schuster UK Ltd, 2013
This paperback edition published by Simon & Schuster UK Ltd, 2014

1 3 5 7 9 10 8 6 4 2

Simon & Schuster UK Ltd
1st Floor
222 Gray's Inn Road
London WC1X 8HB

www.simonandschuster.co.uk

Simon & Schuster Australia, Sydney
Simon & Schuster India, New Delhi

A CIP catalogue record for this book
is available from the British Library

ISBN: 978-1-47111-355-0
ebook ISBN: 978-1-47111-356-7

Typeset in the UK by M Rules
Printed and bound by CPI Group (UK) Ltd, Croydon, CR0 4YY

Making It
Happen

Contents

Prologue

'You have a long time to regret it if you don't get it right.'

Fred Goodwin, 7 June 2004, *Businessweek*

During the boom years, at the beginning of the century, the Royal Bank of Scotland chose an advertising slogan. The words were emblazoned in large letters on billboards at airports, used in television campaigns and appended to mountains of marketing material selling mortgages, insurance and investment products. RBS, the adverts promised, would 'Make It Happen'. The phrase was chosen by the then chief executive Fred Goodwin for several reasons. It not only informed customers that RBS stood ready to help if they were minded to make it happen – whether 'it' was moving house, insuring said house, expanding a small business or trading billions on the financial markets in complicated products. It was also intended to encapsulate Goodwin's 'can-do' determination to build a bank that could take on the very best in the world. All that activity eventually resulted in RBS becoming, briefly, the very biggest of all, just at the moment when being the biggest was the last thing a sensible bank should want to be. Fred Goodwin and his senior colleagues were true to their word, albeit not

1

quite in the way they originally intended. They really helped to make it happen.

The collapse of the bank they ran in October 2008 was not just a corporate catastrophe for those who worked at RBS, or owned shares in the company. It also presaged a severe and sustained downturn in the economy that has had adverse consequences for the prosperity of Britain. In January 2013, five years into the crisis, the UK economy was still 3.4 per cent below its pre-slump peak. The living standards of millions of families have declined.

Of course, in the crisis of 2007 to 2008 RBS was not the only British institution to need rescuing. Plenty of others got into difficulties – HBOS, Northern Rock, Bradford & Bingley. All had to be bailed out or sold, and even the institutions that did not have to be nationalised – taken over by the taxpayer – relied on forms of special support and loan facilities from a government desperate to keep the banking system alive. RBS is a special case, however. Its blow-up was the largest and most spectacular of the lot. When it arrived at the point of failure, the government had to buy £45.2bn of RBS shares and offer many billions more in credit facilities to prevent the bank's collapse. The rescue dwarfed the packages needed for the other UK banks.

The damage done by the crisis goes well beyond simple lost economic capacity. The egocentrism and greed of the 'good' years and the trauma of the downturn that followed so widely shook confidence in the basic precepts of capitalism that it became common to talk of it being in crisis. In this way, our reckless past, troubled present and precarious future are bound up in the incredible story of how a previously modest, Presbyterian, cautious Scottish institution ended up with a balance sheet of almost £2 trillion just when the boom went bust.

Goodwin himself is not an obviously stupid man. But if the former RBS boss had wanted to make himself the epitome of bad boy bankers, the physical embodiment of the British end of the crisis, he could not have done a better job if he tried. His bizarre handling of the aftermath has involved the adoption of an anti-PR strategy in which he offers nothing in the way of explanation. He has even used the courts to try to block mention of aspects of his private life. It has done nothing to aid understanding and has guaranteed that Goodwin be treated as the pantomime villain, a target at which anger over what happened can be channelled. Early on, there was the darkly comic awfulness of his public appearances in front of a parliamentary committee and at the RBS Extraordinary General Meeting held to approve the terms of the government bailout. He apologised for what had happened. He regretted how it had all turned out. He wished he could do something in order to make it different. That was all. There appeared to be no proper reflection or reckoning. 'For Fred to admit he had got something, anything, wrong, that would be incredible,' says a former member of his management team. 'If you were to say to him when something had gone wrong, I saw you do it wrong, I know you did it, Fred would say no, that's not how it was. He is like a little boy who never admits mistakes.'

Former colleagues, friends and enemies all testify to his considerable abilities. Certainly, he did not rise each morning looking for ways in which to ruin the bank he ran and destroy his own reputation, while inflicting epoch-defining damage on the UK economy. So what on earth did he think he was doing? Finding out is not straightforward. Goodwin makes no comment in public, lives in Edinburgh, draws a pension from the taxpayer-owned RBS (of £342,500 per year), sees a few friends, shoots, repairs vintage cars, tries not to read the newspapers and avoids engaging with those who want to question him about his motives, recollections and regrets. 'He has shut out the world,' says a friend. His marriage foundered after it emerged that he had an affair with a member of staff at RBS in the run-up to the financial crisis. His wife, Joyce, only discovered this when he revealed that it was about to be reported in the newspapers. Everyone knows that Sir Fred Goodwin is now plain Mr Fred

Goodwin, but it is rarely mentioned that Lady Goodwin lost a title too when her errant husband was stripped of his knighthood in 2012.

Other than the removal of the Goodwin honour, very few bankers have faced any sanction, which is remarkable considering the scale of the disaster. Johnny Cameron, the former head of the division at RBS which oversaw investment banking, was singled out for criticism in an investigation by the Financial Services Authority (FSA). Cameron is not allowed to take up any full-time position in the City. Peter Cummings, a former banker at HBOS, another bank that got out of control, has been fined by the FSA. Bob Diamond was forced out of his post at Barclays, over the interest-rate-setting Libor scandal, which is only indirectly related to the crisis. Belatedly, Sir James Crosby of HBOS lost his knighthood. A few others have been forced to stand aside from their jobs, and that is pretty much it. At the time of writing, no one has gone to jail.

In the five years following the crisis there were various studies and reports undertaken by MPs, peers and public bodies, dealing with particular aspects of the crisis. Incredibly there was no full report carried out on RBS, although it is a common misconception that there has been, mainly because the FSA published a 450-page document called 'The failure of the Royal Bank of Scotland'. The reality is that the FSA did not investigate the company. It investigated Johnny Cameron to establish whether or not he should face any action and then, when the government applied pressure for more, widened the scope a little, rebadged the findings and issued it as a sober-looking tome. There is very interesting material within its pages but several of the main characters at the top of RBS were not even interviewed, and several others received only the lightest of grillings. Another substantial chunk of the report involves the results of an investigation the FSA instigated into itself. The document is hardly a complete account of what happened.

I became fascinated by these omissions and contradictions in the British response to what had been a national economic disaster on a grand scale, and by the inadequacy of many of the explanations. How and why had Fred Goodwin, his senior colleagues at RBS, other financiers and the political and regulatory class got Britain into this mess?

Goodwin himself has intrigued me ever since I encountered him fleetingly when I was editor of the *Scotsman* newspaper in Edinburgh for three years, from 2001 to 2004. I shook his hand a couple of times at social events, then observed him work the room, and listened over lunch as awestruck people who knew RBS whispered horror stories about the chief executive's behaviour. As an innately sceptical journalist I actually found all this rather baffling and struggled to square his image as a coming titan of finance with the strangely unimpressive, slightly geeky figure in a Royal Bank of Scotland corporate tie and sober suit.

The public-spirited thing for Goodwin to do would be to donate himself to the psychology department of a decent university in order that academics could run years of detailed tests. He is a study. Had he really terrified some of his staff into submission as it is claimed? Yes, some. 'Fill in the complaints book on your way out of the door,' he told one executive who had been eviscerated in his office. 'He had what he called Fred's black book for executives who had displeased him,' says a colleague. 'He liked to say that if your name was written in the book in pencil you were on the borderline. If it was written in ink you were well and truly fucked.'

Yet, although his nickname was 'Fred the Shred' he seems to have fired hardly anyone personally at a senior level. There was little swearing, and not much shouting, as he preferred destruction by logical deconstruction and biting sarcasm. Were fully grown men (they were almost all men) – such as those on the RBS board whose job it was to oversee his tenure – really reduced to shaking wrecks by this and unable to speak up? Of course not. Many of them were experienced and extremely wealthy individuals who did not need the money and had no reason to be afraid. It is simply not credible that they were too scared to urge restraint. Something else must explain their inaction, and I wanted to find out what.

Some in the management team admit to having been frightened, although most developed strategies to cope with his unorthodox approach while taking the money. 'You have to understand,' says another of his closest collaborators, 'that Fred had no interest in or understanding of ideas, even though he was gifted and had sharp insights into how to solve a problem in a deal or a proposal. So you proceeded mainly according to the goals and targets that were set for you and tried not to get tripped up, rather than thinking of the bigger picture.'

Another concludes: 'The job of chief executive wasn't really done by him in the normal sense of someone trying to strategise properly and see the dangers and opportunities ahead. He was obsessed by all sorts of small details and measuring things and all sorts of minutiae and crap in certain parts of the business. We would spend hours in meetings discussing the wrong things. Colours for advertising campaigns, computer systems and targets were what grabbed him. I think he thought that meant he was on top of things when he wasn't.'

Goodwin, an accountant by training and *not* a banker, was fixated on detail. Yet, there was a terribly important and ostensibly puzzling exception. The division of RBS that ended up doing most damage in the run-in to the collapse was its investment banking division, and the chief executive had only a very limited grasp of its activities. Apparently this did not concern him until it was too late. A supposed control freak didn't want to know what he didn't know, until, as we shall see, he smelt trouble and then made belated and insufficient efforts to investigate.

He wasn't alone in this. Although it was extremely unwise

for any ambitious bank executive to admit it, many without a degree in mathematics or a particular kind of investment banking background seem to have been ignorant of a good deal about modern banking. When arguing with a drunken RBS executive from the investment banking arm who had questioned his judgement on the disastrous bid for the Dutch bank ABN Amro, Goodwin called investment banking 'your money-making machine', as though what half the bank he ran did was not his responsibility. In contrast, he spent more time on branding and making RBS a global giant. Says a close colleague: 'What Fred wanted was to get bigger. He was determined that RBS would be bigger than Barclays.'

That the modern Royal Bank of Scotland was only partly Fred Goodwin's creation is often forgotten. It is impossible to understand what eventually transpired without reference to Scotland, and to the man who groomed Goodwin: Sir George Mathewson, his predecessor as chief executive and chairman for more than half of Goodwin's time in post. The nationalistic Mathewson was not a banker either. He was an engineer who became convinced that from the ruins of post-industrial Scotland in the late 1970s and 1980s could emerge a bank under his leadership that would lead a national reinvention. From the late 1980s he gathered together bright young managers, friends from the government economic development agency he had run and executives from Scotland's computer industry, 'Silicon Glen'. With them he set about remaking the Royal Bank of Scotland.

Mathewson's new notion echoed an old idea. The reputation of the Scots as uniquely canny bankers stretched back three centuries, to when a Scot, William Paterson, had helped found the Bank of England in 1694 to lend the money the English government needed to wage continental war. Scotland then established two properly commercial banks serving businesses and individuals – the old Bank of Scotland and the Royal Bank of Scotland – when England did not have even one. Mathewson mined his country's past to forge its future, telling his team that there was nothing to prevent an innovative Scotland from creating the best bank in the world. He chose Goodwin to continue his mission.

Mathewson had begun his extraordinary efforts just as the transformation of modern international finance got under way properly, as banks exploited new technology and grew by lending more and trading in innovative ways. Then a generation of politicians and regulators emerged in the UK and the United States to declare that these developments when allied to the rise of emerging economies, which increased vastly the potential for trade, meant that there was now a new paradigm, a settled period of rising prosperity or the 'end of boom and bust'. The intellectual climate of the time created a dangerous feedback loop in which top financiers could act as though the good fortune was attributable to their genius – hence the need for them to be given ever-better remuneration – while politicians in power could take credit, spend the proceeds and stroke the ego of the financiers they needed to keep delivering growth. Hardly anyone involved paused for a moment to ask the old question: what happens when this stops or there is a reverse?

It was in this exciting climate that a young accountant turned bank executive called Fred Goodwin emerged to run a small but terrifically ambitious bank in Edinburgh. 'I want us to be bigger than J. P. Morgan,' Goodwin told another banker, referring to the giant of US investment banking. For a few months he got his wish, and then in late 2008 it all – the Royal Bank of Scotland, other banks, some of the complex instruments investment bankers had created, the supply of cheap money and the assumptions underpinning the long boom – came crashing down.

It suits many people at or near the scene of the disaster to make the British end of the financial crisis all about Fred Goodwin. Astonishingly, many who were most intimately involved have barely featured in the coverage of the crisis, or have been mentioned only fleetingly and gone on to continue their careers quietly. But Fred Goodwin at RBS did not operate alone, like some deluded young rogue City trader trying to make his first millions. Although his monumental management errors and dud decisions produced an end result that was catastrophic both for the bank he ran and for the rest of us, others shared his ambitions and collaborated each and every step of the way.

While this book has the rise and fall of Fred Goodwin at its heart, *Making It Happen* is not exclusively about him. That would be much too convenient for others who share the blame. Rather, it is the story of how an over-mighty chief executive, corporate vanity rooted in patriotic pride and global ambition, misguided management, regulatory failure, and epic political hubris, all combined to produce a calamity.

A member of his management team throughout his reign at RBS – someone with plenty of cause to dislike Goodwin – put it this way when I was beginning my research: 'When you write this book you must tell everything you can about Fred because he has so much to answer for. He led us into the biggest fuck-up in British corporate history. But there is a lot more to it than that. We on the management team should have stopped him. We failed, I failed. Where was the board of directors? Where were the big shareholders? Where were the regulators? Where were the auditors? Where was the government?'

Where, indeed. In this book we will find out.

London, February 2014

1

Tuesday, 7 October 2008

'You're in a bit of trouble'

Lord Myners to Fred Goodwin

Outside London's Ritz hotel, a chauffeur-driven S-Class Mercedes painted Royal Bank of Scotland blue sits waiting for Sir Fred Goodwin. Shortly after 8 a.m., the RBS chief executive makes his way through the revolving doors of the hotel, walks past the doorman on the steps, emerges onto Arlington Street and gets into the car. The London markets are opening for business and it promises to be another turbulent day. Yesterday, Monday 6 October, RBS shares had stood at just 148p when trading finished in the City, meaning that in six months of wild fluctuations the price has more than halved. The share price is simply a measurement of what investors – from massive institutions that control our pensions to individuals who play the markets – are prepared to pay to own a slice of a company. It is an indicator of a firm's health, monitored on screens by profit-seeking traders who look at moments of crisis such as this for clues as to how ill the patient might be. RBS is about to go into cardiac arrest.

Pulling away from the Ritz, Goodwin's car heads north, through Mayfair. The first appointment of the day is a long-standing engagement from which he is unable to extricate himself. The RBS chief executive has been booked as one of the first speakers at today's Merrill Lynch annual banking and insurance conference, being held in a lesser five-star hotel, the Landmark, on Marylebone Road. Such events, held in front of several hundred executives and banking industry analysts, are standard fare for chief executives, who usually do a bull-ish presentation on their company's prospects, take a few questions and then leave. Goodwin also knows the hosts well, the American investment bank Merrill Lynch. That relationship stretches back to Merrill's richly rewarded advisory work on the £21bn purchase of NatWest in 2000 that had made Goodwin's reputation. Matthew Greenburgh, one of Merrill Lynch's highest-paid dealmakers, had become a trusted counsellor and friend. Anyway, failing to turn up to the conference is not an option. It would suggest panic.

There is a lot to panic about this morning. For months investors and traders have been trying to rid themselves of shares in banks exposed to the sub-prime crisis, which has its origins in years of catastrophically lax mortgage lending in the United States. Merrill Lynch has itself already been swept up in the tumult. Riddled with sub-prime-related problems of its own, it was sold to Bank of America in September. Today, the next bank in the line of fire is RBS, a Scottish institution that has grown rapidly to become a global player. Goodwin and his colleagues have waded into the toxic swamp of sub-prime and are now stuck, up to their necks. It is not just the share price that is a problem. That is merely a reflection of a more fundamental weakness. The bank is leaking money at a phenomenal rate. Just raising the billions it needs every day to keep going has been a struggle for months, and now the situation is deteriorating as large depositors move their money out. A major oil firm is the latest to show that it has lost faith in RBS's ability to survive, suddenly withdrawing more than £1bn in deposits and quietly putting the money somewhere deemed safer.

Fearing that the entire banking system is about to collapse, government ministers and officials have been attempting to work up a rescue plan in collaboration with the Bank of England's governor Mervyn King and the chairman of the FSA Adair Turner. Several senior bankers and lawyers have been drafted in to help. Yesterday evening, Monday, as part of the latest effort to find a solution, Goodwin had gone to the Treasury in Whitehall with fellow chief executives from Britain's other big banks for what was meant to be a private meeting with the Chancellor of the Exchequer, Alistair Darling. Goodwin claimed, yet again, that the problem facing RBS was a temporary one of simple liquidity, or cash-flow, attributable to panic in the markets. The underlying business was sound, he said. Darling and the senior officials in the Treasury see it differently – as a question of capital, and the banks holding too little of it to cover looming losses. RBS is the worst exposed. The government will have to find a way of giving the weakest banks billions more in capital, which will mean the taxpayer owning large shareholdings in the bailed-out institutions. Darling is frustrated by the response and is convinced that the bankers, particularly Goodwin, are refusing to face up to the true nature of the problem. The meeting had broken up without agreement, and Goodwin retreated to his usual room at the Ritz, his London base while the Savoy Hotel is refitted.

News of the Monday evening meeting at the Treasury does not stay private for long. At 7 a.m. on Tuesday morning the BBC's business editor Robert Peston publishes an account on his blog.[1] Peston had been briefed late last night and then again first thing this morning. He knows he has a 'bloody great story', although he is not prepared for the scale of the sell-off on the markets that his report is about to help trigger. Peston reveals that the bankers who had met with Darling were unimpressed; their view is that the government simply does not have a serious plan in place to deal with the crisis and that ministers should get a move on. The message is clear. The bankers think that the government does not know what it is doing. This news takes a little time to ripple across trading floors, where already jumpy traders are looking for reassurance that someone is going to step in and avert disaster at RBS and the other banks. Now the parties supposed to be sorting it out are squabbling. Cue panic selling.

Goodwin takes to the stage in the Empire Room of the Landmark hotel at 8.45 a.m. and begins his presentation. As usual his team has commissioned a series of PowerPoint slides to accompany his talk. In view of what is about to happen, the presentation might as well have been prepared on a different planet. Under the heading of 'Operational Effectiveness', Goodwin explains that RBS has a 'diversified and high-quality' portfolio in the UK and the United States. Yes, the bank has been 'de-leveraging', meaning that it has been battling to reduce its lending and exposure, but there are still opportunities for growth in Asia. Closer to home he admits the outlook is 'challenging', although the bank has the strength to meet these challenges.

Quite how 'challenging' the outlook is becoming is apparent to members of the audience looking at their BlackBerrys and mobile phones for news from the City. The RBS share price is nose-diving. Several members of Goodwin's team are in the audience and are being emailed and texted by frantic colleagues back in the office in the City and in the bank's headquarters at Gogarburn in Edinburgh. One who is in the room watching Goodwin thinks about trying to warn him in mid-presentation, but concludes there is no way to do it without causing a scene: 'I'm looking at these texts and thinking shit, how do I get a message to him, do I run on stage? I know I can't do that. Fred is completely unaware of what is happening while he is speaking.'

After half an hour of this, Goodwin takes questions at the end as agreed with the organisers. A member of the audience gets straight to the point. Is he aware that while he has been on his feet making his presentation, the RBS share price has fallen by 25 per cent? Goodwin blanches, gives a holding answer, takes only a couple more questions and then indicates that he needs to leave. At high speed his staff hustle him out of the Landmark hotel shortly before 9.30 a.m. and back into the car for the journey to the City. Goodwin is straight on his mobile phone to the office. The first of his calls is to Sir Tom McKillop, the chairman of RBS, who is in his twelfth-floor corner office of the RBS building at 280 Bishopsgate. The trading screens are showing the slaughter as a sea of red, with graphs running on the TV news channels illustrating the vertiginous fall of RBS minute by minute.

The sell-off is so rapid that the London Stock Exchange has suspended trading twice. This suspension of trading in shares spells an evaporation of any remaining market confidence and means death for a bank. McKillop and Goodwin discuss their options, which doesn't take long. They have been warning the government in private for months that Mervyn King, the Governor of the Bank of England, is useless and not doing enough to help. Now the government will have to do something. McKillop says he will try to get hold of the Chancellor right away by putting a call through to the Treasury. As his car speeds towards the City a stressed Goodwin rings off and calls Guy Whittaker, the RBS finance director, to check if he thinks there is a realistic prospect of making it through the day.

McKillop's office struggles to raise Darling. The Chancellor is stuck in Luxembourg in a routine meeting of the Economic and Financial Affairs Council (ECOFIN). Instead, it is the Prime Minister Gordon Brown who calls McKillop back, asking: 'How bad is it? What should we be doing?' McKillop thanks Brown for his expressions of support but warns him that it is not about to get any easier. The RBS share price is collapsing, he says, and the Bank of England and its governor Mervyn King are simply not stepping up to do what is needed in terms of helping with liquidity and support for the embattled banks. Brown attempts to reassure him that the government will get RBS what it needs to keep going.

Darling has no desire whatsoever to be in Luxembourg, 300 miles away from the epicentre of the crisis. But opting not to attend would have suggested that he and the others at the top of the government are spooked by the seriousness of the situation, which they are. On Monday the 6th he had updated MPs in the House of Commons on the financial crisis, emphasising that the government stands ready to help the banks while declining to give too many details of what that might involve.[2] This holding statement was designed to calm the markets, while the embryonic rescue scheme is worked on. He left Downing Street on Tuesday at 5.30 a.m. reluctantly, with ominous thoughts about the prospects for the banks filling his head. Accompanying him in the government people carrier on the way to RAF Northolt is a small team of civil servants: his private secretary Dan Rosenfield, special adviser Geoffrey Spence and Steve Pickford, who is there to deal with the standard business of an ECOFIN meeting. Unusually, the undemonstrative Darling has ordered that a small private jet be chartered for the trip to Luxembourg. It is the only way he can be sure of having transport on hand if he needs to get back to London quickly in the event of catastrophe.

Inside the ECOFIN meeting after 8 a.m., Darling has no means of checking what is happening in the markets other than popping out, to see his officials, before returning to talks not relevant to the concerns of the moment. As the meeting progresses, Spence and Rosenfield are outside on their mobile phones, getting reports from the Treasury of the RBS meltdown on the markets following Robert Peston's report. Rosenfield scribbles down the figure of 35 per cent and marks an asterisk next to the news that trading in RBS shares has been suspended twice. They have to get their boss out of his meeting as quickly as possible. For a start, McKillop's call has to be returned. Spence goes to get Darling, waving at him from the doorway, while others locate somewhere quiet where the Chancellor can call London undisturbed. The only place they can find is an anteroom being used by Kim Darroch, the UK's top diplomat at the EU. Spence is now extremely fired up and shouts: 'Clear the room! We need the room!' Darroch complies calmly and leaves Darling to it.

First, while the Treasury switchboard locates McKillop, the Chancellor has to deal with another aspect of the financial meltdown by calling Iceland, to try to glean the latest on the recent collapse of that country's banking system. Many Britons stand to lose their savings in Icelandic banks that have been offering unfeasibly generous interest rates. Darling gets little comfort from his efforts to establish whether the authorities in Iceland will stand behind their banks. After the call Darling is patched through to McKillop. The government, the RBS chairman implores, has to do something: 'This Peston leak is a disaster and the markets are just terrible.' Darling asks how long RBS can keep going and receives a chilling answer from the bank's chairman: 'A couple of hours, maybe.' In soothing tones, Darling attempts to reassure McKillop that the Bank of England will provide emergency funding for the rest of the day while the government comes up with a proper rescue plan this evening. While Darling is doing his best to stay calm, to avoid panicking the RBS chairman further, inwardly he is fearful. The collapse of Northern Rock in September 2007 had been a dress rehearsal for the Treasury in terms of dealing with failed banks, but RBS is a far larger institution. With the McKillop call finished, Darling, not generally known for making theatrical flourishes or melodramatic statements, turns to Spence and Rosenfield and pronounces: 'It's going bust this afternoon.' They need to get back to London as quickly as possible.

Fred Goodwin's journey to 280 Bishopsgate takes little more

than fifteen minutes. Emerging from the lift at the twelfth floor, home to a suite of executive offices, he turns right along a marble-lined hall which leads out to the cream-carpeted reception area. From there he turns left and heads through glass double doors leading to a wide corridor. Off that corridor is the meeting room – positioned between the chairman and chief executive's large offices – dubbed the 'war-room' by staff. Today it will be the setting for a sprawling series of meetings running for hour after hour, with senior executives arriving with news and McKillop and Goodwin leaving at various points to make phone calls to try to establish what they should do next. Members of the board are dialled in and put on loudspeaker. Goodwin himself remains relatively calm at the centre of the storm. There are no histrionics or cursing of the fates today. He is quiet and eventually retreats to the sanctuary of his office. 'Fred knows he's dead, it is over,' says one of those who visits him several times. After his telephone diplomacy earlier in the day, it is obvious to colleagues that a frantic McKillop is struggling to compute the enormity of what is happening to the bank he only reluctantly agreed to chair. There is also the question of historical reputation. A hitherto highly successful career is culminating with a starring role in the collapse of the UK's biggest company and a substantial share of the blame for a national fiasco.

When the Group Executive Management Committee is convened, Goodwin is not around for most of the discussion, which focuses on whether enough money is in the branches of RBS and on what should be said to desperately worried staff. Alan Dickinson, head of the bank in the UK, has recently doubled the cash limits at branches in an effort to ensure that the cash machines remain full and there are no queues.[3] For weeks Goodwin has been phoning him every day to check. The RBS treasury department, charged with making sure that the bank has the billions it needs to fund its balance sheet, is where the immediate problem lies. Without emergency help from the Bank of England, RBS will not be able to transact the basic business of clearing large payments for corporate customers. Other banks are reluctant to deal with it. Making matters worse, large corporate customers and retail customers are continuing to withdraw billions of pounds in deposits. The scene on the twelfth floor is chaotic, although the situation has moved well beyond the control of any of those present. Among the senior executives and staff there is sheer horror at what is unfolding. Not only is there the shared humiliation to contemplate, in seeing an institution they had been so proud of brought to the brink of bankruptcy. Many also have their own money tied up in RBS shares. As recently as January 2007 one share cost £6.50. Today the same share is worth less than a pound. Says one of those who was on the twelfth floor: 'Everyone seemed numb with the shock of it, and we were asking each other how could this happen to us so quickly?'

The work of trying to sort out RBS's immediate liquidity problem, of how to keep billions flowing through it, falls first to Nick Macpherson, Permanent Secretary to the Treasury, the senior civil servant in the department. Darling calls and orders him to get straight on to the Bank of England. They have to avoid Goodwin's team running out of money this afternoon because if they fail there is a risk that the entire UK banking system will freeze. It sounds simple but Treasury officials realise there is a complication. The Bank of England's rules forbid it from giving emergency funding to an institution it judges insolvent, and the Royal Bank of Scotland certainly looks insolvent. A message is passed to Bill Winters at the US bank J. P. Morgan, asking him to carry on transacting with RBS. Ironically, Winters has rather sensibly dodged the chance to move to RBS to become the head of its investment bank and successor-in-waiting to Goodwin. The American wanted too much money, Sir Tom McKillop thought. Others suspected that this was a cover story because Winters had sensed just how much trouble was coming at RBS. Now Winters agrees to help the Treasury. If the UK government really is standing behind the Royal Bank, then J. P. Morgan will carry on dealing with it, meaning that RBS can be regarded as solvent. This, combined with the multi-billion government bailout that is supposed to be coming, gives the Bank of England the cover it needs to turn on the taps. In the following ten days, RBS will need more than £35bn in Emergency Liquidity Assistance.

Inside the Treasury, as midday approaches, and with Darling on the tarmac in Luxembourg, officials and ministers gather for a meeting convened by the chief secretary to the Treasury, Yvette Cooper. If the officials are generally calm, several feeling they have been battle-hardened by the Northern Rock experience, some of the politicians are extremely tense. It is understandable. The banking system teeters on the edge of total collapse and it is ministers, not civil servants, who will have to go to Parliament, and on television, to explain financial Armageddon to the voters. Joining Cooper are Lord Myners, who was only appointed City Minister yesterday, as a final addition to the Prime Minister's ministerial reshuffle that had taken place at the end of last week. He comes with a wealth of City experience, which even includes the distinction of having been shredded by Fred Goodwin. Myners lost his seat on the NatWest board, and then his job, when RBS and Goodwin took over the bank in 2000. With Myners is former investment banker Baroness Vadera, a minister at the Department of Business and close confidante of the Prime Minister. The suspicion in the Chancellor's team is that the fearsome Vadera has been parachuted in to keep tabs on the Treasury on behalf of Gordon Brown. 'Shriti [Vadera] is saying to Yvette and the rest of us, get on with it, this is an emergency, but then she was always saying that, at every stage,' says an official.

This time it really is an emergency. Cooper is told that, as yet there is no final agreement on what should be announced or proposed to the banks. Some Treasury officials are in favour of trying to wait until the weekend if possible before unveiling a bailout, although such a delay no longer looks practical, considering that

RBS might be about to go out of business this afternoon. By the time Darling returns to Whitehall a couple of hours later, following a bumpy landing, it is obvious that at the very least the outline of a bailout deal must be in place by the time the markets open on Wednesday morning. Darling calls another meeting in the Treasury at 3 p.m. and is given a 'rich download' of the options by Macpherson and his deputy John Kingman, the Second Permanent Secretary at the Treasury. Along with Tom Scholar, managing director of International and Financial Services at the Treasury, they will be mainstays of the bailout negotiations that are to come. All three are career civil servants who have worked for governments of both major parties, seeing their fair share of drama, disaster and dispute along the way. However, rescuing the banking system is of a different order.

The outline of a possible bailout package is emerging. Vadera, well connected in the upper echelons of the City, has been working with Scholar for weeks, discreetly visiting City lawyers and investment banks to establish what is possible. Desperate to avoid news leaking of Treasury concerns that RBS might go bust, officials give RBS a code name: Phoenix. With the help of other Treasury officials, Andrew Bailey at the Bank of England and several senior bankers and lawyers, they have drafted proposals for the banks to be shored up with many taxpayer billions in fresh capital, which is what banks need as a buffer to cushion losses and reassure markets. This is in line with the view held by Darling and Brown for months that it is a question of capital. Tom Scholar has also been charged with 'man-marking' Vadera and ensuring that his colleagues in the Treasury are kept fully involved as this work progresses, when there might be a tendency for Vadera to go straight to Brown.

Now – with 'Phoenix', RBS, going down in flames – that work will have to be turned rapidly into a simple set of proposals which can be put to the bankers this evening. There is a discussion about whether or not to make a public statement immediately. It is deemed more sensible to use the time they have until the markets open the following morning to get a plan together, rather than worrying about media appearances. Catherine MacLeod, the Chancellor's media adviser, says that it is better to tell the world first thing the next morning when they – hopefully – have a deal that the banks agree to. It seems clear what they should do, Darling tells the officials. Get the banks in to the Treasury this evening and tell them that the outline offer has three components: £200bn of liquidity funding to provide an immediate lifeline for the banks; a government credit-guarantee scheme underwritten by the taxpayer, to give the banks confidence to lend to each other; and most controversial of all a recapitalisation of the weakest institutions. Darling is told that anywhere between £50bn and £75bn will be needed in fresh capital.

At 5 p.m. Darling is joined in his office by Mervyn King and then a few minutes later by Lord Turner, chairman of the Financial Services Authority, the regulator supposedly overseeing the UK banks. 'Mervyn and the Bank of England have absolutely no regard for the FSA,' says a Treasury official. 'His view has been I'm a world-class economist and Alistair Darling is just finding his way. Now Mervyn is revising his view on Alistair.' King and Darling's relationship had been very fraught. In Darling's mind, King has been cosying up to the Tories because he thinks Labour will soon be out of office. Today, however, the situation has become so serious that they are on the same page. A few days earlier King told Brown and Darling that he thought the banks needed a recapitalisation of £40bn. Turner is in a different position from King. He only arrived as FSA chairman a few weeks ago, whereas King, who sets great store by his academic credentials, has been governor throughout the long boom that is in the process of going bust, spectacularly. Both concur with Darling's plan and the Chancellor walks to Number 10 for a conversation with Gordon Brown where they agree to proceed. For once, with the crisis raging, Prime Minister and Chancellor are working together harmoniously.

On the twelfth floor at 280 Bishopsgate, there is relief among the frazzled executives when trading on the London Stock Exchange ceases for the day. It has been a gruelling final few hours, with RBS shares finishing Tuesday at 90p, down almost 40 per cent on Monday. There has also been a further serious run on deposits, with £6bn removed by customers.[4] An institution used to boasting of dramatic and sustained growth is sinking at a rate that can be measured in hours and minutes.

Goodwin is due to take part in a conference call with the CEOs of the other banks at 6 p.m., and at issue, despite his protestations for weeks that it is simply about liquidity, is capital. How many billions will the government force on the banks? Inter-bank rivalry complicates matters. In one sense the CEOs have to stick together, because even those not in line for recapitalisation need the government bailout to happen because it will underpin the entire system. They may also be next in line in the markets after the Royal Bank if it fails. Treasury officials are particularly suspicious of Barclays, fearing that it is more exposed than it is admitting. For his part, Goodwin hates Barclays. Its boss John Varley – who spoke in the 8 a.m. slot preceding Goodwin at the Merrill Lynch conference that morning – insists that he does not need an injection of capital from the government. Rivalry between the pair had been a significant factor when both charged ahead in 2007 trying to buy the sub-prime-riddled Dutch bank ABN Amro, a race which Goodwin won with disastrous consequences. Now, on the call, Varley and the others turn on Goodwin and start pushing. It is RBS that is the issue; you are the biggest problem. Another old rival is in trouble and is in the middle of being taken over after experiencing its own bank run. Andy Hornby's crippled HBOS, which contains the old Bank of Scotland, RBS's Edinburgh rival for almost three centuries, is being bought by the hitherto cautious and conservative Lloyds, run by Eric Daniels. 'Fred hated the HBOS guys,' says a friend. 'He really enjoyed when they had to be taken over by Lloyds and were humiliated. He said: "Good."'

This unlikely band of brothers, along with the CEOs of the other banks, files into Darling's office on the second floor at the Treasury at 7.30 p.m. and take seats at the table with their backs to the wall. Goodwin sits in the middle, in a seat with arms that becomes known afterwards by civil servants as 'the chair of death'. Darling records in his memoirs his shock on realising that the bankers are not going to accept gratefully and say thank you to the taxpayer for saving their skins. Instead, they start picking holes in the package. The scheme is too complicated, Varley says. The £50bn of recapitalisation is way over the top and he only needs a small amount of it, if any, Goodwin insists. The RBS chief executive looks remarkably relaxed, nonchalant even, for a man who has helped land himself, his bank and the country in the mire. 'Fred was the least emotional of the bankers partly because he obviously realised that the game was up,' says a Treasury official. In contrast, it is obvious that HBOS's Andy Hornby – management whizz kid, top of the class in his year at Harvard but with no prior experience of banking when he moved to HBOS[5] – is in anguish. 'Hornby looked absolutely terrible, sitting there all hunched up. It was clear that he was a completely broken person.'

The bankers are exiled to a room next door ('Can they hear what we're saying?' Darling asks) while the officials in the Chancellor's office discuss what to do. As Darling told the bankers when he sent them next door: this is the deal, there is no other deal, they had better get used to it or 'God help us all'. Darling and the others are hungry, so Dan Rosenfield, Darling's private secretary, orders £350 worth of supplies from the Chancellor's favourite curry house, Gandhi's in Kennington. Treasury messenger Kevin Whelan, veteran of many previous crises at the Treasury, such as the night Britain fell out of the European Exchange Rate Mechanism (the ERM) in 1992, drives to collect it. Several weeks later Rosenfield's unorthodox expenses claim is queried by an official in the Treasury accounts department. They are suspicious that the order for a curry was so large, with no names attached explaining who had eaten the long list of dishes.[6] Could he not list who had had what?

Next door, Goodwin is still protesting that the £50bn figure is excessive. 'It will scare the markets and anyway I don't need anything like that much.' Varley is on this occasion in a stronger position and cannier. Smoother, more conciliatory and better at playing the establishment game, he appears to realise that this recapitalisation is not going to be averted. He is also desperate to keep Barclays out of that humiliating element of the rescue, so it suits him to be seen by the Treasury trying to get the others to agree, broadly, to what Darling wants for RBS and Lloyds/HBOS. They should push the government to make refinements to the way in which the credit guarantee scheme will work, but progress to a deal. By 11 p.m., Darling is exhausted and wants some answers. He has been up since before 5 a.m. and will have to be wide awake again in six hours in order to announce something, anything. The bankers are summoned once more. Again the exchange does not go well. Darling explains that while details can be finalised later they have to agree to the main elements of the plan, now. More objections are raised and Darling, not known for losing his cool, says he is heading off to bed shortly and they had better get on with it. The bankers, rather taken aback, are expelled from his office.

Darling has had enough. 'Alistair is completely fed-up by this point, and no wonder,' says one of his staff. The Treasury team is kept behind while a gloomy Chancellor declares the situation to be 'a complete mess'. The bankers are to be informed that he will be asleep by 1 a.m. and he wants an agreement ready four hours after that, so he can take it to the Prime Minister. Kingman and Scholar know that in conjunction with Myners they are going to have to make speedy progress. The two officials sit down with the CEOs to try to have them clarify their concerns and pin down acceptance of the recapitalisation. How can they move this along? Varley leads for the bankers, explaining that there are complications but they might be surmountable. The idea is emerging that perhaps the £50bn could be split in half, with £25bn promised as recapitalisation now and another £25bn earmarked in case it is needed.

It is now past midnight and the bankers retreat to the office set up for them on the first floor, with Myners in his room on the second, along from Darling's office. Above them, on the third floor, a small group of lawyers and officials is busy drafting and redrafting. Myners, Vadera, Scholar and Kingman call in Goodwin, Varley and the others again, at 2.30 a.m. The chief executives do seem prepared to sign up to the figure of £50bn, if it is announced as two batches of aid and the precise amounts assigned to each bank are worked out later. This is enough on which to hang a statement by Darling and Brown in the morning if it can be cleared with lawyers. At 3.15 a.m., as the other bankers head for their chauffeur-driven cars lined up downstairs, Myners asks Goodwin to stay behind for a discussion along the corridor in front of several officials and a lawyer. In light of the scale of the disaster, thoughts are obviously turning to how Goodwin's departure will be handled, although it has not yet even been mentioned and the RBS chief executive himself offers no acknowledgement that he must be put through the corporate shredder. Is Goodwin thinking of the negotiation to come? Crumble immediately in a fit of emotion and he risks the many millions to which he is contractually entitled. Myners, who eight years before lost his place on the NatWest board when Goodwin swept in after the Royal Bank completed its £21bn takeover, opts for understatement: 'You're in a bit of trouble.'

'Fred disagrees and is completely normal,' says one of those present. 'He just says that the markets are awful and that is it.' Goodwin heads downstairs to his waiting Mercedes, to be sped back to the Ritz on nearby Piccadilly. Darling is woken at 5 a.m. and greeted by panda-eyed officials including Scholar and

Rosenfield in the downstairs sitting room in Number 11. After a few minutes Brown joins the exhausted group. The Prime Minister and Chancellor have the makings of an outline deal to sign off and announce. It involves a bailout fund so astonishing in scale that they hope it will buy them some time. How much time is not clear. At this stage Scholar tells colleagues they now have a few weeks, rather than a few days, in which to work out the precise details. As it turns out, they will actually be back in the Treasury for more late-night and early-morning negotiations by the weekend, in less than seventy-two hours' time. Before 8 a.m. on Wednesday 8 October 2008, Brown and Darling host a joint press conference in Number 10 to announce that they will recapitalise Britain's weakest banks to the tune of £50bn – meaning £25bn now, with another £25bn available if more is needed, which it will be. The stricken RBS will require by far the biggest chunk of this enormous sum.

How has it come to this shameful denouement, with mighty banks flattened and tens of billions of public money needed to pick them up, when the government has claimed so confidently for so long that the country is in the middle of a new golden age? We will come back to Gordon Brown later. First, consider the rise and fall of the Royal Bank of Scotland. For most of its 281-year history it proceeded prudently. A healthy entrepreneurial streak was balanced by an emphasis on careful financial husbandry. Then, somehow, it morphed from a conservative, small bank into a financial monster. Its near £2-trillion balance sheet made it the biggest bank in the world, yet it was so polluted with toxins and questionable assets that it was having to be rescued by the British taxpayer with vast sums of emergency state aid.

Which forces and personalities had propelled RBS towards this calamity? There was Fred Goodwin, but he was not flying solo. For years, those at the top of the Royal Bank presumed that success in the increasingly globalised world of finance depended on their institution being prepared to change and, if necessary, grow much bigger. Eat or be eaten, as the phrase of the time had it. Like plenty of others, their calculations were rooted in widely held and mistaken assumptions that were the prevailing wisdom of the age. Those in the biggest banks – whose salaries and bonuses became so gargantuan – were hardly likely to question whether the system they were a part of was soundly based, not when it was making them rich.

But while there are certainly people in this story and in the wider world of banking for whom avarice seems to have been the main motivation, greed on its own is an insufficient explanation for why the blow-up of the Royal Bank of Scotland was quite so spectacular.

Says a senior figure in the City who came to know Goodwin: 'Fred was building a monument and he was bloody proud of it.' In making his monument he was building on foundations laid hundreds of years before by men who were financial innovators and patriots. Those who cared about the Royal Bank could point to an exceptional heritage and claim plausibly that it was no ordinary company, not some here today gone tomorrow firm willing to be treated as a chattel by asset-stripping foreigners. Its very history seemed to endow it with a special status. Indeed, to understand properly why RBS and the rest of us ended up where we did on that cold, grey dawn on 8 October 2008 we have to examine the story of Goodwin's rise, and go back to the man who hired him, his immediate predecessor, whose extraordinary reinvention of the Royal Bank was motivated by patriotic pride and a desire to build the best bank in the modern world out of a Scottish institution which first opened for business in 1727. We begin just a little before that, towards the end of the seventeenth century, when inventive and profit-hungry Scots are agonising, not for the first or last time, about how their country might make its way in the world.

2

Company of Scotland

*'If we were all Scotchmen, I believe the unlimited issue of
one pound notes would be an excellent measure'*

William Jevons, economist, in *Money and
the Mechanism of Exchange* (1875)

The Royal Bank of Scotland had its origins in the wreckage of
a previous financial disaster that humiliated a nation. On
the coast of the Isthmus of Panama, the thin strip of land joining
North and South America, is Punta Escocés, or Scottish Point.
There, in the late seventeenth century, several thousand Scottish
settlers set up camp hoping to found a trading empire that
might rival those of bigger countries, such as England. It didn't
work. Instead, the audacious adventure, complete with a pirat-
ical postscript, ended up draining Scotland of a large part of its
wealth, in the process clearing the way for political union with
England. This ill-fated moneymaking venture, the Darien
Scheme, had another important legacy. It also led to the creation
of the Royal Bank.

The foreign adventure had been meant to improve Scotland's

standing. In the late seventeenth century the place certainly needed a lift. Perched on the edge of northern Europe and lashed by rain, Scotland had a predominantly rural economy that had recently experienced waves of emigration, persistent crop failure and famine. Originally, the Scots had hoped that the Union of the Crowns with England in 1603 might somehow improve the position, by opening up more English markets to Scottish traders. Under the arrangement, the two countries were united under one monarch, James VI of Scotland and I of England, while both kept their own parliaments. Economically, it simply didn't work. English merchants remained protective of their own markets and Scotland still struggled to compete and trade with its powerful neighbour. As the 1700s approached, frustrated Scots looked for opportunities for urgent national improvement.

William Paterson, a Dumfriesshire-born trader and imaginative financier who had spent time in England and the Caribbean, thought he had the answer. Paterson wanted Scotland to colonise the area then known as Darien, where goods might be transferred overland from the Pacific to the Caribbean. The historic gap between east and west would be bridged and Paterson, and Scotland, would become heroically wealthy. That was the theory.[1]

The architect of this adventure clearly had an inventive brain and an appetite for risk. In London, Paterson had already helped to found the Bank of England in 1694, which was established to enable the government to raise funds for its military campaigns. The institution then became the world's prototype central bank, issuing notes and eventually underpinning the entire British banking system. For his next trick, Paterson tried and failed to raise funds on the continent to support his Darien initiative. Then the Company of Scotland was established in 1695 by a Scottish Parliament keen to invigorate foreign trade. At the same time parliamentarians also authorised the establishment of the country's first bank, the Bank of Scotland, which almost three centuries later ended up as part of HBOS and then Lloyds. The Company of Scotland, the new national trading company, would, it was hoped, give Scotland an outfit to rival the English-owned East India Company by challenging it in Africa and the Indies.

The East India Company was obviously not keen on this new competitor and King William in London was persuaded to withhold his support for Scottish colonial expansion. Outraged by the king's snub, and in an atmosphere charged with patriotic fervour, the Company of Scotland took up Paterson's Darien idea. A great public subscription drive was mounted to raise funds and the affluent in Scottish towns rushed to invest.[2] Rivals Glasgow and Edinburgh, competitive even then, both contributed £3000. The burghs of Irvine, Inverness and Inverkeithing raised £100 each, while Renfrew, Ayr, St Andrews Ayr, Paisley, Linlithgow, Haddington and Dumfries were in for more. Perth committed £2000. The noble families of Scotland were heavy investors, with the Duchess of Hamilton handing over £3000. Andrew Fletcher of Saltoun, the philosopher, politician and soldier, staked £1000 of his fortune. Merchants, lawyers, lairds, landlords and clergymen also subscribed. The amounts involved sound small by the standards of our age, loose change to modern investment bankers, but in a pre-industrial economy they were very significant sums. In all, more than £400,000 was raised from more than 2000 subscribers, an investment which it is estimated constituted at least a fifth of Scotland's then cash wealth. If the expedition was a success everyone would get their money back and make large profits. Trebles all round. Alas, the possibility of failure does not seem to have been contemplated.

As the historian William Ferguson[3] wrote of the Darien Scheme: 'In theory this was a brilliant idea, which if realised would have generated a great trade, cutting out as it would the long stormy voyage around Cape Horn.' Indeed, in 1914 the Americans opened the Panama Canal, vindicating Paterson's original vision. If the theory sounded good, in practice Darien turned into a disaster for the Scots as a dream of national rebirth became a pestilent nightmare. From Leith, five ships left on the initial expedition on 14 July 1698, with as many as 1200 settlers on board, including Paterson. He played only a limited role in the mission after being removed from the management of the Company of Scotland. There had been a scandal when a colleague he had brought into the company was found to have embezzled funds entrusted to him for investment in London.

The eager settlers had been persuaded, by pamphleteers and publicity, that Darien was an undeveloped paradise which would easily generate riches. It does not seem to have occurred to Paterson or his colleagues that while the Spanish had colonised parts of the neighbouring areas they had long since abandoned any effort to settle in Darien. The land was now christened Caledonia and a main settlement was built called 'New Edinburgh', where tropical diseases started to kill off the settlers. Exacerbating an already difficult situation, there was little trade to be done, with King William's representatives warning English merchants to stay away for fear of riling the Spanish. A further expedition set off with another 1300 settlers on board, even though the tattered remnants of the first expedition were already heading home via New York. The second wave of Scottish arrivals initially defeated Spanish forces on land and were then blockaded by the much stronger Spanish fleet. The stragglers agreed to leave, capitulating on 31 March 1700 and abandoning Darien forever the following month.

A miserable postscript followed when the Company of Scotland sent two ships – the inappropriately named *Speedy Return* and the *Content* – out to the Indian Ocean so that they might carry out some more conventional trading on the west coast of Africa in the hope of making up some of the huge losses from the failure of Darien. Both ships were taken by pirates, and ended up burned.

Back in Scotland the impact of these events on national morale and economic confidence was absolutely shattering. Of fourteen ships commissioned by the Company, eleven were lost. As many as two thousand settlers and crew had lost their lives and there was initially little compensation for the many who had invested. English obstructionism was blamed, because the king had not backed the venture and had refused to organise a rescue mission when it became clear that the settlers were under attack by the Spanish. In truth, blaming the English seems like a convenient excuse. The Scottish failure was as much a result of poor planning, inept leadership and an unnecessarily rapid expansion rooted in patriotic fervour and blind optimism about the prospects.

Of course Darien was not the sole cause of the full Union with England that followed a few years later. At the same time the English government had become concerned that Jacobite Scots loyal to the Stuart line, which had been removed and replaced by the Protestant King William III, might rise up and seek to restore the old king with the support of the Catholic French. The English did not want a hostile power to the north, so the Whigs – the architects of the post-Stuart settlement who had set about dominating national affairs – looked for a way to subdue Scotland. The economic distress caused by Darien also suggested that perhaps Scotland could no longer afford to go it alone. If the Scots wanted to improve their economic prospects and stand any chance of extending their trading into the exciting New World, then they would surely be better doing it in partnership with the English, rather than relying on their own pitiful navy. It had only a handful of ships. After negotiations, and despite considerable public opposition, involving rioting in several towns, the Treaty of Union between England and Scotland came into effect on 1 May 1707. Britain was born.

Justifiably the Scots wanted compensation, because now they would have to contribute to funding England's national debt. A sum of £398,085 10s, known as 'the Equivalent' was agreed, and crucially a large slice of the compensation fund was also to be used to assist those who had invested in Darien and lost money in the defunct Company of Scotland. Commissioners were appointed in 1707 to handle these payments, although the process descended into years of bitter squabbling and it was only in 1719 that the Westminster Parliament in London finally made proper arrangements to pay all those who held certificates. Two separate societies were formed, one in London and one in Edinburgh, to protect the interests of those due money.[4] William Paterson, who had understandably moved back south after the abject failure of his Panamanian scheme, was one of the directors in London. The mastermind behind the Bank of England and Darien died in Westminster in 1719.

While a stream of income from the Equivalent was all very well, eventually the directors wanted more. They began to issue loans and with the establishment of the Equivalent Company in 1724 they looked to move formally into banking. Their overtures for a merger with the old Bank of Scotland having been rejected, on 31 May 1727 the Equivalent Company was instead allowed by the government in London to establish a brand-new bank. This was the Royal Bank of Scotland. The failure of Darien and the Act of Union had sown the seeds.

The Royal Bank opened for business with only eight staff in 1727, from a house in Ship Close on the north side of Edinburgh High Street, in premises which the directors rented for the sum of £65 a quarter on a three-year lease.[5] Refurbishment was undertaken and a vault built where the 'strong boxes' were placed. Individual loans were not to exceed £5000, and the directors had to adjudicate on all loans requested above £800. The Royal Bank's total authorised capital was just £111,347.

The prime mover in this new enterprise in 1727 was an Eton-educated aristocratic schemer who was fast becoming the central figure of the age in Scotland. Archibald Campbell was the Earl of Ilay and later 3rd Duke of Argyll after the death of his elder brother. His portrait, as the bewigged first Governor of the Royal Bank, still appears on RBS banknotes. Hugely ambitious and commercially minded, Ilay was an adept political climber and the natural figurehead for a new financial enterprise. Ilay not only ran the Royal Bank, he also ran the country and was dubbed 'King of Scotland'. In the decades immediately after the Union, Scotland remained a wild place that was extremely difficult for London to govern. Ilay offered to administer it in return for influence over patronage and public and judicial appointments north of the border. Shortly before becoming the first Governor of the Royal Bank, Ilay had been appointed Minister without Portfolio responsible for Scotland by Sir Robert Walpole, the Whig statesman regarded as the first holder of the office of Prime Minister. In addition Ilay was also Keeper of the Privy Seal and Lord Register of Scotland, appointments which meant he embodied Whig power in Scotland.

Scotland was logistically nightmarish to tame. In the early 1700s, as much as half of the population lived in the Highlands within the hierarchical clan structure, in rural communities rooted in hand-to-mouth agriculture. Support for the Jacobites was strong among various Highland clans and there was an entirely justified fear in London of plots and a Jacobite invasion of England. Indeed, in 1715, James Francis Edward Stuart, known as the 'Old Pretender', had tried to take back his deposed father's crown by instigating a rising both north and south of the border. Ilay's brother, the 2nd Duke of Argyll, played a central role in putting down that rebellion.

The politics of insurgency and loyalty to the Crown mattered a great deal to a new bank established in Edinburgh in the 1720s, mainly because the old Bank of Scotland was deeply distrusted by the Whig establishment in London. Correctly, it was suspected of Jacobite sympathies, as some of its officers had close links with the rebels. In contrast, the Royal Bank would be the Whig bank, an instrument in Scotland of the then newly formed British elite with its directorate and customers drawn from the ranks of Edinburgh lawyers, judges, landlords and crown officials.

The Scottish capital of the 1720s and 1730s in which these men lived was much less than half the city of today. Edinburgh was then restricted largely to what is now known as the 'Old Town', where tourists go to see the Castle perched atop volcanic rock, and to walk down the Royal Mile at the time of the arts jamboree that is the Edinburgh Festival. In the early eighteenth century the famous New Town, with its exquisite Georgian architecture and neatly laid out streets, had yet to be built. Edinburgh, or 'Auld Reekie', was the Old Town, a maze of ancient alleys, or 'closes', and tall tenement buildings bedevilled by poor sanitation. However, these unpromising surroundings were soon to be the focus of great energy and intellectual excitement, when the Scottish Enlightenment took hold in the city's university and taverns. Improvement – be it educational, agricultural, scientific or financial – became the new obsession of the elite and the emerging middle class. These were the Royal Bank's customers.

The Bank of Scotland hated its younger rival and the ill feeling was reciprocated. Both institutions now spent decades trying to put their rival out of business in a banking war. This was waged by securing substantial amounts of the other's notes, 'promissory notes', and suddenly presenting them and demanding 'specie', hard currency or coins, in return. The idea was to drain the rival of funds, or to demand more than could be produced by the other bank so that it would disrupt their activities. The banking both provided was pretty basic; it involved taking deposits and lending it out in sensible quantities to those it thought would pay it back (an approach that some of today's bankers might usefully revisit). In the mid-eighteenth century there was no network of branches, just offices in Edinburgh's

Old Town and eventually agents in other parts of the country who agreed to represent the bank. Formal branches would come later, another of the innovations stemming from the so-called 'Scotch' system of banking which was later copied widely. From the start the Royal Bank was innovative. It even has a good claim to have invented the modern British overdraft. In 1728 customers were offered the chance to go overdrawn if they could show good faith and undertake to return their accounts to credit later. The Royal Bank was growing, extending lending and demonstrating that the monopoly enjoyed by its rival, the Bank of Scotland, had needed challenging.

War threatened to disrupt this progress. The outbreak of the final Jacobite rebellion in 1745 was an extremely dangerous moment for a bank favoured by the ruling Whigs in London, especially if the rebels were going to occupy Edinburgh. Bonnie Prince Charlie, Charles Edward Stuart, arrived from France aiming to raise an army from the clans still loyal to his cause. He landed on the west coast of Scotland in August 1745, with only a handful of men and little in the way of funds. He hoped to per-suade his allies in France to join the fight if he took Edinburgh and then launched an invasion of England.

In one of those quirks of history that proves that Scotland is a village, the ancestor of one of Fred Goodwin's most senior lieu-tenants was pivotal in the rising. Johnny Cameron, head of RBS's investment bank arm at the time of the financial crisis of 2008, is a senior figure in Clan Cameron, whose leader is traditionally known as Cameron of Lochiel. Today, Johnny Cameron's brother has the title and the ancestral lands in the western Highlands. In 1745, the Jacobite Donald Cameron, 'the Gentle Lochiel', ran the show. In the hierarchical old Highlands, the clan chief could command the men on his land to follow him into battle, and without Cameron there would have been no 1745 uprising. Prince Charles was struggling to recruit an army and when he 'raised his standard' at Glenfinnan, in Inverness-shire, it looked as though hardly anyone would turn up. His rising might have been over before it had begun. And then, around the corner of the Glen, came Lochiel and the Camerons.

As several thousand Jacobite rebels arrived in Edinburgh in mid-September, the leaders badly needed money to pay their troops and buy supplies.[6] For the increasingly nervous directors of the Whig-backed Royal Bank of Scotland this posed a problem. Would they comply if the Prince asked them for funds by producing Royal Bank notes and demanding coins in return? The directors moved the bank's cash, and gold reserves, into a vault in the safety of the government-controlled Edinburgh Castle, and waited. Just a month after landing, Prince Charlie had control of Scotland and Cameron of Lochiel was made Governor of the capital. He deployed guards on the approach to the castle, an impregnable stronghold from which the well-armed Hanoverian garrison held out, taking potshots at the Jacobites who held the City below.

The small group of Royal Bank directors who remained in the Old Town to look after the bank's affairs did not have all that long to wait for the knock on the door. A Jacobite returned from Glasgow with coins and notes for the war effort. Of £5500, £857 of it was in Royal Bank notes. On 1 October 1745, an emissary of the Prince gave the Royal Bank directors forty-eight hours to redeem the notes in coins. If they failed to cooperate, 'the effects and estates of the directors and managers should be distress'd for the same'. In other words, if the bankers did not hand over the coins, the Prince's men would take an equivalent sum by raiding the homes of those who ran the Royal Bank. Here, the bank was blessed to have John Campbell in charge. From relatively humble beginnings, 'John of the Bank' had joined as one of the first employees in 1727 and risen to the position of cashier, equivalent to general manager or chief executive.[7]

Approached by the Prince's emissaries, Campbell initially played for time, explaining that it was difficult because he could not gain access to the Castle. The Jacobite leaders grew restless and the Prince's demands on the Royal Bank rose to upwards of £3000. Campbell would have to get inside the Castle to retrieve what the Prince's men wanted, without the commander of the government's garrison realising he was aiding the rebels. Campbell met Cameron of Lochiel in a tavern, Mrs Clerks, and over drinks they made arrangements. In this way, the ancestor of Johnny Cameron – investment banker and a pivotal figure in Goodwin's RBS – arranged safe passage for John Campbell through the Old Town on the way to the Castle at 9 a.m. Carrying a white flag, Campbell and his colleagues went to get the Prince's coins.

A meeting with the generals in command of the castle followed, at which Campbell explained vaguely that the Royal Bank needed access to the vaults to conduct essential business. They were permitted to enter. Campbell and several colleagues then spent six hours collecting the coins for Prince Charles and destroying piles of unissued banknotes so that they would not fall into the hands of the Jacobites later. All this happened against a backdrop of exchanges of fire between the Jacobites in the town down below and the government forces in the castle. On finishing their work, Campbell and his colleagues left the castle, passing back through Cameron of Lochiel's guard and handing over the coins to the Prince's waiting representative. It was a murky episode. The Bank of Scotland – with its Jacobite sympathies – had gone unmolested by the rebels while the Royal Bank had been pressurised by Bonnie Prince Charlie's forces. Of course, John Campbell and his colleagues could have refused to help. Instead, they deceived the government's generals in the Castle and provided the Jacobite leaders with some of the coin they needed for the attempted invasion of England that followed.

The aftermath might have proved embarrassing to the Royal Bank, especially once the Jacobite rebellion had ended in humiliating defeat in April 1746 at Culloden. Luckily for Campbell, the Royal Bank's role was hushed up. The deputy governor, Lord Milton, returned to Edinburgh and was furious with Campbell, who was now suspected of secretly having Jacobite sympathies. Yet Milton could not risk any scrutiny of the affair for fear of the government in London noticing what had been happening. Campbell prospered, by continuing as cashier until his death in 1777 and fathering fourteen children. A portrait of him, resplendent in full tartan, still hangs in the Royal Bank in Edinburgh. The defeated Prince fled the battlefield for exile in France. Donald Cameron of Lochiel followed him, joining the French army and dying in battle in 1748. His brother Archibald, another relative of Johnny Cameron's, was the last Jacobite to be executed. He was imprisoned at Edinburgh, then taken to the Tower of London. In June 1753 at Tyburn he was hanged, not until dead, and then beheaded.

In the final Jacobite crisis, the Royal Bank had gone through an important stage in its evolution. Tied to the Whig political cause when it was founded, it had now shown that what really mattered to the bank above all else were its interests and its survival. Campbell had responded pragmatically under pressure and carried on the business of the bank, giving the customer, Bonnie Prince Charlie, what he wanted but keeping it quiet.

Scotland, and the Royal Bank, prospered in the peace that followed, when there was a dizzying intensification of the revolution in ideas that became known as the Scottish Enlightenment. The Scottish conceit, of a small country defying the odds and punching well above its weight, stems in part from the startling intellectual and financial developments of this period. ('Here's tae us, wha's like us?' as Robert Burns put it.) This intellectual explosion was fuelled by Scots having unusually good access to basic education, thanks to the innovation of schools introduced by the 'kirk', or church, meaning abnormally high literacy rates for the time. Upwards of 70 per cent of Scots were able to read and write by the mid-eighteenth century. At a time when England had only two such institutions, Oxford and Cambridge, Scotland had four ancient universities in the shape of St Andrews, Aberdeen, Edinburgh and Glasgow. From the latter intellectual hothouse came Adam Smith, the great classical liberal author of *The Wealth of Nations* (1776). Smith taught at Glasgow, gave popular public lectures in Edinburgh and became the father of modern economics. The ideas of philosophers including David Hume and Adam Ferguson, and scientists such as Joseph Black, helped shape our world. Even the modern insurance industry can be traced to Edinburgh and the establishment in the 1740s of the 'Fund for a Provision for the Widows and Children of the Ministers of the Church of Scotland', which created the model, with the use of actuarial tables, whereby a mutual insurance company could ensure that it had sufficient funds to insure against early death.[8]

It was in this innovative climate that the Royal Bank and the old Bank of Scotland pioneered what became modern British banking. It wasn't just the Royal Bank's simple individual overdraft. There was the refinement of the entire cash-credit system, in which merchants could open an account, pay bills and deposit their takings secure in the knowledge that the bank allowed the balance to fluctuate each day within agreed limits. This made it much easier for firms to plan ahead, to order stock, to make payments and to grow. Most importantly, the two Scottish banks were from the start examples of what is known as joint-stock banking. They were owned by a wide range of shareholders. The banks could use the money brought in by issuing shares to increase their pool of capital and expand lending. Shareholders could sell their holdings on, creating a secondary market in the bank's shares. Such banks only became commonplace in England after an 1826 Act of Parliament.[9]

The Royal Bank and the Bank of Scotland gained another edge when they sued for peace in 1752 – agreeing at a clandestine meeting to cooperate. They would now accept each other's notes. Eventually they developed the issue of small notes, creating the £1 note for smaller transactions and gradually all but eliminating the need for large amounts of 'specie' or coins of the kind that Bonnie Prince Charlie had needed to pay his troops a generation earlier. With sound institutions the customer could trust to look after their money, paper money was deemed sufficient for many transactions. The idea of the Scots as Britain's instinctive bankers – their canny financial husbandry sometimes caricatured as meanness – was soon an integral element of popular perceptions about the country.

There were some spectacular reverses. The dour Presbyterian ethic, which sprang from the Scottish Reformation and its violent rejection of Catholicism, involved the veneration of hard work, education, modesty and prudence, all highly commendable virtues. In this way the post-Reformation Scots were perhaps tailor-made to be Britain's prototype bankers. Yet there seemed to be a flip side, as though all that Scottish emphasis on sound money management suppressed desires which occasionally spilled over into mad projects and wild endeavours.

John Law, the swindler, womaniser, cardsharp and economic theorist who almost bankrupted France in 1720, was a Scot. After killing his opponent in a duel he escaped from prison in London, established the Banque de France, introduced paper money and created an enormous bubble that gulled French investors. His purchase, on behalf of the French government, of the Mississippi Company in Louisiana was designed to boost trade. It was inspired in part by the Company of Scotland and the mania for joint stock companies and trading in shares. Law fled France once his bubble burst. In Scotland too, periodically, restraint would also vanish in a miasma of financial innovation and greed. The Ayr Bank had liabilities of more than £1m and crashed spectacularly in 1772, stalling the Scottish economy for a while and ruining many farmers and merchants. Established just three years previously, with the aristocracy of Ayrshire and surrounding counties heavily invested, the Ayr Bank had expanded too fast, made too many loans and became overextended. To fill the gap it started borrowing ever-larger amounts from elsewhere. Then came disaster, with the sudden collapse of the London-Scottish banking house of Neale, James, Fordyce and Downe, with which the Ayr Bank had done business.[10] Adam Smith, writing in *The Wealth of Nations*, several years later, described the Ayr Bank's reckless approach to running its affairs in the following terms: 'The project of replenishing their coffers in this manner may be compared to that of a man who had a water-pond from which a stream was continually running out, but who proposed to keep it always full by employing a number of people to go continually with buckets to a well at some miles distance in order to bring water to replenish it.'

Despite occasional crashes, the general trajectory was upwards for Scotland and the Royal Bank. The country's trade soared in tobacco, textiles, manufacturing and eventually coal. William Paterson's vision of Scotland as a great trading nation began to be realised in the Industrial Revolution and push for Empire of the late eighteenth century. With its share of the proceeds, the Royal Bank opened larger and much more salubrious premises in Edinburgh. The Enlightenment desire for improvement had reshaped the Scottish capital, with the creation of the New Town in the late eighteenth century, which still stands as one of the finest examples of Georgian architecture and refined town planning. In 1821 the Royal Bank abandoned the cramped Old Town, with its romantic memories of the bank's birth and the 1745 rebellion, and moved to an elegant headquarters in St Andrew Square. In February 1825 it purchased the Italianate Dundas House next door, the former mansion of Sir Lawrence Dundas. Later it attached a spectacular domed banking hall topped with a star-adorned roof. This was a temple to Scottish bankers, to their values, ethics and achievements and these buildings would remain the headquarters of the Royal Bank until 2005 when Fred Goodwin moved the flagship office to a vast new complex built on the distant edge of Edinburgh at Gogarburn.

In the nineteenth century, ensconced in its new offices, the Royal Bank was the ultimate Edinburgh company: careful, deeply conservative and embedded in the clannish Edinburgh establishment. Scotland's compact capital then, as now, is most unlike London. The senior lawyers, bankers, actuaries and insurance professionals who ran its affairs tended to live in close proximity, either in the smart Georgian houses of the New Town or in Victorian villas not far away. And many of them tended to know each other. The more junior staff the Royal Bank employed were given security and a route for advancement, if they accepted the ethos underpinning a bank embodying self-proclaimed Presbyterian values of hard work, modest behaviour and loyalty.

Scottish banking blossomed. Rival outfits opened in Dundee, Ayr, Aberdeen and Perth and banks such as the Bank of Scotland started to develop national networks of branches – another innovation well ahead of England. There were more periodic panics, as there usually are. In 1857 the Western Bank in Glasgow failed spectacularly in the middle of a bank-run, going down with liabilities of almost £9m. Its shareholders were wiped out. In 1878 there was an even worse disaster when the City of Glasgow Bank folded, following its botched investment in the Racine and Mississippi railroad in America. A difficult situation was exacerbated by extensive fraud on the part of the bank's management. Amid great public excitement there was a trial, resulting in the imprisonment of the manager and directors. These recriminations were followed by much introspection and soul-searching. Scotland was famed for its skill in banking, so why had it produced a banking collapse? The government's failure to regulate properly was identified as a factor, although the incompetence and greed of some of the directors was held to be key.

The Royal Bank had had its own more modest difficulties in the 1830s when it became overextended, lending too much in a boom. It survived the fall-out and continued gradually accumulating customers, taking over other banks such as the Dundee Banking Company in 1864 and widening its branch network. There were some conflicts with English bankers, as the Royal Bank and the Bank of Scotland fought off attempts by the Bank of England to end the practice of the Scottish banks issuing their own notes (which they still do). The directors, tentatively at first, started the bank's move into London, in 1863 buying property in the City in Lombard Street, near the Bank of England, and opening an office. The Royal Bank, fortified by the famous reputation of Scottish banking, was broadening its horizons.

So exalted was the standing of Scottish banking, that William Jevons, one of the most influential economists of the nineteenth century, wrote in *Money and the Mechanism of Exchange* in 1875:

Englishmen and Americans, and natives of all countries, may well admire the wonderful skill, sagacity and caution with which Scotch bankers have developed and conducted their system. There is no doubt that Scotch bankers are guiding the course of development of the banking system in England, India, and the Australian colonies, and elsewhere, with conspicuous success. If we were all Scotchmen, I believe the unlimited issue of one pound notes would be an excellent measure.

By 1927, when the Royal Bank of Scotland celebrated its bicentenary, this had long been the settled view. Scotland had played a disproportionately large role in the development of British banking and could be justifiably proud of the independence of its robust financial institutions. The Royal Bank saw itself as being by far the most prestigious of these companies. Prudent management had resulted in the gradual growth of deposits and profits, all conducted at a manageable pace over many decades. In contrast to recent developments, it took many decades to grow. In 1865, deposits were only £8,127,791 and the annual profit was £177,941. In 1927 deposits had climbed to £44,186,574 and profits stood at £481,977, still under half a million pounds. It was a result of solid, steady development concentrated on taking in deposits and trying to lend only what was prudent.

On the evening of Friday 3 June 1927, 300 guests gathered in Edinburgh's North British Hotel (now the Balmoral Hotel), to celebrate these achievements and mark two hundred years of the Royal Bank.[11] At the top table sat an eminent cast list, which included Montagu Norman, Governor of the Bank of England, and Earl Haig, commander of British forces in the First World War and by 1927 a director of the Royal Bank. The Duke of Buccleuch, the governor of the bank, chaired proceedings. Not one woman was present.

Winston Churchill, then the Chancellor of the Exchequer, sent apologies for his absence. His telegram celebrating the anniversary was read out to the assembled directors, senior staff, branch managers and a sprinkling of guests. The Duke of Buccleuch, responding to the toast to the health of the Royal Bank, noted that 'the banking system of Scotland is probably the greatest and most original work which the practical genius of the Scottish people has produced'. Following further laudatory speeches, punctuated by laughter and applause, and rich with historical references to events such as the 1745 Jacobite rebellion and the old rivalry with the Bank of Scotland, Sir Alexander K. Wright stood to reply to the toast made to the staff. Some six hundred of the bank's 1270 staff were stockholders, or shareholders, and the sense of pride in shared ownership and achievement is still palpable in Wright's concluding remarks: 'I venture to express the hope that when our successors meet together to celebrate the bank's tercentenary (in 2027), the institution will still be occupying a high position in the life of the country and that on the evening of the dinner there will be a Duke of Buccleuch in the chair.'

As the guests on that June evening in the 1920s filtered out of the ballroom of the North British Hotel and on to Edinburgh's Princes Street, there seemed every reasonable expectation that such hopes would be fulfilled.

3

New World

'Our dream is to create an international bank run from Edinburgh'

Charles Winter, group chief executive of
the Royal Bank of Scotland (1987)

The Royal Bank at which George Mathewson arrived in 1987 had been living off its proud past for years. The hiring of pugnacious 'wee George' had been ordered by elements of the management and board who realised that something had to change, and quickly. It seemed as though the Royal Bank might not even have a future as a stand-alone entity and that its history would culminate in an ignominious swallowing up by a foreign giant. Goodness, the buyer might even be English. The thought appalled the nationalistic Mathewson.

The Royal Bank was not alone in suffering an existential crisis. Outwardly, in the decades immediately after the Second World War, the Scottish economy, like the UK economy, appeared to be doing relatively well. This obscured the looming reality of deindustrialisation as old businesses with roots in the distant

Industrial Revolution struggled to adapt. Ships could be made more cheaply in South Korea. Germany and others were dominant in chemicals and car manufacturing. Meanwhile, Scotland, like its banks, seemed to be relying increasingly on a fading and self-congratulatory version of its fabled past.[1]

Not that the Royal Bank had stood still in the period since it celebrated its bicentenary in 1927. In 1930 it had followed up its 1924 purchase of Drummonds in London by buying Williams Deacon's Bank Ltd, and then came Glyn, Mills & Co in 1939. The purchase of these English banks offered a glimpse of what an expanded UK-wide operation could look like. In 1960 a new international operation was born, with the opening of an office in New York. Offices in other American cities and in Hong Kong followed. At home, the managers of the 1960s introduced early computer systems and new products aimed at attracting savers and customers. Williams & Glyn's were fused together. The industry also went through a wave of consolidation, mergers and takeovers, as smaller institutions were swallowed up, and the remaining players attempted to improve and professionalise their businesses. Ultimately, in the case of the Royal Bank, it was all rather unsatisfactory. The 1969 purchase of the National Commercial Bank of Scotland made the Royal Bank Scotland's biggest bank, but it did not produce the efficiencies and dynamism that had been hoped.

The Royal Bank looked tired, like a target for takeover, which it duly became. Lloyds had tried first, in 1979, having built up a shareholding. The notion of surrender to an English bank appalled the board and scandalised Edinburgh opinion. The offer was turned down. When, the following year, Standard Chartered came calling with the offer of a merger, it sounded much more appealing to the board. Although it was registered in London, most of Standard Chartered's activities were abroad, in Asia, Africa and the Far East. The Royal Bank would have the security that comes from being part of a large international group, while being dominant in terms of the proposed combined company's UK activities. Standard Chartered agreed that the UK bank could be run from Edinburgh. The board approved the deal and the Bank of England's governor, Gordon Richardson, gave his blessing.[2] Without the intervention of the Hong Kong and Shanghai Banking Corporation it would most probably have happened.

The then head of overseas operations at what is today known as HSBC was Willie Purves, an old-school Scottish banker who had joined his local branch of the National Bank on leaving school in Kelso at sixteen. During national service in 1951 he had been awarded the Distinguished Service Order, and if he hadn't been a national serviceman it would likely have been the Victoria Cross. Then he returned to banking, moving east, to Hong Kong. Purves and his colleagues thought that Standard Chartered was getting the Royal Bank for a steal, so they came in with a higher offer.

There was an almighty row. Political pressure was applied, with MPs demanding intervention and a Scottish 'ring fence' so that the country's banks could not be bought by foreigners. The Monopolies and Mergers Commission ruled against the HSBC takeover as well as the merger with Standard Chartered.[3] In its report in January 1982 the Commission declared that: 'The degree of control and management exercised by Scots from Edinburgh, the size of the company and the importance of it and its industry for Scotland lead us to conclude that removal of management and control of the group from Scotland would be a serious detriment.'

Relief in St Andrew Square was tempered with embarrassment. The board, in toying with a merger, had exposed the company to a takeover and revealed that they did not have a good enough plan to protect and grow the institution. By the mid-1980s the truth was unavoidable. The Royal Bank was looking like a tired bit-part player, overly reliant on invoking receding memories of distant glories, which had only avoided takeover thanks to a political campaign and the work of the competition authorities.

Elsewhere, finance was being revolutionised. The so-called Big Bang, the radical deregulation introduced by Margaret Thatcher's government in 1986, was designed to allow London to compete properly in a new age of international finance.[4] Computerisation swept away the polite old world of the City with its sedate institutions operating, mostly, according to the motto of the Stock Exchange: 'my word is my bond', a promise that obscured considerable amounts of skulduggery and some insider trading, meaning trading on privileged information to which the general investor was not privy. With Big Bang, the traditional way in which stockbroking business had been conducted – on the floor of the exchange with buying and selling done verbally and on paper – was replaced by computer trading and various restrictive practices were abolished. It wasn't just share dealing that was metamorphosing. The clearing banks – the institutions, of which the Royal Bank was one, who were authorised to clear each other's cheques – were being allowed to sell mortgages in large numbers. Until now this activity had largely been restricted to the building societies. In turn, these societies would soon be allowed to 'demutualise' and many would turn themselves into banks. Finance in all its manifestations – the funding of companies, the scale of borrowing, the types of deals done by bankers and basic banking for consumers – was changing. Would the old Royal Bank be capable of keeping up?

The man who thought that it could, who would transform its fortunes and then hire Fred Goodwin as his successor, was Mathewson. He wasn't even a banker. By education and inclination he was an engineer. Born in Dunfermline in 1940 and schooled at Perth Academy, George Mathewson graduated from St Andrews University with a degree in maths and physics. A PhD followed but he was restless. The Britain of the late 1960s did not seem to him to be a place for an ambitious young man wanting to make his mark: 'I joined the brain-drain,' as he puts it. Five years spent working for Bell Aerospace and living in

Buffalo, New York state, introduced him to America's enterprise culture. It was a revelation. In contrast to 1960s Scotland, America seemed invigorating, exciting and open to change, a country where a young engineer could glimpse the possibilities of wealth creation. Mathewson studied in the evenings for his MBA and looked around for business opportunities. But by 1972 he missed Scotland so much that he wanted to go home to build a career. Not one of life's natural mandarins, he turned down an offer to join the civil service and instead accepted a job that would give him his first experience of finance, with the Industrial and Commercial Finance Corporation, which later became the private equity firm 3i. He knew nothing about finance; he just thought it sounded interesting, intellectually stimulating and potentially rewarding.

Mathewson was attracted by the chance to get involved in the boom that was under way in oil production in the North Sea. Aberdeen was being reinvented as a boom town and in London the deals were being done that helped fund exploration. Here was a can-do industry on the move, while much of the rest of Scotland was visibly decaying. Other than oil and a nascent computer industry, the Scottish economy by the late 1970s and early 1980s was in poor condition. The nation's industrial heritage, hewn in the days of the Empire and the Industrial Revolution, was in steep decline. As in parts of the North of England, shipbuilding, coalmining, steel production and other heavy manufacturing were all but dying. In many cases what was to blame was a fatal combination of poor management, trade union intransigence and a failure to modernise stretching back many decades. But the human cost, in terms of rising unemployment and distress, was enormous when the reckoning came.

With UK unemployment rising above 2.5m in 1981 and heading for 3m, the Conservative government was under intense pressure in Scotland to look for ways to encourage the growth of new businesses that might replace the old dying industries. In

1981 Mathewson was recruited to head the Scottish Development Agency, the taxpayer-funded quango originally established in 1975 by a Labour government. It was supposed to solve the riddle of what Scotland would do once it didn't make so many ships or extract so much coal from the ground. The answer appeared to be that it would extract oil instead, make computers (in the emerging industry known as 'Silicon Glen') and possibly expand financial services. Mathewson's mantra as boss of the SDA was that he would make any public sector money available go as far as possible, whether it was in trying to kickstart the attempts at regenerating Glasgow or persuading foreign businesses to invest in Scotland. He also wanted to use his muscle and expanding network of connections to save grand old companies if they were worth saving. The SDA and Mathewson were pivotal in the 1980s when Weir Group, the engineering giant, encountered difficulties and needed rescuing.

For most of the period when Mathewson ran the SDA, the Secretary of State for Scotland was George Younger, Scotland's man in Margaret Thatcher's cabinet. Younger and Mathewson clicked; they worked well together. The politician was prepared to let the ambitious quango boss get on with it and in turn Mathewson found Younger – a pillar of the Scottish establishment – calm and supportive. Soon, they would collaborate to dramatic effect at the Royal Bank of Scotland. After six and a half years spent trying to help rescue the Scottish economy, with partial success, the impatient Mathewson wanted another challenge. Sir Robin Duthie, chairman of the SDA and a director of the Royal Bank, was wrestling with the question of succession. Who could he find to help shake up a bank that was struggling to adapt? George Mathewson.

In 1987 an approach was made and Mathewson became the bank's new director of strategic planning and development. He was clear in his mind that in order to survive the Royal Bank needed its own version of the financial revolution under way in

London. This Scottish nationalist who didn't care for the City, who had no time for the new breed of loudmouth traders and investment bankers who were starting to dominate the dealing rooms and wine bars, had a different philosophical creed. It was a punchy patriotism, which expressed itself in repeated declarations that there was no reason on earth why a Scottish bank could not become the world's best, if only it would change in order to compete with the English banks and others. Highly energetic, blunt and magpie-like in his enthusiasm for new ideas and technical innovation, he was far removed from the traditional image of the cautious Edinburgh banker.

Charles Winter, Mathewson's new boss, was an old-fashioned bank manager who was known as 'the banker's banker' because he had done it the old-fashioned way, starting in the Dundee branch straight from school, rising to the top by dint of hard work, loyalty and application. He was the organist in his local church, near Edinburgh. The Royal Bank Winter ran was chaired by Sir Michael Herries – of Eton, Oxford and the King's Own Scottish Borderers. He was awarded the Military Cross for gallantry in 1944 and had run Jardine Matheson, the great Hong Kong-based venture that began by trading in tea and opium in the early nineteenth century. It had been started by two Scots and retained strong ancestral links. Ambitious Scots keen to travel and work abroad found it a good place to make their way. Yet, for all his accomplishments, the old-school Herries was not a banker. He had joined the board of the Royal Bank in 1976 and didn't seem particularly suited to the cut-throat era of modern banking.

There was some important innovation under Winter and Herries, including the launch of Direct Line, the UK's first telephone-only insurance business, created in 1985.[5] Williams & Glyn's – with its branches in England – was also subsumed by the Royal Bank brand in the October of that year. But the hope was that Mathewson would bring energy and ideas. Announcing the hiring of their new head of strategy, group chief executive Charles Winter said: 'Our dream is to create an international bank run from Edinburgh and we are well on the way to doing that.' Mathewson loved the sentiment, but found the institution he landed in hopelessly old-fashioned and ill suited to turning Winter's dreams into reality. An impatient Mathewson appreciated that Winter had strengths but some of the rest of the senior management weren't up to it. The Royal Bank seemed slow, staid and lacking in sophistication. Profits were measly.

Then an opportunity for the beginnings of global expansion presented itself. In purchasing the American bank Citizens in 1988, Winter – encouraged by Mathewson – hoped eventually to go much further than establishing a mere outpost in the United States. Citizens Bank had begun life in 1828 as a savings institution, a small mutual firm, much like a British building society, based in Providence, Rhode Island. Run by George Grayboys, in the 1980s it had demutualised, turning itself from a mutual society into a stockmarket-listed company. Grayboys wanted the backing of a bigger partner to facilitate expansion and he had a meeting with Winter in 1987. On his trips to Edinburgh, where he and Mathewson strolled down the Royal Mile, immersed in conversation about the possibilities, he fell in love with Scotland.[6] Think what could be accomplished if the two institutions came together. Citizens would get the backing from a new owner who wanted to grow and the Royal Bank would get new access to American expertise and markets. Grayboys, impressed by Sir Michael Herries with his war record and immaculate manners, wanted a deal. The Royal Bank paid $440m for Citizens.

In Edinburgh, Mathewson was growing concerned that the basic business of the Royal Bank was so decrepit that collapse or takeover was likely. It simply did not make enough money. The branch network was inefficient and the early adoption of computerised technology had not been followed up with sufficient verve. In the Royal Bank's loan book there were also some horrors lurking. Mathewson had concluded that the situation needed to be confronted. With his customary bluntness, he sought out Herries in his office and told him: 'We are going to go bust unless we do something.' Winter concurred, although the Royal Bank old guard below him resisted Mathewson's early talk of change. At a meeting with two of the leading executives of the period, the director of strategy was astonished to be told that the Royal Bank simply could no longer make money from its branch network in Scotland even though the Bank of Scotland seemed to manage it. This bank really is in trouble, Mathewson thought. The more he saw it from the inside the more he believed a total transformation of structures and culture, led by him of course, was required. Luckily for Mathewson, at that point an ally arrived, someone he knew well and liked from his days running the SDA. Sir George Younger had by now tired of being a cabinet minister and had given a commitment that he would become chairman of the bank while Herries remained chairman of the Royal Bank Group. After three years as Defence Secretary, preceded by seven years spent as Scottish Secretary, Younger told Margaret Thatcher that he wanted to step down, although he would remain an MP until the 1992 general election.

Younger became a director of the Royal Bank of Scotland on 1 October 1989, shortly before opponents of Margaret Thatcher attempted for the first time to unseat her as Tory leader. That autumn he was immediately drawn back into the fray at Westminster, with the Prime Minister asking Younger to run her leadership campaign when a stalking horse candidate – Sir Anthony Meyer – emerged in November 1989. She would be victorious, on that occasion. Her luck would not last long. Younger was trying to help keep Thatcher in Number 10, but in his office in the Royal Bank headquarters in Edinburgh he was becoming convinced of the need for a leadership challenge at the bank. As anticipated when he joined, in January 1990 he became deputy chairman of both the Royal Bank Group and also of the bank itself. In June Mathewson was elevated to the post of

Deputy Group Chief Executive, retaining responsibility for strategic planning and development. By July Younger was chairman of the bank, but not the Royal Bank group, and he agreed with Mathewson that bolder action was required. Younger's reputation as a creature of the establishment might suggest that he would have been happy to see the chairmanship of a grand Scottish institution as a comfy sinecure before retirement. Instead, he and Mathewson began plotting and pondering how to proceed with dramatic changes.

Every Friday, Mathewson began meeting in secret with a select group of colleagues to prepare a management clear-out and reorganisation. The office of Cameron McPhail, brought from the SDA by Mathewson to work on strategy, was swept for bugs, so that each week Mathewson, Norman McLuskie, Miller McLean, Frank Kirwan (another strategist) and McPhail could gather there and plot without being spied on. They chose a code name – 'Novo Redo' – meaning 'new rethink' or 'redesign' in Portuguese, because one of their number was doing some work in Portugal, although they argued about what the correct spelling should be. The discussions resulted in a confidential paper that autumn – written by McPhail and Kirwan, and edited by Mathewson – which advocated a wholesale reorganisation. To save it, the Royal Bank would be divided up into much simplified divisions: the Branch Banking Division under Tony Schofield, the Corporate Bank, eventually under Mathewson's friend Iain Robertson who was hired from the SDA; Direct Line reporting to its founder Peter Wood; and Citizens in the United States, run by Grayboys. Winter, who approved of the plan, remained as chief executive but real power was passing to Mathewson, the deputy. More than half the existing senior executives would be cleared out and all of this would be sprung in one day when the board met in November 1990 to give the go-ahead. Mike Mosson, the head of personnel, was brought into the plot to help prepare the coup.

Here the Royal Bank's history intersects with the removal from office of a British prime minister. At just that moment, in November 1990, the Tories were preparing their own dramatic management reorganisation. Thatcher's coiffed rival for the Tory crown, Michael Heseltine, finally made his move and triggered a contest amidst feverish excitement at Westminster. Younger, busy scheming with Mathewson at the Royal Bank, was caught up in the fallout of the Conservatives' civil war just when he was trying to concentrate on the Royal Bank's looming, and still secret, internal revolution. At first he declined the request to manage Thatcher's leadership campaign, telling his Tory colleagues that he could not spare the time because of his work in Edinburgh. Then loyalty to his old boss meant that unwisely he caved in to pressure and tried to do both, shuttling between Edinburgh and London, with the plodding, shambolic, and frequently drunken Peter Morrison MP as his deputy on the Thatcher campaign. Earlier in the year Younger had tried to warn the Tory leader just how perilous her position was, asking her to tone down her rhetoric on Europe. Thatcher would not listen.

From Thatcher's point of view Younger's handling of the second leadership campaign was disastrous. He said later: 'MPs did what constituents do in by-elections. As we guessed, at least fifteen told us they would vote for Margaret and then did the opposite. This was the simple reason why our forecasts proved to be wrong.'[7]

On Tuesday 20 November Thatcher won, but fell four votes short of the total she needed to avoid a second round. Two days later she would resign. Famously, she was at the British Embassy in Paris when the result came through and went outside to say that she would fight on, delivering a holding statement that her supporters had persuaded her to make. On the night of the vote, Younger, her campaign manager, was not even at the count at the House of Commons in London. Astonishingly, he was in his office at the Royal Bank in St Andrew Square, watching events unfold on television. He wrote later: 'I was in Edinburgh when the vote was announced and was shocked and horrified that it had not been possible to get the extra four votes – although even these would not have been enough to give her the full confidence to remain in power. Even so, I was devastated, partly for her personally but also because I felt that the Conservative Party had made an enormous blunder.'

What Younger was really doing in his office that evening was meeting Mathewson to make the final arrangements ahead of the Royal Bank's own 'night of the long knives', which would start the following morning when the board met. The pair sat and watched Thatcher's televised humiliation and then got back to work. On Wednesday the 21st, the members of the group board were called in early to hear the proposals and then approve the palace coup. Within weeks many general managers and senior executives had been removed. The old-fashioned Royal Bank title of 'general manager', dating back to the eighteenth century, was abolished and the terminology modernised. Mike Mosson got to his desk one morning to find new headed notepaper in which he was listed as 'Human Resources Director' rather than 'General Manager, Personnel'. These small tweaks were designed by Mathewson and the group who had led 'Novo Redo' to signal that much bigger change and modernisation was coming.

There were tears and considerable anger when the firings began. A quarter of the senior executives were forced to retire or depart almost immediately. The polite Royal Bank had never seen such corporate carnage. And then, for a while, it passed. For the first half of the following year it seemed to executives that the changes would not mean all that much. On the surface, the Royal Bank was still the model of Presbyterian reserve and civic-minded Edinburgh politesse. The location of its headquarters in St Andrew Square meant that it was plugged into the heart of Edinburgh. As chairman, Younger often made a point when he was leaving the headquarters building of going through the elegant main banking hall so that he could be approached by any customers who wanted to express an opinion. Edinburgh ladies accosted the chairman and politely made their latest complaints or observations about the bank's services. The Royal Bank was, in its way, grounded.

If the facade still looked fine, behind it the bank was in an even worse condition than Mathewson had realised. The reorganisation of November 1990 was not going to be anything like enough on its own. In the summer of 1991, to the horror of its customers and shareholders, the Royal Bank issued a profits warning. A property downturn had revealed how inept and incontinent the bank's lending policies had been. In 1992 it just about scraped a profit of £20.9m, which the following year was marked down and shown to have been only £12.6m.

The danger was obvious immediately. The Royal Bank might go bust, and even if it did not, it needed to make itself big enough to resist more attempted takeovers by any much larger bank that might be on the prowl looking for weakened prey. To avert such a disaster, Mathewson sanctioned Project Columbus, named for the 500th anniversary of the explorer's voyage to the New World in 1492. The implication in the name was obviously that the Royal Bank was setting sail on an exciting voyage of discovery to a new world. At that point any echoes of the Darien Scheme seemed very distant.

Initially thirty or so of the bank's best and brightest were put to work on Project Columbus in an office above the old bus station, next to the headquarters in St Andrew Square. The numbers involved gradually swelled to almost 200. They were shepherded by Cameron McPhail, a Glasgow University economics graduate and part of Mathewson's small team who had worked on the original reorganisation leading to the night of the long knives. He would report to Tony Schofield and to Mathewson. Prior to joining the Royal Bank, McPhail had been living in San

Francisco, promoting Scotland as an investment location and imbibing the spirit of the coming computer age.

Mathewson wanted modern thinking to imbue their deliberations. The Royal Bank should be reorganised from top to bottom, he told them, in ways that controlled costs of course. The management consultants McKinsey were hired to assist the effort. In terms of the bank's staff, a premium was put on having non-bankers involved, outsiders who had worked in other industries and who would not be swayed by old loyalties and ingrained traditions. Among them was Steve Rick – who grew up in a children's home, worked as a draughtsman, became a personnel director and was then headhunted by the Royal Bank. The Project Columbus team was in 'the crappiest office' but it was refreshingly open-plan and they had great IT. The atmosphere was collaborative, egalitarian and exciting, although many of their colleagues viewed those in the project with great suspicion.

Rick was tasked with working out how to handle the considerable disruption there would be as older managers and staff in branches were encouraged to leave to reduce costs. The aim was to allow new talent through that would be open to innovative ideas in middle management. That meant more promotion for women, who had hitherto found it difficult to get on in a bank where the local management was almost exclusively male. 'In the past, selection for promotion quite often had a lot to do with your golf handicap,' says another member of the team. 'RBS was like a golf-club.'

One of the core failings was that the existing structure put far too much power in the hands of branch managers who were expected to know every aspect of banking. One minute they were offering advice on savings accounts to pensioners, the next they were discussing large potential loans with local companies whose needs, and capabilities, might easily outstrip their experience. In one sense customers liked the idea that they could call on their neighbourhood bank manager. But McPhail's team found that it was inefficient, particularly when it came to allocating capital, or putting to work the money deposited by customers. Too much of it just lay in the individual branch vaults or strongrooms, when it could have been lent to businesses and earned a return. Those managers not hoarding cash too often made unwise lending decisions that resulted in the bad debts which had shown up in 1991. Now vans were dispatched by head office to gather up some of the excess and the money was passed to the Corporate Bank, where it could be put to more profitable use, lending to business consumers.

There would be a much tighter grip on lending decisions. A major missing ingredient in the old set-up was the extraordinary absence of proper credit controls, which scored those customers applying to borrow. Alan Dickinson, who had started in banking the old-fashioned way on the counter at Williams & Glyn's, before going off to university, was drafted in from south of the border to fix it. Other basic banking processes were judged to be broken too. Payments were given to Jim Rafferty to sort out and sales and service to Bob McInnes. A centralised machine – for administration, IT, product creation, sales and the setting of performance targets – was being constructed, that would drive efficiency and profit.

It was, Mathewson told them, more than about simply saving the Royal Bank. His sense of patriotic ambition was infectious. In the weekly sessions held to review progress with McPhail and the others he pushed and praised, declaring on more than one occasion: 'I want us to be the dominant force in British banking.' The relatively young team revelled in the competitive environment and became increasingly loyal to Mathewson. Says one: 'It was high pressure. Of course initially he could be frightening as he had a style that people weren't used to, but when we got depressed and thought this is going to be a disaster, he would come in and give us a strong push. George went out of his way to praise and thank you. He was an incredibly strong leader. It was afterwards that he made mistakes.'

Columbus took four years to complete and when it was finished in 1996 the Royal Bank was a very different company. Profits started to boom. Those on Columbus had talked in terms of 'deskilling the branches', meaning that as much as possible would be done centrally to restrict costs, using telephone banking and direct mail to sell financial products and computers to manage customers accounts. Mathewson was innovating out of necessity, although other banks went in a similar direction. All this did come at a cost. Some of the caution and conservatism that had served the old Royal Bank well down the centuries was being traded for dynamism. And while it was thrilling for those in that Columbus office, who saw their ideas for synergies and efficiencies rolled out, for many who were moved on it was much less of a thrill. McPhail loved the way they had taken the old established Royal Bank marque, the brand, and reinvented it. But a 'sales culture' had been created, with many employees in the bank now measured according to rigorous targets dictating how much they must sell in the way of products to customers. 'We created a monster,' McPhail told friends.

The reforms might have been essential and sometimes they might even have been good for customers. But the basic business of banking and the public's understanding of it were being altered. Customers used to thinking in terms of asking nicely for credit started to find that banks were competing to give them more credit than perhaps they needed and trying to sell them products. It certainly wasn't just the Royal Bank. This happened, at varying speeds, across much of the banking industry and in the thrift-driven building societies that turned themselves into banks. This so-called financialisation of the economy – meaning that finance, banks and the City were becoming a larger part of the nation's life, and that more leverage or debt were merely natural by-products of what it was to be a modern consumer –

was accepted widely as the new norm. As many of the banks were getting bigger it seemed, for a while, as though their very size was a virtue, a comfort even. Would it always remain so?

In the 1990s, it did the trick for Mathewson and the Royal Bank. In 1993, profits before tax had been just £265m, an amount that twenty years later looks like little more than a rounding error in the context of the multi-trillion-dollar financial crisis. In 1994, Royal Bank profits leapt to £532m; to £602m the following year; and to £695m in 1996. In 1997, the year Labour's Tony Blair and Gordon Brown swept to power, the Royal Bank made £801m. At that rate it would soon break the billion pounds in profit barrier. A confident Younger, by then Lord Younger of Leckie, beaming in the portrait of the board taken inside St Andrew Square for the annual report in 1997, could tell investors: 'This group will continue on its course of consistent and profitable expansion.'

It almost turned out very differently. Although it was never disclosed, Younger and Mathewson had actually held top-secret discussions a year before with another bank. In 1996 the Hong Kong and Shanghai Banking Corporation, which had been prevented from buying the Royal Bank in the early 1980s, came calling again. By now it was headquartered in London ahead of the handover of Hong Kong to the Chinese and had been rebranded as HSBC. Willie Purves, the boy from Kelso in the Scottish Borders who had risen to be global CEO and chairman, had never quite given up on the idea of HSBC owning a Scottish bank. There were discreet discussions over lunch in Younger's flat in London. Younger was open to the idea of a deal. He and Purves got on well. Both had fought in Korea in Scottish regiments. HSBC might be good custodians, if they undertook to preserve the Royal Bank brand within a larger group. Mathewson was less keen, having made such play of growing the Royal Bank to keep it wholly independent and thinking that it had a way to go yet in terms of growth. The HSBC team indicated that they would even be prepared to station the combined group's headquarters in Edinburgh. The secret discussions foundered when HSBC gleaned the impression later that Mathewson would want to be chief executive of the whole show. This struck HSBC as ludicrous. They were the much bigger bank. Why would they hand the top post to an executive of the bank that was effectively being taken over? In this way a chance for HSBC to be headquartered in Edinburgh was lost.

Anyway, Mathewson was soon hailed as the architect of the Royal Bank's incredible recovery and there was a knighthood for him in the 1999 New Year Honours list. In the parts of wider Edinburgh and Scotland that paid attention the turnaround seemed slightly unfathomable. The profit numbers were suddenly, by the standards of the time and in a small country, so big. There was considerable pride in Scotland as newspaper profiles lauded the rebirth of an institution that had managed to combine exciting modernisation with authentic patriotism. The staid old Royal Bank, which only a decade before had appeared lost, was becoming what Mathewson had said it could become. Why couldn't a Scottish bank rise to be one of the best in the world? Where was it written that there must be a cap on ambition? The City of London, which Mathewson instinctively disliked, also loved what he was doing. The share price rose. Up, up and up it went. At the end of 1992 one share cost an investor 208p. Just four and a half years later in May 1997 it had trebled to more than 600p.

Steve Rick, who left the Royal Bank in 1996 as the Columbus Project came to an end, counts Mathewson as the best CEO he ever worked for. Rick went on to a successful career in the technology industry and still he regards what the Columbus team did as groundbreaking. At the time he did have a concern, however. As an Englishman living in Edinburgh in the mid-1990s he was slightly discomfited by the huge surge of patriotism in Scotland that greeted the release of Hollywood films such as *Braveheart* and *Rob Roy* in 1995. He discussed it with colleagues.

The new Royal Bank seemed to relish being the financial embodiment of a nation's assertiveness. Might the spirit of nationalistic pride that Mathewson loved to invoke eventually get out of hand? Says Rick now: 'I blame *Braveheart*, I really do. I think it had a lot to answer for when it came out. *Braveheart* gave those guys in the Scottish banks too much confidence.'

For all the plaudits, Mathewson, who was fifty-seven in 1997, wanted to find a potential successor to widen the bank's choices when he opted, eventually, to move upstairs to become chairman. The moment would soon come for Younger's retirement from public life. Chief executives in large publicly owned companies tend not to play the major role in choosing their successors, for good reasons. Ego may cause them to confuse their interests with those of the company and its owners, the shareholders. They might see it too much in dynastic terms and be keen to recruit someone who will continue with their agenda, giving their work imperishable meaning when otherwise their reputation might be mouldering in the corporate graveyard. Usually, in successful companies, a chairman and the board will take the lead on such a succession, deploying external recruitment specialists to help find a new chief executive.

Mathewson's position was highly unusual, and for the resurgent and increasingly international Royal Bank it was all new territory. This strong leader with unconventional methods, who was not a banker by profession, had saved the organisation and seemed to have an understanding of what was needed next. Mathewson himself cast around for options and wondered who would best grow the Royal Bank and protect its status as an independent institution. He needed someone Scottish, someone who would understand, or could learn, what he, Mathewson, had been trying to achieve with the Royal Bank. How about an ambitious young accountant turned chief executive at a rival Scottish bank? Mathewson's mind turned to hiring Fred Goodwin.

4

Paisley Pattern

'Disce puer aut abi' (Learn, boy, or get out)
Paisley Grammar School motto

Frederick Anderson Goodwin, always known as Freddie in his youth, was born in Paisley on 17 August 1958. The myth is that he was raised on a tough council estate and even though it has been repeated many times, first when he was riding high and then after the financial crisis when he was the singled out as the alleged 'world's worst banker', it is simply untrue. Goodwin always seemed content to let the false impression linger, however. Even at the height of his powers he professed to loathe the scrutiny involved in being interviewed for personality profiles. Although he was happy to talk about the rise of RBS, requests made to the Royal Bank press office for more intimate access were generally declined and he made it clear to subordinates that he was not interested in talking showily about school, family and his rapid rise. Revealing his 'back story' was of no interest: 'I hate that stuff.' The image he projected instead was the one that he had created for himself through his work, of someone who was self-made, competitive, professional and unsentimental. Anyway, letting his background in Paisley seem much earthier than it was certainly helped him sound tough.

The truth is that thanks to his ambitious parents Freddie had a comfortable middle-class upbringing. Fred Goodwin Snr was a product of Britain's post-war boom in social mobility, the son of a policeman, a draughtsman by trade who worked hard and became one of the bosses in a fast-growing local electrical engineering firm, James Kilpatrick.[1] It became Balfour Kilpatrick and part of Balfour Beatty. In the 1950s the firm offered the opportunity for travel and promotion as deals were signed for work in the Middle East and on the Indian subcontinent. Fred Snr travelled to Iraq and also supervised a project in what is now Bangladesh. Having helped manage such breakthroughs, he became the well-paid head of special projects. He met Mary (known as May) Mackintosh through work, a Paisley girl who worked in the office at Balfour Kilpatrick. Their colleagues were astonished when it was revealed that the bright, kindly and approachable May was romantically entangled with Fred. He was quiet, acerbic and buttoned up in his sports jacket and tie ('not a braw man', meaning handsome, as one of their colleagues puts it). In contrast, May was good company and widely liked. Certainly, Fred Snr does not seem to have been the easiest of men to work with. According to another member of staff: 'There is no way to explain it I'm afraid other than to say that Fred Goodwin was a bit of a bastard. He was a very cold man.'

Fred Snr and Mary were married in 1957 and did live initially in Paisley's Tannahill Terrace, which is in Craigilee on the edge of Ferguslie Park, then already one of Britain's most notorious housing estates synonymous with poverty, social breakdown and violence. But the residents of the little enclave in which the young married couple resided were at pains to point out that they were not actually in Ferguslie Park proper. Anyway, they did not stay long. By the time Freddie was a toddler they had purchased a plot of land in Lounsdale, a mile and half away near the local cricket club, where they had a bungalow built. Two more children followed: a sister Dale and a brother Andrew, both of whom still live in the Paisley area.

The Paisley in which the Goodwins then lived was still thriving. There were certainly large pockets of serious deprivation, but in the 1950s and 1960s it was also a prosperous, self-contained town with textile and engineering industries.[2] Its proud residents made great play of rejecting the common misconception that it was merely a suburb of its bigger neighbour, ten miles up the River Clyde. Glasgow was looked down on as 'gallus', or brash. Paisley residents felt they lived somewhere that was a distinct place in its own right, with a history that marked it out and an abbey dating back to the twelfth century. Thanks to the wealth creation of the Victorian era, in which textile mills were the powerhouses of the local economy, there was some decent architecture and a legacy of thriving civic institutions. Like similar towns in the industrial heartland of England it has since suffered from a hollowing out after the disappearance of most of its industry, with the middle-class section of its population living comfortably on the periphery, often commuting to jobs in Glasgow or Edinburgh as the centre of Paisley declines. In the 1950s it was flourishing.

School for Freddie was Paisley Grammar, a choice that indicated immediately that Fred and May had aspirations for their son. It involved a modest fee and was where the children of the professional classes tended to go, along with those whose parents wanted their offspring to climb the ladder. The school was partly selective and with its Latin motto *Disce puer aut abi* (Learn, boy, or get out) and school debating society, the culture was hard-working, academic and aspirational. The headmaster of the senior school when Freddie arrived was R.Y. Corbett, a strict disciplinarian who encouraged high expectations and was an admired figure in the town. As a pupil Goodwin was always in the 'top stream' or top class of the school, an academic achiever, although not in a stand-out way, who was socially unremarkable. 'He was bright, able and very diligent,' remembers a school classmate. 'Freddie was inherently a very conventional person who would never, ever express a controversial opinion on anything.' As a teenager Goodwin played golf, at the course at Ralston in Paisley, had a girlfriend, played rugby for the school (not in the first XV) and was obsessed by cars.

Family life was more explosive. Fred's highly competitive father is described by one acquaintance as 'a complete bampot', a Scottish phrase denoting a tendency to wild behaviour. Says another: 'He was a very difficult man who was forever getting into arguments with people and starting fights over things. Fred's father was an absolute tyrant.' When his son was bullied at school, his father went to locate the bully and held him down while Fred filled in his tormentor with his fists.[3]

By the early 1970s, with Freddie in his teens, Fred Snr was making more money, and the family was on the up again, moving to a large bungalow in Southfield Avenue in the salubrious Potterhill area of Paisley. The house was gutted and refitted – with the help of workmen from Balfour Kilpatrick – before the family moved in. In contrast to her pugilistic husband, Fred's mother, who still lives in Paisley, is regarded as someone public-spirited and decent who has had to cope with her eldest son's transformation from Businessman of the Year to pariah of the decade. She is described by those who knew the family as the steadying force when her bright, but introverted, son was growing up. After the death of Fred Snr in 1992 she remarried, to someone much calmer: an accountant.

It was expected that the brightest from Paisley Grammar would go to Glasgow University, which Freddie did at the end of the fifth year in 1975. Says a classmate: 'The question was not what will you study at university, it was what will you do at Glasgow? Only occasionally would someone do something exotic such as go to Edinburgh University.' Freddie chose law, although contemporaries say he had no obvious desire to be a lawyer. It just seemed like a sensible choice for an undergraduate uncertain on the career front. By the standards of the time there was something notable that Freddie had achieved. He had acquired a car, bought, it was assumed by friends, with parental assistance and the proceeds of a summer job. His gold-coloured Rover 2000 made him the daily designated driver for a small group of friends who had been at the grammar and were now at Glasgow University. Showing an early and keen interest in finance, at the end of each week he made a point of asking for petrol money from those who had accepted a lift.

The Smart brothers – Ian and Alan – were among those who were regularly in the car. They liked Goodwin, although they were interested in radical left-wing politics, the revolutionary Marxist struggle and Scottish devolution. This was, Fred explained self-deprecatingly, all too complicated and confusing for someone like him when discussions on such subjects got under way. He was an anti-devolution unionist Tory and when there were arguments on the journey to university about which radio station should be played, somewhere it might be possible to hear the sounds of the emerging punk movement or a more conservative station playing the songs of middle-of-the-road bands such as the Eagles, Freddie argued for the Eagles. At Glasgow, says another contemporary, it would have been impossible to pick him out as a future high-flyer and banker: 'Out of our law class of 100 we would never have chosen him as the man most likely to.' He was obsessively competitive in the Glasgow University Union – the men's union as the two were still segregated – but not in the field of debating, politics or sport. Hours were spent between lectures playing the pinball machines in the basement. He could drink too, when the opportunity arose. He was developing a decent capacity for it.

Goodwin had decided that he did not want to become a lawyer, he told Ian Smart. He wanted to be an accountant, which by the standards of his surroundings and upbringing counted as an unconventional choice. He finished the three-year basic law degree, joined Touche Ross in Glasgow as a trainee and dropped the 'die' from his name, becoming Fred. Accountancy suited Goodwin. It was something he was instantly good at, says a colleague; he had found his calling. Not only did he seem to find understanding the numbers very easy, his brain worked methodically, quickly and logically. He could spot patterns and problems in spreadsheets and balance sheets, and he could think creatively about business opportunities. For some time accountancy had been growing steadily more sophisticated, as the big firms moved beyond straightforward auditing of a client's books so they complied with company law. Now they were also advisers and consultants aiding companies, and banks, who wanted to do a deal, or needed help with the financial engineering involved in expansion.

In school and at university Fred had been anonymous and barely worthy of note. Here he was a star performer. After qualifying as a Scottish chartered accountant in 1983, he worked between 1985 and 1987 as part of the team at Touche Ross sent in by the government to Rosyth Dockyard, near Gordon Brown's constituency in Fife. He managed the contract awarded for the running of the yard. Coming into the orbit of the accountant John Connolly was also a lucky break. The sharp-elbowed partner would go on to run Deloitte, the firm with which Touche Ross later merged. Connolly took a relentlessly meritocratic view of promotion and was prepared to elevate the young if they were deemed talented enough. His second wife, Odile Griffith, had been the first female partner in the firm's history. Goodwin became the youngest partner, shortly after he turned thirty.

He got married too, in 1990, to Joyce McLean and settled down in Quarrier's Village, near Kilmacolm, in the countryside to the west of Glasgow. Her career in finance had involved time at Citibank and the French bank Compagnie Bancaire, which became part of BNP Paribas. She also did an MBA at Strathclyde University. When they were dating Joyce was furious to discover that the firm she worked for was on the same piece of business as Touche Ross. When she found out that Goodwin had not told her about this potential conflict of interest he got the 'sharp-end of her tongue'. Fred was drawn to a strong woman who was prepared to speak back, robustly, to him.

Goodwin had toughened up, a lot, and found an outlet for his competitive streak. At Touche Ross the hours were long and a steely gift for office politics was required. It all seemed to unleash in him, says a contemporary, a drive that had been pent up. The unremarkable Paisley boy was becoming a hard-driving executive trained to spot and prosecute weakness. Accountancy also gave him experience of the aftermath of a banking collapse. When the Bank of Credit and Commerce International (BCCI) went out of business in 1991, Deloitte and Touche was appointed to unscramble the mess on behalf of creditors. Goodwin was put in charge of the effort, leading various teams across the Middle East, Europe and America who were trying to find out where the money had gone. Goodwin was prospering and increasingly ambitious but, says a colleague, he was in a crowded field. A career change might mean the opportunity for more rapid elevation than staying in a large firm. How would he like to run a bank?

The Clydesdale Bank had been established in Glasgow in the late 1830s.[4] A smaller rival to the two much grander Edinburgh-based rivals, the Royal Bank and the Bank of Scotland, it had nonetheless prospered, expanding into the north of England in the nineteenth century before being sold to an English institution, the Midland Bank, in 1919. Then – after the Midland got into difficulties – it was sold to the National Australia Bank in 1987. The new owner of the Clydesdale flew in Australian executives to inspect their purchase and found a nice, gentle, largely harmonious operation that was somewhat lacking in dynamism. 'We were collegiate and good with customers but it was a bit sleepy and it needed updating,' says a member of the management team. The environment was not remotely cut-throat. Richard Cole-Hamilton, the chief executive since 1982, came straight from Scottish Establishment central casting.[5] After Loretto (one of Scotland's top public schools), Cambridge and National Service with the Argyll and Sutherland Highlanders he had joined the Clydesdale. When he stood aside there was a search lasting a year. In late 1993 the board chose a well-respected and relatively young Scottish banker, Charles Love. Only a year into the job, aged just forty-eight, Love died of a heart attack on a family skiing holiday in Méribel, France.

But for this accident, Fred Goodwin might never have joined the Clydesdale. The sudden death of Love meant that the Australians needed an interim replacement. Frank Cicutto, an Italian-immigrant Australian, was flown in to Glasgow, although what they really wanted was someone else to complete what they had hired Love to do, meaning modernise the bank and inject some urgency into its dealings. The Australians liked the look of Fred Goodwin. They had had plenty of opportunity to observe the ambitious young Scotsman as he had helped do the due diligence on the Clydesdale when NAB was buying it. His untangling of BCCI had also been judged highly impressive. Don Argus, the chief executive of NAB, was a fan and Fred joined the Clydesdale in 1995.

Obviously Goodwin was an accountant not a banker by training, an oversight which was later to have important consequences for RBS and the British economy. The work of bankers and accountants overlaps to such an extent in a modern economy that it is often forgotten that originally they were envisaged as distinct types of work requiring contrasting worldviews. A veteran banker describes it this way: 'An accountant exists to examine the numbers, take measurements, assess the situation and then put his or her signature to a piece of paper declaring that on a particular date everything claimed to be there is there. A good banker knows that ultimately what he or she does rests on a benign white lie. The customer lends the bank money in the form of a deposit and the bank then lends that out multiple times. That is the basis of banking. It is a construct built on trust. It all rests on creating sufficient confidence in order that everyone does not get worried enough to ask for their money back at the same moment. Because if they do the bank is probably sunk. Accountants and bankers should be different.'

To National Australia Bank in the mid-1990s Goodwin's lack of experience was not deemed a problem. Perhaps banks such as the Clydesdale needed to become more like the big accountancy firms. The partnership culture of Touche Ross and similar firms was certainly very different from a then sleepy small bank. A bright graduate joined one of the large accountants, worked incredibly long hours scrutinising numbers, wrote documents for the partners in charge and often took so-called 'dog's abuse' in the process. They would either leave after a few exhausting years equipped for a role in a business, as say a finance director, or stay and rise to be a very well-paid partner putting the next generation of youngsters through their paces. It was competitive, ruthless and stressful. This had suited Goodwin, because he excelled at manipulating situations to his advantage and was not squeamish about being extremely robust with those who worked for him.

What attracted the Australians to Goodwin was his ferociously logical approach to problem solving and the capacity to learn quickly which he had demonstrated at Touche Ross. A spell as deputy chief executive of the Clydesdale was deemed suitable preparation. That way he could familiarise himself with the banking business before he eventually assumed full control within a year or so. Cicutto[6] was very much a backroom banker, lacking sufficient flair for running an organisation and finding it a struggle to communicate. Says a Clydesdale banker: 'Fred made clear he had no time for Cicutto as chief executive. He was putting down a marker that soon things would be done his way.'

Goodwin's colleagues on the management team in Glasgow were fascinated by the newly arrived prodigy. 'He was clearly hugely ambitious but it was not obvious to what end and I don't think he burned to be a bank chief executive. We used to ask Fred about him going into politics and running the country but he just laughed it off,' says one. Another Clydesdale banker said he was refreshing: 'My first impression when he arrived was of great intelligence. Here was someone incredibly quick and decisive. If you gave him a problem he could go through A to Z and come up with a solution quicker than anyone. Nine out of ten times he was right.' Meanwhile, the new arrival was trying to adjust to being in banking, a profession superficially similar to accountancy but in those days very much a different world requiring other skills. At his first office Christmas night out, held at the Amber Regent Chinese restaurant in Glasgow, he confided to colleagues that the Clydesdale was most unlike the business he had been trained in. At Touche Ross, he said, people were here today and then gone in an instant if they didn't shape up. In a bank, many people joined from school and stayed for their entire careers.

There was no doubt that the Clydesdale needed to modernise. Younger executives agreed that it had to sharpen up, to make bigger profits and improve its market share. Maybe Goodwin was just the man. Perhaps it would be exciting and invigorating when he took over. Says one Clydesdale banker who had had high hopes at the prospect of Goodwin's promotion: 'Isn't that the thing about sociopaths? That at first they

convince you and you go along with them. And then oomph ...
they've got you.'

Executives noticed an immediate chilling in the atmosphere
when Goodwin was elevated and Cicutto – who later went on to
run NAB in its entirety – left for another post. The 8.30 a.m.
Monday morning 'week ahead' meeting, billed as a 'chit-chat'
over coffee, became an occasion to be dreaded, as Goodwin set
about briskly enforcing discipline. Says a regular attendee: 'If
you were slightly late or something hadn't worked quite the
way intended he would berate you in the most humiliating way.
Not by shouting, you would be pilloried.' Deemed even worse
was the Tuesday morning 8.30 a.m. meeting, in which a dozen
or so senior executives had to report on the major projects they
were responsible for. Goodwin dealt with his team alphabetic-
ally, although he did once spring a surprise and start at the other
end and work back. 'This came as a shock to Graeme Willis who
for once got the most terrible kicking, which cheered us all
up,' says a regular attendee. Willis, the chief operating officer at
the Clydesdale, later surfaced as head of Group Enterprise Risk
at the Royal Bank of Scotland between 2006 and 2009, the critical years encompassing the financial crisis. Getting a shredding
from Fred was not always an obstacle to being employed by
him in the future.

It was only when it came to the production of the first annual
strategy paper for NAB that his management team witnessed
the full force of Goodwin's personality and grasped the nature
of his talent for organisation. The management in Australia
demanded a yearly plan from each of its divisions, explaining
how they would grow or improve their part of the business.
Goodwin initially refused, deeming the exercise a formulaic
waste of time and resources and failing to spot that his bosses
were serious. The head of NAB in the UK flew to Glasgow to tell
Goodwin that the delivery of such a plan was non-negotiable.
With only a week until the deadline, Goodwin snapped into

life, setting up camp in the executive meeting room and holding an almost continuous rolling series of meetings in which senior executives and managers below them were tasked with coming up with ideas for how to overhaul or improve the Clydesdale. They were then sent away to get better answers. Goodwin was using his accountancy partnership training; he was drilling colleagues, interrogating their numbers, ideas and assumptions and terrifying the weaker members of the team from 7.30 a.m. until 2 a.m. the following morning. Clydesdale executives who had been used to civilised hours were suddenly working into the early hours in a bid to satisfy his demands. The shell-shocked bankers later suspected it had all been deliberate, that Goodwin had left it as late as possible to test his team in adversity and expose those who couldn't cope with the stress. In this way he had established total authority over his team. By the Friday at 4 p.m., when the finished paper had to be sent by fax to headquarters in Australia, there was no doubt who the chief executive of the Clydesdale was.

As if to emphasise his strength, Goodwin made a warlike addition to the Executive Committee room. The film *Braveheart* was then popular in Scotland.[7] In it Mel Gibson plays William Wallace, cries 'Freedom' and fights the English in a romanticised epic that takes considerable liberties with the history of the late thirteenth and early fourteenth centuries. On the wall, behind the chair in which Goodwin sat when he was hosting meetings with his team, he hung a replica 'long-sword' similar to the one William Wallace wielded to such brutal effect in the film. 'It looked very impressive,' says a witness. 'You really couldn't fail to make the connection.'

His staff noticed that his extraordinary attention to detail manifested itself in unusual ways. Goodwin seemed to have very little interest in the traditional components of a bank chief executive's activities. Questions of credit and risk, the basics which govern how much is lent and to whom, seemed to hold little appeal. He was much more fixated on subjects such as the cleanliness of branches. A mass tidy-up was ordered across the Clydesdale and Goodwin took to mounting patrols, springing surprise inspections on unsuspecting staff. The alleged scruffiness of the branches became a particularly vexed question. Goodwin complained that there was too much paper lying about piled up in front of customers or in the strongrooms at the back, where old ledgers were stored. He had a particular hatred of any public use of Sellotape. If it was used to put up a notice in a branch, and he spotted it, a sharp rebuke followed. In the middle of a meeting with one executive, Goodwin took a call. It was May, his mother, on the phone. She had been walking past the Clydesdale head office in St Vincent Street, Glasgow, where Fred was based. She had noticed that on the steps outside someone had dropped a cigarette butt. Goodwin thanked his mother and immediately phoned another senior executive, ordering him to have the offending piece of litter removed from the premises immediately.

Although these concerns, such as cleanliness, were legitimate, his colleagues thought they were taking up an inordinate amount of his attention. On 17 July 1997 the divisional and district managers were even ordered to appear in front of Goodwin to report on what they had done to further the aims of the great clean-up. Some appeared to be terrified, while others struggled to keep a straight face. Goodwin was once even apprehended by the police when pursuing his cleanliness campaign. On a Sunday morning he drove to his local branch in Bridge of Weir and was taking photographs of the exterior ('He thought the area around the cash machine looked messy,' says a colleague) when a passing police officer spotted him. His assurances that he was the chief executive of the Clydesdale were given short shrift and he was taken by car to the police station, where his story was checked out and he was allowed to go.

The Clydesdale Bank tie was another obsession. Goodwin

always wore his to work, regarding it as a badge of corporate pride. He thought that his colleagues should do the same, although he stopped short of making the wearing of it and a white shirt mandatory. Some executives thought the bank tie looked cheap and avoided putting it on whenever possible. One manager who was summoned for a dressing down over mistakes made by a subordinate in handling an account arrived minus the Clydesdale neckwear, sporting a tie of his own. As he got to security at head office he discovered that his pass no longer worked. This, the receptionist told him, was because Goodwin's secretary wanted to know the instant he was in the building so that Fred could be alerted. Understandably unnerved by this, he made his way to Goodwin's recently extended office. It seemed vast, the size of a cricket pitch, and on a much larger scale than the previous chief executive's office. The manager sat down and Goodwin entered the room from behind. 'I tried making some small talk but he didn't want to know. He didn't sit down, he stood gripping the back of his chair. I tried to apologise and say that it had all been sorted out as soon as I had found out and that he, Fred, wouldn't hear anything more about it. I was travelling to meet the customer and to apologise in person for what had gone wrong. I was sorry and it would all be fine. At this he became furious, banging his fist on the table and saying: "It is not fine!" I decided to shut up and take it. It was horrible.' As the manager subsequently made for the door and safety, Goodwin noticed that his visitor was not wearing the Clydesdale neckwear: '"Where's the tie today? Tie at the dry-cleaners?" I said, "Absolutely Fred, my bank tie is at the dry-cleaners." What I was thinking was, "Oh please fuck off."'

His colleagues from that time, even those who are critical or still baffled and fascinated by his foibles, recognise that there was much to admire in his approach. The Clydesdale seemed to be a better-run and more efficient business. Goodwin grasped that the old way in which the branches had excessive autonomy was not sustainable, although perhaps too much centralisation then followed. There was also too little access to up-to-date information technology, or even decent word processing, something he set about changing by forcing the IT team which catered for the Clydesdale and its sister bank, the Yorkshire, to take his demands seriously. 'There is no doubt that change was needed,' says a colleague, 'although the way Fred did a lot of it was so unnecessary. Rather than taking people with him he too often terrorised them. I seriously don't think I ever saw him be compassionate in that period. I don't think that compassion is in his make-up.' Says another member of the then management team at the Clydesdale: 'He manufactured fear.'

Someone unexpected who was on the receiving end of a dressing down was a very close friend from Glasgow University days. In 1990 when Goodwin had married Joyce, David Thorburn had been best man. Thorburn had joined the Clydesdale in 1978 and by the time of Goodwin's elevation he had risen to be a district manager at the Clydesdale, responsible for the north-east of Scotland. This led to some awkwardness, with their colleagues knowing of their friendship and imagining at first that it might have protected Thorburn from a shredding. Not a bit of it. At one of the bank's management 'away day' gatherings, Goodwin asked Thorburn, in front of fellow executives, why he had moved a statue in one of the Aberdeen branches and not told him. Goodwin was not satisfied with the explanation. 'Fred gave David a kicking. He went absolutely mental,' says a friend. The mild-mannered and well-adjusted Thorburn would later become the Clydesdale bank's chief executive, although his colleagues said that quite understandably his friendship with Goodwin suffered.

The annual 'away days' organised by Goodwin and held at Gleneagles Hotel in 1996, and Turnberry Hotel in 1997 and 1998, were generally not occasions to be looked forward to. The idea, then very much in vogue, was that the top 150 or so people in the bank would get away from the pressures of the office and 'strategise' for a couple of days in the comfort of a five-star Scottish hotel. Having set it up, Goodwin seemed uncomfortable with discussion, which some of his colleagues thought he seemed to confuse with dissent. At Gleneagles an after-dinner speaker had been booked, to lighten the end of a long day with some gentle jokes. One of those present remembers a decent speech being greeted with little laughter. 'The atmosphere was so awful that hardly anybody laughed because we were so depressed.' Only Sheena McDonald, the tough-minded Scottish broadcaster and former news anchor at Channel 4 who was booked to chair and facilitate proceedings, seemed able to constrain Goodwin in the discussion sessions, where Goodwin was on stage and executives made contributions from the floor. 'She was a strong woman who wouldn't take any nonsense from Fred. He thought she was wonderful and she tried to let other people have their say.'

And then in the bar afterwards Goodwin would be transformed into good company who could comfortably drink others 'under the table'. He was witty, almost urbane at points, with a dry sense of humour. An executive who that day had been clinically 'machine-gunned' by Goodwin in one of the sessions was astonished to be accosted by a cheery chief executive who insisted on buying him a drink as if nothing had happened. It was, his colleagues whispered, as though he had an on/off switch by which he could move at will, quite suddenly, from cold tyrant to jovial late-night companion.

Back in head office in Glasgow, the atmosphere was getting steadily more oppressive. Goodwin's various trips around the country, involving 'roadshows' designed to allow him to explain to staff the latest developments in the bank, meant that he sometimes returned with the names of middle managers who had asked awkward questions. When their names came up at one of the executive meetings, he would declare, with a wave of the hand: 'Oh, he is toast.' It was noticed, however, that as much as Goodwin liked talking about people being fired he didn't like sacking them face to face. He preferred others, such as the human resources manager Neil Roden to quietly arrange an 'exit'. The nickname 'Fred the Shred' comes from this period, despite claims it was invented later. Clydesdale executives remember it being used at the time, after it was coined by a branch manager who got on the wrong end of Goodwin: 'Fred used to say it was just because Fred didn't rhyme with nice. But he liked it really.'

At the Clydesdale, some of his colleagues called him names much less polite than Fred the Shred, particularly when they got the most dreaded call on a Friday afternoon. Each week Goodwin's secretary would ring and ask various frazzled members of the management team if they would like to join the chief executive to wrap up the week with a beer in his office. Some of those invited worked out that the trick was to try to distract the boss, by switching the subject to vintage cars or sport and keeping it there. Sometimes that wouldn't work and Goodwin would instead start methodically cross-examining one of those present on what progress they had made on a particular item that had come up at the morning meetings. This was not regarded as the ideal way to finish a busy day when the weekend beckoned. 'After several hours off Fred would go, quite happy, to be driven home by his chauffeur while we went to get the train home to explain to our wives why we were late.' Perhaps it was Goodwin trying to be friendly. Some thought it a deliberate tactic, to ensure that executives were reminded that another round of morning meetings was less than seventy-two hours away and they should spend the weekend thinking about where they might be vulnerable.

Outside the Clydesdale, others were starting to notice the rising star of Scottish banking. The energetic Goodwin had attracted the attention of George Mathewson at the Royal Bank of Scotland. When the assorted chief executives of Scotland's banks gathered for lunch several times a year, Mathewson was much taken with Goodwin's directness, youthful ambition and obvious analytical skills. On the fringes of those meetings, in 1997, the pair got talking and liked each other. At a subsequent party held at the National Gallery of Scotland, Mathewson broached the possibility of Goodwin moving to the Royal Bank: 'I need a finance director, why not come and join us?' said Mathewson.

Goodwin wasn't sure, he responded. At the Clydesdale he had a good deal of autonomy, pretty much running his own show with his ultimate bosses 11,000 miles away. For their part the Australians were keen for him to move his family to the other side of the world, so he could be in the running for the top post at NAB. Negotiations with Mathewson stalled while Goodwin embarked on a six-month secondment to Australia. It was a chance to tour the business and decide whether or not he would be able to make the move permanently. But he found that Australia simply wasn't for him and close up NAB was even more dysfunctional than it appeared from Glasgow. On his return he told Mathewson he missed Scotland, evidence of strong patriotism that appealed to the nationalistic Royal Bank CEO. Perhaps, Goodwin agreed, Edinburgh and the Royal Bank might be the better move.[8]

Mathewson had effectively been in charge for more than seven years, which amounted to a long and successful spell even by corporate standards of the time. Even though this period had involved remarkable changes – the Project Columbus overhaul and steeply rising profits – eventually there would come a moment when a new chief executive would be required. Rather than waiting for others to suggest it, such as large investors or commentators in London's financial press that Mathewson had little time for, he would get ahead of the game and choose his own successor. This should be someone young and energetic who shared his vision of growth and turning the Royal Bank into the world's best financial institution; someone who was committed to the bank remaining Scottish in line with its proud history stretching back to 1727; someone who wouldn't dream of moving the headquarters to England; maybe someone like Fred Goodwin.

Mathewson had initially wanted Goodwin to be the leading contender in a small pool of rivals. Also hoping to be considered for promotion was Johnny Cameron, whose Jacobite ancestor Cameron of Lochiel had provided the guard for the directors of the Royal Bank when they went to Edinburgh Castle to collect money on behalf of Bonnie Prince Charlie. Cameron had just agreed to join the Royal Bank to run the Corporate Institutional Bank and had been given the impression by Mathewson that he was in with a shout for the top job, eventually. There was the young outsider Benny Higgins who had recently joined the bank with a view to running its retail operations. He might be a longer-term prospect.

Goodwin had no desire to be part of a succession race. He stipulated that he would only join the Royal Bank on the clear understanding that he was the heir apparent. He would come if he were deputy chief executive not just finance director. Mathewson, wowed by Goodwin, agreed. The pair would work as a duo. He could not absolutely guarantee the post of chief executive, although if they enjoyed success together in the next few years, it was as close to being a certainty as these things can be. 'Fred played George like a fiddle,' says a colleague. 'He negotiated brilliantly.' That summer of 1998, early one morning, Goodwin rang the press office at St Andrew Square. He wanted to make doubly certain that the press release announcing his appointment made it plain that he was deputy chief executive, and not simply finance director. 'Fred was determined that everyone should know. He wanted it to be clear to all of us when he arrived that he was the coming man.' He was also determined to get a good deal on his pension arrangements, insisting on being able to bring with him the funds he had built up at Touche Ross and the Clydesdale, but being treated as though he had been in the Royal Bank scheme from the start of his career. 'George said "Oh that'll be fine",' says one of those involved in sorting it out later.

In the Royal Bank, news of the impending arrival was a shock to many of Mathewson's top staff. Several telephoned friends and counterparts at the Clydesdale to ask what they might expect. Neil Roden, the HR director who had been at the Clydesdale and had moved to the Royal Bank, in part it was said by colleagues to get away from Goodwin, was pressed for information. Another member of the executive team phoned a Clydesdale senior manager and got a worrying response: 'Fred is the brightest guy you will ever meet and he is also a total bastard.' One high-flyer at the Royal Bank volunteered the view to a friend at the Clydesdale that Goodwin would find it much more difficult at St Andrew Square, where there was considerable competition and a string of worldly potential rivals who would 'take care of Fred': 'I wouldn't be sure of that,' his friend who had been working for Goodwin countered. 'I don't think you've ever met anyone like Fred.' At the Clydesdale Bank in August, when Goodwin departed, there was jubilation. Says one senior banker: 'Oh, when he left we partied for about three weeks.'

5

Battle of the Banks

*'What we're saying is, "Thank you very much, but
bye-bye."'*

Sir David Rowland, chairman of NatWest,
November 1999

In August 1998, when Fred Goodwin arrived at St Andrew Square, the inner sanctum of the Royal Bank still ran much as it had for decades. Although Mathewson had radically reordered the bank's various divisions, the revolution had not yet reached the executive toilets inside the Georgian building. In the washroom designated for the top management there were still individual pegs, with name-tags, on which hung each executive's towel. If the tags and towels were moved at any point, it indicated elevation or a shift in the balance of power. Of course such facilities were for men only, while secretaries to executives had to trek down a floor to their own toilets. It was never quite clear what that rarest of breeds – a visiting female senior executive (and there were still very few) – should do.

For the most exalted executives there was also still 'the

mess' – a wood-panelled dining room – where the leading members of staff were expected to lunch together. New arrivals learned quickly that they should only get up from the long table, laid out immaculately and decorated each day with fresh flowers, once the chairman, the charming Lord Younger of Leckie, had finished his lunch and was ready to leave. The gatherings were male and collegiate. There tended to be one polite conversation at lunch, which offered those present a chance to gossip about business, finance and rivals the Bank of Scotland, the favourite topic of all. In keeping with the Royal Bank's Presbyterian history, the group at lunch was overwhelmingly Protestant.

Despite his fearsome reputation and new nickname of Fred the Shred, the forty-year-old Goodwin slipped in quietly, somewhat baffling his new group of colleagues. One intrigued rival found him monk-like and distant. Others regarded this tall bespectacled figure, bookish in appearance, as puzzlingly quiet for someone who had risen so fast, although he had a dry wit if prodded. At the management morning meetings, when he did have to intervene he was sharp and capable of making his points in a crisp manner. Says a subsequent critic: 'You very rapidly got the impression that Fred was the smartest guy in the room.'

Initially, for much of his first year, it was unclear exactly what he did with his time each day. He was supposed to be the finance director, as well as deputy chief executive, although he did not seem to do much directing of anything. As it had been early on at the Clydesdale, Goodwin seemed to be waiting for the top post to become available. Mathewson was delighted, though; he had found his successor. The two contrasting types, Mathewson restless and mercurial, and Goodwin disciplined, endlessly logical and somewhat shy, were forming a strong bond. The question was what this partnership might produce together before Goodwin took full control.

In Edinburgh it was a period of excitement and seemingly limitless opportunity. The staid old Scottish capital was suddenly resurgent, with the banks embodying a new confidence, or over-confidence. Inevitably, as both the Royal Bank and the Bank started to make bigger profits it was also good for Edinburgh's lawyers and the other firms that fed off their growth. Property prices began a steep upward climb. The rises in Edinburgh out-stripped anywhere else in Scotland and in terms of the rate of increase the Scottish capital was even competing with London.[1] Goodwin moved his family from the West of Scotland and bought a six-bedroom house in the Grange in Edinburgh. The Georgian houses and vast high-ceilinged flats of the New Town, along with the villas in the most expensive suburbs, were increasingly desirable for the most senior bankers who were beginning to be much better paid. For senior executives such as retail banker Benny Higgins, group secretary Miller McLean, communications chief Howard Moody and the others the success of the Royal Bank equalled personal good fortune: 'These guys were suddenly being paid hundreds of thousands of pounds with the prospect of a lot more. In a place like Edinburgh it meant they had more money than they knew what to do with,' says an executive. Junior members of staff also started to see their bonuses and share options boom.

New restaurants opened and upmarket shopping improved, reflecting Edinburgh's reinvention. In this period Harvey Nichols, the epitome of the era's *Absolutely Fabulous* approach to fashion, chose the city as the location for its second store in the UK outside London. It opened next door to the Royal Bank's headquarters on St Andrew Square.[2] It felt as though Edinburgh, already one of the most agreeable places to live in Britain, might be on the cusp of another exciting golden age, underwritten by its banks. This wasn't quite a second Enlightenment, but the city did seem poised to benefit from a boom based on financial services, shopping and rocketing house prices.

The new confidence could also be attributed in part to dramatic political changes in the same period, changes in which Edinburgh took the lead. Scotland in the late 1990s was experiencing a constitutional upheaval bigger than anything since the Union with England of 1707 and the era of the Earl of Ilay, the Royal Bank's founder. After a campaign by politicians and activists, the Scottish Parliament that had disappeared with the Act of Union was revived. If the Scots did not then want to be fully independent, they did desire the halfway house of devolution, often called home rule. Opponents were swept aside. On 1 July 1999 the Queen opened the new Scottish Parliament in Edinburgh in its temporary home, a building on loan from the Church of Scotland, the austere General Assembly building on the Mound diagonally opposite the headquarters of the Bank of Scotland.

The Scottish nationalist Mathewson was initially invigorated by devolution and pleased by Edinburgh's reawakening. Already though, his mind was elsewhere. For all the Royal Bank's growing profits and new assertiveness, he was worried that this success would encourage complacency. If Scotland wanted to have strong banks for more than a few years, the Royal Bank needed another dramatic increase in scale and profitability. There was a realisation that what had been achieved with Project Columbus might not be sufficient to ensure survival. 'If we don't do something else, we are going to be taken over,' he told his executives, echoing what he had said to Sir Michael Herries almost a decade before when he and Younger prepared their initial 'night of the long knives'.

Institutions which chose to remain small risked being vulnerable to a bid from rivals or foreigners. Even the Halifax – yes, the Halifax, a former building society from England – had toyed in October 1998 with buying a stake in the Royal Bank as a prelude to a potential takeover.[3] Mathewson warned his team that to maintain itself as a proud Scottish bank, headquartered in

Edinburgh, where many of its senior executives lived, they needed to be ready to get bigger and better. How it would be done exactly, the chief executive didn't yet know. In spite of Mathewson's patriotic vision and his desire to create a legacy, he remained at root restless about how he would make the Royal Bank 'the best in the world', as he repeatedly intoned. Says one of his management team: 'George didn't believe it was his job to lay out a precise vision of the future, because you don't know what it will look like. He believed it was best to be fighting fit, able and opportunistic, ready to take on whatever the future might throw up.'

Before the arrival of Goodwin, Mathewson had tried a spot of expansion and been rebuffed twice. In the summer of 1997 the Royal Bank had made a bid for the Birmingham and Midshires building society. Mathewson's team offered £630m and the deal was all set to proceed when in March 1998 the Halifax appeared with a rival offer of £780m.[4] Mathewson also flirted with the thought of a bid for the much bigger Barclays, although he backed off. When news of his overtures emerged there was opposition in the City to the idea of a tiny Scottish bank taking over a big English bank. He was frustrated, although he felt the time and effort had not been wasted. The next time an opportunity emerged his team would be ready.

This time what the future threw up was NatWest, a struggling bank two and a half times the size of the Royal Bank. England's NatWest had for some time been a troubled institution. More than a decade earlier the chairman and three directors had resigned following the notorious Blue Arrow affair. The company's investment banking arm, County NatWest, was accused of deceiving the Bank of England over an £837m share offering. In 1997 the bank was hit by scandal again when it was left with a £90m trading black hole in its dealing operations. NatWest was fined £320,000 and there were resignations. Profits were disappointing for a bank of its size; its share price lagged; costs were higher than those of its rivals; the management seemed unsure what to do next and City analysts speculated about a possible takeover. Still, the thought of it actually being bought by one of the two relatively small Scottish banks seemed a remote and bizarre notion. By the standards of the day NatWest was huge. It had assets of £186bn, 64,400 staff and 1730 branches. Those profits, deemed disappointing by shareholders, still amounted to £2.1bn before tax in 1998. The Royal Bank was a minnow in comparison, with assets of only £75bn, 22,000 staff and 650 branches. Profits had only recently broken the £1bn barrier. The Bank of Scotland was even smaller, with £60bn in assets, 21,000 staff and just 325 branches, although its profits of £1bn were the equal of the Royal Bank's. Mathewson's team whispered that this was because the Bank of Scotland's procedures were too lax and its property lending, even then, seemed a little racy.

The centuries-long rivalry between the Royal Bank in St Andrew Square and the Bank of Scotland on Edinburgh's Mound – still intense, with the two managers of the banks tending to measure their institutions against each other rather than against the achievements of outsiders – was about to be resolved. It was extraordinary then that Mathewson and his opposite number at the Bank of Scotland, the golf-obsessed Peter Burt, should begin secret talks in the summer of 1999 on a possible joint bid for NatWest. This was the Scottish business equivalent of Rangers and Celtic, Glasgow's bitter footballing rivals, combining to plot a joint venture. Burt and Mathewson felt that a battle for control of NatWest could be messy and destructive, when their organisations might more usefully unite against a common enemy, the English banks. He told Burt: 'If you bid, we'll have to bid.' Couldn't they devise a way of instead jointly capturing NatWest in a cross-border raid and somehow dividing the spoils?

Mathewson's recently arrived deputy, Fred Goodwin, much

preferred the idea of the Royal Bank doing it alone. He was opposed to a joint bid for NatWest, he told Matthew Greenburgh, when the Merrill Lynch investment banker went to visit him in his office in the summer of 1999. Greenburgh was in the process of becoming one of the most influential and best-paid dealmakers of his generation in London. Shortly after Goodwin joined the Royal Bank, Greenburgh had telephoned the new arrival and suggested a meeting. They hit it off immediately. That initial call was to prove a smart investment by Greenburgh, who became a key figure in the Goodwin coterie. Small, tenacious and ultra-competitive, he had a confident manner that did not appeal to Mathewson, who disliked investment bankers on principle. In contrast, Goodwin liked Greenburgh and valued his counsel.

If the Royal Bank was going to do a deal it would need help. When high street banks, or large companies, are trying to buy a rival, or when they are taking a significant step such as raising money, they appoint one or more investment banks to advise. Teams of investment bankers such as Greenburgh then descend to crunch numbers and help dream up ways of making the deal work, all in return for large fees. The potential flaw in this set-up is that investment bankers have only one interest: pushing a deal through to earn themselves millions. Merrill Lynch's Greenburgh was involved in all of the major deals the Royal Bank did subsequently. Much later, in 2007, Merrill Lynch helped Goodwin design the disastrous bid for ABN Amro on the eve of the financial crisis. That year Greenburgh pocketed a £10m bonus. When the British banks went down in the financial crisis of October 2008, Greenburgh was drafted in by Lloyds/HBOS to help to advise it on the terms of the £17bn bailout it needed from the taxpayer.

In August 1999, no one was thinking about systemic collapse. At the Royal Bank the increasingly urgent question was what it would do about the possibility of NatWest that autumn. Mathewson felt affection for Burt and didn't want a falling-out, so the talks continued for a time. Against the backdrop of that year's Edinburgh Festival, Burt and his senior colleagues had a meeting with Mathewson. However, the discussions got nowhere. A joint deal seemed excessively complicated and the potential for infighting and resentment on both sides was too great. The talks foundered. If there was going to be a race for NatWest, there would have to be only one winner.

NatWest then made a big mistake. To show that it had a plan for growth, and to make itself too large to take over, the management attempted to buy the insurance and unit trust company Legal & General for £10bn. Investors and the City establishment hated the idea. Within a fortnight NatWest shares were down by a quarter and its bid stood no chance of being successful. It was directionless and suddenly very vulnerable.

Burt at the Bank of Scotland spotted his chance and struck first, in a dawn raid. His timing was designed to create maximum surprise, as most bank chief executives and chairmen were getting ready to travel that weekend to Washington ahead of that year's IMF and World Bank meetings, which are customarily attended by the world's top financiers. Before the markets opened on Friday 24 September 1999, Burt announced a bid of more than £21bn. In the shower that morning, Merrill Lynch's Greenburgh heard it on Radio 4's *Today* programme and exclaimed: 'Oh fuck.' A furious Mathewson was already in the United States, at the Country Club in Brookline, Massachusetts, preparing to watch that year's Ryder Cup, a piquant detail that the even more golf-mad Burt relished. The Royal Bank's chief executive had to hide behind a bush to call Edinburgh and find out what was going on. While he seethed on a subsequent flight back to the UK, he admired Burt's panache and nous in getting in first. 'Clever old Bank of Scotland,' he told his deputy, Goodwin, when he got off the plane. At NatWest's headquarters in the City there was incredulity mixed with blind panic. The chairman, Sir David Rowland, a City grandee, was appalled. The bank's share price rocketed in anticipation of a takeover and the NatWest board met in emergency session to reject the Bank of Scotland offer, calling it 'unsolicited, unwelcome and ill thought-out'.[5]

Goodwin was calm, even though the pressure on the Royal Bank to make an immediate offer of its own was soon intense. Investment bankers were desperate for the juicy fees that could result from a contest for NatWest. A race would mean the rivals might have to increase their bids in a rush to persuade shareholders to choose their offer. The City press loves nothing more than the excitement of being able to report on an enormous takeover battle.

That Sunday Mathewson summoned investment bankers, lawyers and his own senior executives to a secret meeting in London at the offices of Freshfields, the City law firm. The deal-hungry Greenburgh's team from Merrill Lynch was joined by Andy Chisholm, representing Goldman Sachs. Oliver Pawle's unit from UBS, the Swiss bank, was also on hand. Everyone should calm down, there would be no unseemly rush to a bid, Mathewson said. The Royal Bank would take its time, do its homework and see what the next few weeks brought. To some of those present it seemed as though City-sceptic Mathewson was taking considerable pleasure in telling the investment bankers who was boss. 'The attitude from them was, right, now you Scottish guys are in the big time, move aside and we'll take it from here,' says a Mathewson staffer. 'But George said no, we do it our way. The investment bankers were going bananas because they were hungry for us to bid. They stood to make a lot of money.'

Mathewson was uncertain. 'Forget the hype afterwards, George wasn't entirely convinced about bidding. Fred wanted to bid,' says a then adviser. From members of the board pressure was growing too. Emilio Botín, the president of Spain's Banco Santander, a friend of Mathewson and a board member of the Royal Bank, was wildly enthusiastic when he flew in from

Madrid. Banco Santander and the Royal Bank were allies, each owning shares in the other. As a board meeting discussing NatWest dragged on, the Spanish banker was urgently in need of a cigarette. He declaimed with a flourish that it was imperative to bid. 'You must do it! I will give you the money!' Banco Santander did help to fund the bid.

Other board members also liked the idea. Angus Grossart, Scotland's pre-eminent merchant banker, a founder of Noble Grossart, the boutique outfit stationed in a tastefully decorated town house in New Town around the corner from St Andrew Square, urged Mathewson on. At this point Goodwin's role became central. Goodwin and Mathewson agreed a clever compromise. The Royal Bank would bid, but it should take its time and create the most detailed, fully thought-through bid document possible, rather than being rushed into a quick counter-offer that might suggest panic. Goodwin would handle the process of preparing the document.

The City, meanwhile, was agog at the raid on an English institution by Scottish bankers who had long been best known for their self-proclaimed prudence and caution. The *Economist*, the London free-marketeering magazine increasingly becoming the house journal of the rising global business elite, did offer a different perspective. It welcomed the attempted takeover.[6] It told its readers: 'NatWest has been a limping, troubled, formerly great British institution for far too long. Which is why the great British bank auction is such good news.' Presciently, it warned the City not to be so quick to dismiss the cross-border raiders from Scotland: 'The London financial establishment has long looked down on its Edinburgh cousins – an attitude epitomised in the dismissive comment by Sir David Rowland that there was a big difference between running a corner shop and running Tesco.'

Rowland tried to get on the front foot against the invaders. On 8 October, with the bid in from Bank of Scotland, the Royal

Bank considering a move and the attempted Legal & General purchase unravelling, he appointed himself as executive chairman and fired Derek Wanless, NatWest's chief executive, who walked away with the rather unkind nickname of 'Witless' and a £3m pay-off.[7] Wanless was a seemingly old-fashioned banker, a genial Geordie who had started with a Saturday job in the Westminster Bank, studied maths at Cambridge and then risen to the top of his chosen profession. An avowed Labour supporter, he would subsequently write a report on the future of the NHS, commissioned by Gordon Brown. It recommended increased spending funded by higher taxes.

High finance is wonderfully – for those involved – circular. In 2000, after being axed by Rowland, Wanless joined the board of a then small bank in his native North East of England and chaired its audit and risk committees until the crash of 2007. That bank was called Northern Rock. To replace Wanless at NatWest in 1999, Rowland made Ron Sandler chief operating officer. The tough, Zimbabwean-born former boss of Lloyd's insurance market was charged with helping Rowland fight off Mathewson and Burt. In a much later incarnation, Sandler would follow Wanless once again. He was hired by the Labour government to oversee the nationalised Newcastle-based Northern Rock after Wanless and others were forced to resign following its collapse in 2007.

In October 1999, it was NatWest that Sandler was battling to save. He and Rowland were forced by investors to announce the formal abandonment of the doomed Legal & General bid and on 27 October they revealed a plan to sell off Ulster Bank, and three other parts of the NatWest business. The hope was that this would generate some cash, which would go to shareholders. In this way they might be persuaded to reject the advances of the Scottish banks.

Goodwin's work was progressing. His job was to come up with a plan which could convince the shareholders who owned

NatWest that they stood to make more money if they let the Royal Bank take over their institution, rather than the Bank of Scotland. With teams of advisers and analysts in Edinburgh and London on hand, he buried himself in spreadsheets and papers on synergies, efficiencies, staff numbers, growth patterns and IT systems. Iain Allan, the Royal Bank's head of strategy, was a key figure helping with the work. This was the kind of painstaking, methodical exercise which Goodwin had already shown he excelled at when he worked for the Clydesdale and Touche Ross. At the Clydesdale he had shown that he could drill a team and marshal the facts to create a coherent plan. Here he could replicate the procedure on a much, much bigger stage. His new colleagues noticed that he was obsessed with the detail. This was the first time many of them had seen him operate properly and they were impressed.

The Bank of Scotland offer for NatWest, Goodwin told Mathewson, was too narrowly concentrated on cost-cutting alone. There were efficiencies to be had, of course. But the real point of doing the deal should be to create growth, a lot of growth. The Royal Bank would endeavour to persuade NatWest shareholders that, thanks to its scale, a merged company could expand a lot more than either could on its own. The Bank of Scotland had moved first, but springing a surprise had come at a cost. Its proposals struck some City analysts as vague. In contrast, Goodwin set about producing an extraordinarily precise plan. The Royal Bank would keep the NatWest brand and concentrate on expansion. Initiative was piled upon initiative, with forty-three in total, all aimed at increasing revenue across the new group. There would be a lot of job losses, 18,000, as the back-room functions were merged with the creation of a giant new 'manufacturing' division to provide all of the support services and create the banking products that the group would sell. Thirty-nine 'efficiency improvement' schemes were proposed, saving £580m. Another £600m could be saved by 'de-duplication' in seventy-two areas. Overall, Goodwin claimed his plan would realise £1420m in increased profits. Within the first thirty days of closing a deal the Royal Bank committed to implementing an entirely new structure, with all divisions finalising three-year expansion plans. It was immensely ambitious.

It would also mean the promised promotion for Goodwin. If investors were to have confidence in the Royal Bank's plan for integrating NatWest, then Mathewson and Younger realised they needed to explain that its architect would stick around. On Friday 26 November, just days ahead of bidding, the Royal Bank announced a timetable for Lord Younger stepping down as chairman, with George Mathewson earmarked to take his place and Fred Goodwin ready to become chief executive.[8] The transition was scheduled to take a year, with Goodwin busy running the teams that would manage the integration. He was booked to become chief executive in his own right on 18 January 2001.

On Monday 29 November, the Royal Bank finally launched its hostile bid for NatWest, matching the Bank of Scotland and publishing Goodwin's proposals in full. Sir David Rowland at NatWest was immediately dismissive, in a way that Mathewson found intensely insulting. Rowland was on friendly terms with Lord Younger, who privately tried to persuade the NatWest chairman to do a deal and recommend shareholders sell to the Royal Bank. But Rowland declared that the bid was based on overestimates of the benefits of a merger.[9] Customers, he warned, would not like the disruption. 'The more I have thought about it, the more the risks have seemed apparent,' he told shareholders. 'What we're saying is, "Thank you very much, but bye-bye."' Goodwin and Mathewson had no intention of waving bye-bye. On 16 December their offer cleared competition concerns and the clock started ticking on a sixty-day period in which the two banks would compete to get the owners of NatWest – the large institutional investors, fund managers and those running pension funds – to vote for them rather than their rival.

All of the historical enmity between the two Edinburgh banks stretching back centuries, and put on hold during their abortive talks about cooperation in the summer, now resurfaced with renewed intensity. Both Mathewson and Burt knew that the winner would most likely emerge in a heroic light, whereas the loser's bank would become a target for takeover itself. No matter that the pair got on well, the bankers thought they were fighting for the existence of their institutions as independent entities. The testosterone surged.

Burt zeroed in on fears about Goodwin's management style,[10] even invoking his nickname: 'The question for NatWest shareholders is who do you want, Fred the Shred or a team of 80 people led by Gavin Masterton.' A much more emollient character than Goodwin, Masterton was the chief operating officer of Bank of Scotland. Mathewson was contemptuous in response. 'The reality,' he told his team back at St Andrew Square, was that the two banks were 'simply not in the same class. Bank of Scotland just isn't big enough, it doesn't have the management, it has no experience of England.'

After Christmas, and the dawn of a new millennium, Younger, Sir George and Fred Goodwin began their campaign to win over investors, to get them to choose the Royal Bank rather than the Bank of Scotland. Long days were spent trudging around London – and in America – making presentations. It was not an entirely happy experience, with the chief executive so obviously no good at faking flattery. 'Wee George' could be prickly to the point of downright rudeness, even to people whose help he needed. Why, Mathewson asked, did they have to be so nice to fund managers and those who managed the shareholdings for large institutional investors? To Mathewson's mind they behaved like sheep following the market. Goodwin was better at it. He had his integration plan distilled into a calmly delivered spiel in which he could run through any of the initiatives in great detail. With some in the City sceptical that the

Royal Bank's promises were deliverable, his half of the double act became critical. After a day of pitching the pair would return to wind down at the Savoy Hotel, the five-star hotel off London's Strand.[11] It became their unofficial campaign head-quarters. George Younger was also instrumental. His contacts book, compiled during a long career involving the army, business, the City and Conservative politics, was so good that he could lift the phone and talk in relaxed terms to his contemporaries who sat on the boards of large investors.

On 31 January 2000, both the predator banks moved to improve their offers. The deadline by which shareholders must choose was less than a fortnight away and the excitement was dizzying for those involved. Two relatively small banks, with annual profits not much more than £1bn each, were prepared to pay around £24bn for NatWest. The Royal Bank's offer actually gave NatWest shareholders a little less per share, but Goodwin had proposed a new piece of paper, a so-called 'additional value share', offering an extra dividend for NatWest shareholders. Greenburgh and the other investment bankers were impressed; it suggested Goodwin could think creatively as well as cut costs.

The mood in the rival camps swung wildly and in the decisive final week there were moments of dark depression in the Royal Bank team. On Monday 7 February, rumours swirled that another bank, Lloyds TSB, was ready to mount a takeover of the Royal Bank if it lost the race for NatWest. Even though Lloyds TSB issued a statement denying the claims, it seemed to Mathewson that his fears were about to be realised. Defeat would most likely result in the eventual end of autonomy. That Monday evening it looked as though Bank of Scotland might have the edge with large shareholders. Phillips & Drew, which owned more than 2 per cent of NatWest, declared that it backed the Bank of Scotland. Led by Mathewson, the Royal Bank team retreated to the pub opposite their London head office in Waterhouse Square, Holborn, before heading for a late dinner in an Italian restaurant near Covent Garden. More troubling news came as the red wine flowed. Howard Moody, the head of communications and colleague of Mathewson's since their days at the Scottish Development Agency, took a call from the *Financial Times*. The influential Lex column, widely read by investors and fund managers, would the next morning endorse the Bank of Scotland bid, he told his colleagues.[12] That day Mathewson and Goodwin had gone to the *FT*'s office, and spent time giving an interview, conducted in the canteen, in an effort to win support. It hadn't worked. Gloom enveloped the group.

Yet within twenty-four hours the picture had been transformed. Fund managers working for Schroders, the second-largest single shareholder in NatWest, spent the Tuesday morning discussing which Scottish bank would get their backing.[13] After a final tour of other investors, Mathewson and Goodwin retreated to Waterhouse Square to make calls and wait for news. Schroders broke for the Royal Bank. Next up was Mercury Asset Management (MAM), the third-largest shareholder in NatWest. Mathewson was on the phone to Patience Wheatcroft, then the business editor of *The Times*, when Goodwin popped his head round Mathewson's door with more good news: 'We've got MAM.' Mathewson punched the air and relayed the news to Wheatcroft: 'How about this for a headline? Wham, bam, thank you MAM ...'

The next morning a trickle turned into a flood. Investors wanted to be on the winning side, and a third had soon sided with the Royal Bank. By that afternoon they had effectively done it. At Waterhouse Square senior executives who had not been much involved in the bid, but who knew they were about to be part of a much bigger outfit, gathered excitedly. The air fizzed with possibilities of promotion, bigger profits and bonuses. Drinks were served and Lord Younger, Mathewson and Goodwin basked in the praise of their colleagues. Tired and excited, the chief executive and his deputy retreated again to their favourite haunt, the Savoy Hotel. Like two boys from the sticks let loose in the big city they decided to treat themselves to a sugar-rush. They ordered an ice-cream knickerbocker glory each.

The battle was over. Burt wrote to his staff on the Thursday conceding defeat and trying, somewhat unconvincingly, to sound upbeat. After fluctuations in the share price of the target and the winning bidder, the Royal Bank offer was worth £21bn. At NatWest headquarters, Sir David Rowland was initially reluctant to cooperate with the new owners. It wasn't until Friday 11 February that he would finally concede that he had lost. Mathewson found his foot-dragging baffling and unbecoming, even though the Royal Bank chief executive made upbeat statements to nervous investors which suggested that relations were cordial.

In reality, when Mathewson and Goodwin travelled to NatWest headquarters to inspect their prize for the first time, there was no greeting party. A security guard simply handed over the keys, saying half-jokingly: 'Here, it's all yours.' The Scottish pair had a look around 41 Lothbury, a colonnaded building right behind the Bank of England in the heart of the City. Goodwin in particular couldn't believe how lavish it was. A cavernous main banking hall had been adapted by NatWest to showcase some of the bank's collection of contemporary art and the wine cellar was stocked with the best vintages from Bordeaux and Burgundy. Like a Scottish medieval monarch, leading a successful raiding party over the border, Mathewson ordered the wine to be shipped to the Royal Bank's headquarters in Edinburgh. A few days later, he returned to NatWest headquarters with his team for a more cordial meeting with senior executives, to explain how the integration would proceed. One of the first decisions taken was that the Royal Bank would have no need of 41 Lothbury. Shortly afterwards it would be closed for redevelopment and then sold in 2006 for £115m at the height of the property boom.

Mathewson and Goodwin were hailed as conquering heroes in Edinburgh, home to the new Scottish Parliament. The *Scotsman*[14] declared of the NatWest deal: 'Scotland has emerged a winner. A native talent for reliability in the moving and making of money, coupled with a certain audacity, has been rewarded. Edinburgh, meanwhile, has reasserted itself as a financial centre.' In the City some presumed that the Royal Bank would naturally now want to be headquartered in London. Mathewson was contemptuous. He hadn't spent all these years trying to create a Scottish banking behemoth only to move south. Although a far larger proportion of the bank's activities would by necessity have to be carried out in London, the headquarters would stay in Edinburgh. A Fleet Street reporter asked Mathewson and Goodwin whether they were really serious about remaining north of the border: 'Of course we are. Just look at my record and then tell me I am not committed to an Edinburgh HQ. One of the biggest banks in Europe – centred in Edinburgh – can only be a good thing.'

Goldman Sachs and Merrill Lynch, which had both earned nice fat fees on the deal, were keen to organise a celebratory private dinner. It would be in Edinburgh, naturally. A house was hired for the occasion, complete with chef and aristocratic owner who rather awkwardly appeared at various points during proceedings. The whole thing wasn't to the meritocratic Mathewson's taste and the dinner came close to being a disaster. One of the Goldman Sachs team made speeches and handed out presents, although the jokes rather misfired. Goodwin was given an Airfix kit model of a car, to reflect his automotive obsession. It looked as though the chief executive in waiting was being mocked for his relatively youthful geekiness. Merrill Lynch gave the Royal Bank team engraved silver plates. There was the consolation of exceptionally good wine at dinner, however. The sommelier uncorked bottles that had been liberated from the NatWest cellar and with their glasses full of Château

Latour 1970 (price in 2000: £370 a bottle) the Royal Bank and its advisers proceeded to toast their success.

Goodwin had enjoyed an astonishing rise. Just five years previously he hadn't even been a banker. Now, with Mathewson due to become chairman, he was about to become chief executive and one of the most powerful financiers in Europe sitting astride a banking colossus. NatWest wasn't just a retail bank with its named branches. It also owned Ulster Bank, which was well placed to capitalise on the coming property boom in Ireland. Across the Atlantic there was the potential for growth too. In Connecticut in the United States NatWest had a trading house, Greenwich Capital, an expert in mortgage securitisation and US government bonds. Even the Queen was now one of Mathewson and Goodwin's customers. The monarch banked at the private bank Coutts, that establishment paragon of financial discretion. It was owned by NatWest and hence was now a Royal Bank company. Hadn't Mathewson long said that a Scottish bank could be among the world's very best? Now it would fall to his hand-picked and anointed successor to continue their shared quest to make the old Edinburgh institution one of the greatest names in global finance. Fred Goodwin readied himself for the top job.

6

The End of Boom and Bust

*'This is the time to set the British economy on a new long-
term course that will deliver high levels of growth and
employment through lasting stability.'*

Gordon Brown, 6 May 1997

The phrase 'son of the manse' might have been invented
for James Gordon Brown. Plenty of other successful Scots
have been raised in the tied houses, manses, in which Church of
Scotland ministers live with their families, but the former
Chancellor and Prime Minister embodies what it is to be the
ambitious offspring of a Presbyterian preacher. Decades later
Brown still described his parents as his inspiration and cited his
father's sermons, with their invocations on the value of hard
work, duty, responsibility, fairness and social justice.[1] The
message preached from the pulpit in St Brycedale, in Kirkcaldy,
by the Reverend John Ebenezer Brown, was that we are not
atomised individuals selfishly seeking to further our own interests. We are cooperative beings. The highest possible calling,
the young Gordon was taught by his parents, involved helping

those less fortunate than ourselves, whether it be through service in the church or in politics.[2]

The Fife town of Kirkcaldy, which lies across the River Forth to the north of Edinburgh, was rather similar to Fred Goodwin's Paisley on the other side of the country in the late 1950s and 1960s. Both places were home to close-knit communities. They had an industrial heritage that was beginning to be eroded and pockets of severe poverty. In Brown's case he saw the evidence of it on his own doorstep. The very poorest often turned up at the family home seeking the help and comfort dispensed by his father and mother. To be the son or daughter of a Church of Scotland minister in such a town in that period was to be marked out from the beginning as special. There was a weight of expectation in the wider community that achievement would follow, and from an early age Gordon Brown was known for hard work and his precocious academic ability. His two brothers, John the elder and Andrew the younger, regarded him as the prodigiously gifted one, someone who was bright but who needed regular assistance with life's practicalities. Both have fussed over their high-achieving brother ever since. Fast-tracked through school, with a select band of similarly bright contemporaries, Brown went early to study history at Edinburgh University, becoming the youngest student in the modern era to achieve a first-class degree there. In the interim he had dealt with adversity, losing the sight in one eye as the result of a rugby accident at the age of sixteen, after which he was confined to hospital for weeks.

Fired by this searing experience, with his ambition to make a difference increased, Brown wanted to do only one thing. He entered politics, becoming the long-haired student rector at Edinburgh in 1972 on a reforming left-wing ticket, backed by 'Brown's Sugars', a group of miniskirt-clad female campaigners. After university he fixed on getting into Parliament as quickly as possible, managing it in the 1983 election when Labour was crushed in the landslide re-election of Margaret Thatcher.

Initially Brown was a standard-issue socialist of the era, who believed that the Thatcherite Tories were on a mission to destroy British industry and make society less equal by encouraging the individual pursuit of greedy self-interest. He had written a biography of James Maxton, the glowering socialist firebrand MP from the 'Red Clydeside' period in the early decades of the twentieth century, when radicalism and industrial strife dominated Glasgow working-class politics. Gradually, however, Brown also became more interested in the literature on markets. He still despised Tory policies but nationalisation and the control of the economy traditionally advocated by the left didn't seem like a suitable response to the needs of an era that was going to be increasingly global. It also didn't seem like a good way of getting a Labour government elected for the first time since 1979, given that it needed to win in the south and Midlands of England. Brown's views started to evolve.

Adam Smith, the eighteenth-century philosopher and father of modern economics, the inspiration for pro-market economists and free-market Thatcherites, was a fellow son of Kirkcaldy.[3] There was a side to Smith that appealed to Brown all along. As well as teaching that markets were essential for economic efficiency, hadn't Smith also appeared to argue in *The Wealth of Nations* that the rich should pay higher taxes to support the poor? As Brown's views shifted away from old-style socialism there were areas he was determined to protect from markets; the National Health Service was the obvioius example. He regarded it as the collectivist glue holding society together, which embodied the nobility of common endeavour and the enduring nature of 'British values'. More broadly the old left's hostility to markets seemed to be a dead end, Brown concluded. Successful markets – in goods and services – were essential to create the growth that government needed, in order to collect taxes that leaders devoted to public service, leaders such as Gordon Brown, could then spend to help the needy.

The United States, where he liked to spend summers in Cape Cod, playing tennis, reading voraciously and mixing when he got the chance with the Democratic Party elite, influenced his thinking. America's economic dynamism and optimism were highly appealing, especially when compared with the sterile arguments he was forced to have with trade union leaders in Britain who did not want Labour to deviate from the true socialist path. On trips to Washington, with his fellow Labour moderniser Tony Blair after another defeat for Labour in the 1992 general election, Brown's developing worldview was reinforced.[4] In the November of that year the Democrats had succeeded in doing what Labour seemed incapable of managing. They had won an election. Bill Clinton prised the presidency away from the Republicans, which gave the visiting Labour leaders hope that they too could win if their party changed.[5] As well as studying the marketing techniques – including spindoctoring – that would soon be copied by New Labour in Britain to such startling effect, Brown and Blair also learnt ideological lessons from the senior members of the Clinton team. The trick, it seemed, was to accept that middle-ground voters were generally keen to get on in life, and were relaxed about markets, as long as you promised to manage the public finances sensibly in a way that guaranteed stability for them and their families. What mattered after that was to use the proceeds of growth to alleviate poverty and make society more equal. It was possible, it seemed, to square the circle. If Brown became Labour leader he could fuse two elements of his Kirkcaldy past: the social concern of his father's sermons and the market dynamism described by Adam Smith. The latter would fund the former.

Brown seemed to have become the dominant intellectual force in Labour, and his bravura performances in the Commons reinforced the idea that he was the party's future. Then Brown got the shock of his life when he lost out on the Labour leadership, shortly after John Smith died suddenly in May 1994. Being deprived of the leadership by Blair – a friend regarded by Brown as very much his intellectual inferior – was simply not in the script. In life, he was used to coming first. To compensate, a grief-stricken Brown threw himself into devising an economic platform that the shadow Chancellor thought would put Britain on a new path. If he could not be Prime Minister, yet, he would be a great, reforming Chancellor first. He didn't want the New Labour government to end in disgrace, ruined by out-of-control spending and mismanagement. To avoid that outcome he planned a revolution in policymaking. If Labour had to gain and maintain economic credibility, allowing it to win election and re-election, everything must be anchored by two watchwords: stability and prudence. As a downpayment, he pledged that for the first two years after the election Labour would stick to the relatively tough spending limits of the outgoing Tories.

Brown also started to wonder about the possibility of giving away control over interest rates, in order to prove that a new government would be committed to continuing the fight against inflation. Alan Greenspan, the chairman of the US Federal Reserve and by then already regarded as the world's most impressive central banker, certainly thought that it was a great idea. In March 1997, just a few weeks before the May general election, Brown met Greenspan on another trip to the United States and sought his counsel.[6] Would it be wise, Brown asked the man who would become his guru, to make the Bank of England independent? Greenspan was enthusiastic, and pointed to the success of the arrangement in America where politicians could not interfere in the setting of interest rates. The endorsement of so widely respected a figure helped convince him.

In opposition Brown had been turning this matter over in his mind for months, and discussing it in great secrecy with his young economic advisers Ed Balls and Ed Miliband. If New Labour won the looming election, he was looking for ways to emphasise that he could be trusted to avoid manipulating interest rates for political advantage, something previous governments of both major parties had tried. Granting the Bank of England independence on interest rates would reassure the voters and the markets. The wider City of London did pose a problem for Brown, however much he and Balls knew that it had to be wooed and neutralised as a source of opposition. Labour had been seeking to do this since Smith's leadership with a series of missions known collectively as the 'prawn cocktail offensive', so named because Labour's shadow ministers would travel to the 'Square Mile' and break bread, or consume canapés, with senior City figures. This was designed to emphasise that the Labour leadership was not composed of radical socialists hell-bent on nationalising either the Stock Exchange or the banks.

Despite these efforts, the Presbyterian Brown seemed initially distrustful of the City's culture. A little like his fellow Scot George Mathewson at the Royal Bank of Scotland, the Chancellor was an outsider in that world and correctly detected the hand of various old-boy networks. If New Labour won power there would have to be changes in the way the City of London and financial services were regulated, in order to make them fit for Brown's new era. City scandals certainly suggested change was necessary. In 1991 BCCI, the Bank of Credit and Commerce International, the London-based international bank, imploded. Then the historic merchant bank Barings (founded 1762) was brought down in 1995 by the 'rogue trader' Nick Leeson. The answer, Brown concluded, was a dose of New Labour modernisation, and a shift to new systems and regulators not dependent on what he saw as the dominance of the old school tie and suspect connections.

On Tuesday 6 May 1997, the new Chancellor made his first move. Less than a week before, Blair and Brown had not merely defeated a tired Tory Party contaminated by allegations of sleaze. They had eviscerated their enemy. New Labour enjoyed a majority of 179, the bedraggled Conservatives were in shock and Brown's native Scotland was now a Tory MP-free zone. Brown was eager to get going. He wanted his first major announcement, on granting the Bank of England independence, to be a coup de théâtre, and when it came on the Tuesday after a weekend of intense work it certainly wowed the press and impressed the financial markets. It had all been agreed with Blair, at a meeting held on the Sunday after the election in his Islington home as he and his wife, Cherie, packed for the move to Downing Street.[7] Blair loved the audacity of Brown's grand gesture on the Bank of England. Number 10 civil servants who offered to work up papers examining the potential consequences and implications were rebuffed. Blair simply asked Brown if it was the 'right thing to do'. His Chancellor responded that it was.

On Monday 5 May, Brown squared 'Steady Eddie', the Governor of the Bank of England, Eddie George.[8] The Chancellor handed him two letters, the first dealing with central bank independence. The chain-smoking George, a Bank of England lifer who joined in the early 1960s, was delighted as it meant a strengthening of powers for the institution he loved. He paid less attention to the second letter.

The other letter would eventually have grave consequences many years later, in the period running up to the financial crisis of 2008. Brown told George that he wanted to remove from the Bank of England its powers to supervise the UK's banks. At the 6 May meeting Eddie George sought – and believed he had received – assurances that this would not be rushed. He told his staff at Threadneedle Street that he would be fully consulted if Brown proposed any further changes.

Two weeks later, Brown summoned George to another meeting in the Treasury to inform him that he was pushing ahead and would announce legislation the next day. The Bank of England would be stripped of all its powers on banking supervision and a new super-regulator established, on the foundations of the existing Securities and Investment Board (SIB). A spectacular bust-up in Brown's office ensued, with George raging that he had been betrayed. In the car on the way back to Threadneedle Street, George began dictating a resignation letter. It seemed as though Brown's modernising zeal, which was meant to show how New Labour could be trusted on the economy, was going to result in the resignation of a widely respected Governor of the Bank of England only three weeks into the new government. Blair was appalled. Senior civil servants in Number 10 and at the Treasury – including the Permanent Secretary Terry Burns, who Brown was keen to push out – attempted to calm the situation. Eventually a compromise was brokered that would allow both George and Brown to save face, with Alistair Darling, the emollient chief secretary to the Treasury, smoothing the way.

The eventual outcome was an awkward division of responsibilities on banks and financial stability. The SIB, or the Financial Services Authority as it became, would do the day-to-day regulation, which meant checking that the banks' products complied with consumer rules and ensuring that bank bosses were running their affairs in line with the rules laid down by the regulator and set by Parliament. But the Bank of England would after all retain overall responsibility for the loosely defined stability of the financial system. Government would take an interest, obviously, and the new three-way set-up was dubbed tripartite regulation. The risk was surely that this political fudge might create the scope for a dangerous amount of confusion. If one or more large banks were ticking all the boxes and apparently complying with every one of the FSA's rules, but still taking big ill-defined risks that might somehow eventually threaten wider financial stability, whose job exactly was it to spot this and intervene? It was never completely clear.

In late 1997 what seemed to matter more was that Bank of England independence was very popular. City and big business leaders in particular were reassured that they could trust New

Labour after all, and the changes on setting interest rates were widely welcomed by many prominent Tories, shell-shocked after their defeat. The changes to regulation of banks were more problematic. Ken Clarke, the Conservatives' recently departed Chancellor, accused Brown of acting too hastily on creating the FSA.[9] Lord Lawson, Thatcher's reforming Chancellor, warned that while he approved of Bank of England independence, the shift on regulation was a mistake. When the Bank of England had banking supervision removed from its control and handed to Brown's new FSA, the bank would lose its clout. The danger was that the City of London and banks would no longer take its warnings seriously.

The old arrangements had been far from perfect – as various scandals down the decades demonstrated – but it was said that an effective governor could have an impact merely by raising an eyebrow. The City, and the banks, feared his displeasure and tended to look to Threadneedle Street for guidance about the condition of the economy and what was deemed acceptable behaviour. Under the new tripartite set-up, the FSA would be stationed away from the traditional heart of the City in an office down the river in Canary Wharf. Howard Davies, who had been a deputy governor of the Bank of England under Eddie George when Labour arrived in office, was given the task of establishing the new regulator and finding a way to make it work.

In the Commons, the Conservative Peter Lilley, then the new shadow Chancellor, one of seven Tories who held that post while Brown was at the Treasury,[10] expressed worries about the way the old set-up was being dismantled. On 11 November 1997 he told MPs: 'We have no objection to the objective of trying to bring greater simplicity and one-stop shopping to the business of financial regulation, but we fear that the Government may, almost casually, have bitten off more than they can chew. The process of setting up the FSA may cause regulators to take their eye off the ball.'

Brown swept aside such concerns. At the despatch box in the Commons he dealt with critics in the manner of someone driving a steamroller armed with a machine-gun. Over the next few years he would perfect this approach. Those opponents not hit by a slew of statistics spewed out rapid-fire style would instead be flattened with extravagant rhetorical claims about the brilliance of New Labour's economic stewardship. The economic weather was certainly sunny. As the old century gave way to the new, the UK was recording impressive annual growth numbers. It had started under the previous government, but under Brown progress continued and confidence rose. UK GDP grew 4.2 per cent in 2000, 2.9 per cent in 2001, 2.4 per cent in 2002 and 3.8 per cent in 2003.[11]

In this boom financial services were also prospering. In fact, the success of banks and other financial firms was one of the drivers of the economy's expansion. This created a slight problem for the Chancellor. The question of how to handle the British banks was initially awkward. In opposition before 1997 he had been keen to present himself as a consumer champion and friend of the disgruntled customer who was tired of being ripped off by rogue elements in the financial services industry. He had been particularly adept at using tabloid newspapers to communicate this message. In 1997 Brown was still minded to encourage much more competition so that the big banks which dominated the market faced a challenge from smaller operators, to the benefit of consumers. In 1998 he appointed Don Cruickshank, a businessman who went on to chair the London Stock Exchange, to prepare a report on how it might be done.

Yet even as Cruickshank was finalising his report on 'Competition in UK Banking', the takeover battle at NatWest was approaching a dramatic climax and the industry was heading for much less competition, not more. In mid-February 2000 the Royal Bank beat the Bank of Scotland and swallowed NatWest. Just a few weeks later, in March, the Cruickshank report was published. It suggested the FSA should actively promote much greater competition and stated that banks should be prevented from becoming too big. With the Royal Bank at that moment taking over NatWest it was all a little embarrassing. Brown knew Fred Goodwin, the boss of the newly enlarged Royal Bank, and liked him. Brown said in his Budget speech days later he would implement Cruickshank's 'main recommendations', but some in the upper echelons of the Treasury thought this impractical. Banks were doing well in the burgeoning boom and as they grew in size they became even more useful sources of employment and tax revenues. Steve Robson, the Second Permanent Secretary at the Treasury, who was also managing director of the government's Finance and Regulation Directorate, was credited by some with leading the effort against the implementation of Cruickshank's recommendations.[12] Robson later joined the board of RBS.

Whoever killed it off, the Cruickshank report was given a quiet burial against a backdrop of booming banks. A ministerial colleague from that period thought Brown's reluctance to force more competition understandable in the circumstances: 'Here in the banks you had the rise of these great national champions, something which, a few big manufacturing businesses aside, we had for a while lacked in this country. I suppose Gordon thought, why knock it?'

Bank profits really were powering ahead now. In 2003 Barclays' profits before tax were £3.8bn, up 20 per cent from £3.2bn the previous year, while those of Lloyds climbed 66 per cent to £4.3bn. Another star performer was the Royal Bank of Scotland. In 2003 it made a then startling £6.2bn before tax, an increase of 29 per cent on the previous year. Not everyone was impressed. Vince Cable, the Liberal Democrats' Treasury spokesman, thought that these profits were being made on the back of exploited customers: 'It is hardly surprising that banks are making such huge profits when consumer debt is approaching a record of £1 trillion,' he observed in February 2004, when RBS announced its record figures. At £1 trillion, total personal debt still had quite a way to go. This was all the more remarkable considering that consumer debt – made up of mortgages, overdrafts, loans and credit cards – had been below £500bn as recently as 1996.

This was only a problem, of course, if there was any prospect of cheap credit ending at some point, but that wasn't deemed particularly likely. Even though interest rates might go up a little, the environment was benign, with low inflation. Consumers could afford to splurge. Could it really be that the end of boom and bust was in sight? Used remorselessly, the claim – 'no return to boom and bust' – became Brown's catchphrase as quarter after quarter – with only a few minor deviations – the economy carried on growing strongly. On Monday 27 September 2004, in his speech at the Labour Party conference, he declared that the UK was: 'No longer the most inflation-prone economy. With New Labour, Britain today has the lowest inflation for thirty years. No longer the boom-bust economy, Britain has had the lowest interest rates for forty years. And no longer the stop-go economy, Britain is now enjoying the longest period of sustained economic growth for 200 years.'

In these circumstances, it was deemed safe for the government to start spending much more on public services. In 2000 to 2001, annual total UK government spending was £341.5bn. By 2007 to 2008, as the financial crisis got under way, the government was spending £583.7bn. During this period some commentators attempted to challenge the orthodoxy and suggested that the economic miracle of the moment might be a mirage, but they didn't get very far. New Labour easily won another landslide majority of 167 in June 2001, squashing Tory leader William Hague in the process. Subsequently the party secured a much reduced but still healthy majority of 66 in May 2005 in Tony Blair's last election as Labour leader.

It was hard to get a hearing for scepticism when house prices continued their giddying rise in a manner that was so gratifying, at least for those who already owned houses or could afford to buy. The leitmotif of this period was the emergence of the property show on television. *Location, Location, Location* – the movement's signature show – first aired in 2000, with its upwardly mobile presenters scouring the country for properties on behalf of the aspirational and ostentatious. Yet somehow the show *Grand Designs*, which first aired in 1999, managed to eclipse its rival in terms of boom-time smugness. If the worthy intention was to celebrate good design and highlight beautiful houses that were being built or restored imaginatively, it tipped over at points into a parade of preening consumerist self-obsession and interior design-driven dottiness. The British had long made a fetish of property, compared with the more cautious Germans or relaxed French, but it was as though the obsession with buying and selling houses was turning into a national mania, or illness.

In June 1987, when Margaret Thatcher won her second landslide election victory preaching the virtues of a property-owning democracy, the average house price in the UK had been £45,809; in April 1992 when John Major beat Neil Kinnock it stood at £64,509 and in May 1997, at the time of Blair's victory, it was only a touch higher at £68,085. Then under Brown's stewardship as Chancellor it soared as the economy raced ahead. By August 2007, and the first public stirrings of the credit crisis, the average house price in the UK was £199,612. A year later it was £174,241. By August 2012 it had fallen back to £160,142.[13]

Early in the first decade of the twenty-first century, Christopher Fildes, City sage and Fleet Street veteran who had witnessed many booms, and subsequent busts, was notably concerned about house prices. In May 2002, on the fifth anniversary of Brown's decision to grant the Bank of England independence, he issued a warning in the *Daily Telegraph*: 'The most visible signal of trouble ahead (in Britain) comes from house prices, which are having a boom of their own.' The Bank of England's Monetary Policy Committee, dedicated to keeping inflation at 2.5 per cent, focused on studying retail prices and did not include house buying, even though the Nationwide Building Society reported that house price inflation was running at 16.5 per cent. This was not a cause for excessive concern, the Bank of England said. 'Now that is worrying,' said Fildes. 'It is true that the committee was set to aim at retail prices, not house prices, and was told to ignore mortgage payments. All the same, anyone who can leave the cost of housing out of the cost of living must have bought himself a tent.'

Fildes cited asset price inflation. A bubble was being blown and if it burst it might send the economy into recession. Perhaps surprisingly, Brown showed no sign of being perturbed by these developments. Cautious by inclination, he was normally not a naturally reckless type. He was, noted colleagues, obsessive when launching initiatives or planning a Budget, asking how will this look in tomorrow's papers and what if this doesn't work? What then could have caused him to believe that boom and bust, an observable cycle in human affairs, had been ended? A close colleague of Brown's from that period pins some of the blame on his advisers: 'Gordon listened to Ed Balls a lot.' Another agrees: 'Ed Balls had a lot of theories about how the world had changed and how policy makers, including him and Gordon, had solved some of the big problems that had bedevilled the West. It suited Gordon to believe it.'

And crucially, by 2003 Brown's attention was elsewhere. Says a Labour cabinet minister from that period: 'What you have to remember is that Gordon was now on an entirely different mission. He was focused on getting Tony out. Look at the contrast, when after 2003 Tony was seen to have failed in Iraq whereas what he, Gordon, was doing on the economy was going so well.' There was still 'more to do', as Brown put it, but he could imply that he had accomplished his end of New Labour's original mission and was ready for the next challenge.

The success of financial services and the growth of banking in Britain were important because they helped vindicate his claims. The global nature of the rise of banking also appealed to Brown, who was increasingly interested in globalisation and the interconnectedness of the world's economy, which obviously created fresh opportunities for global leaders to enact their ideas on the international stage. Brown had also been vindicated on his determination to keep the UK out of the European single currency. Even though Britain was not in the euro, the City of London did not suffer. Quite the opposite, in fact. It asserted its dominance as the financial capital of Europe, where business in euros and other currencies was transacted.

The overhaul of financial services regulation in the 1980s had also attracted outsiders, ambitious bankers and traders from abroad who wanted to work in resurgent London. The result, it was said, was the 'Wimbledonisation' of the City, in which the British provided the charming venue while the game was played mostly by globetrotting foreigners. This was an exaggeration; there were plenty of British success stories too. Still, the influx of bonus-hungry bankers suggested that the British economy was at the forefront of exciting international developments. Under Gordon Brown, foreign investment banks were more keen than ever to have a strong presence in the UK, with its growing reputation as a global banking centre. Since Thatcher's Big Bang of 1986 the UK capital had been judged perfectly placed in terms of time zones for investment banks who wanted to do business around the clock. The plan announced by Lehman Brothers for a new building in London was just more evidence of British success. The US bank had had a presence in London since 1972, although it had scaled up dramatically after Big Bang in the 1980s. Lehman had headquarters in New York, London and Tokyo. Now it had such a large operation in Britain that it needed a vast new building. The steel and glass tower, thirty-seven storeys tall with one million square feet of office space, proved the firm's commitment to the UK, said Dick Fuld, chairman and CEO of Lehman Brothers.

Fuld knew London well. After all, in 1986 he had been part of the original American invasion which had so shocked the sleepy City old guard. Lehman's then management had sent him across the Atlantic to spearhead the firm's push into Europe from London. His new colleagues explained that the firm should also be thinking about expanding elsewhere on the continent. An office in Frankfurt, West Germany, should be considered: 'No way,' declared the aggressive Fuld. 'We're never going behind the iron curtain.'[14]

Richard S. Fuld Jr had since risen to be a Wall Street king-maker able to call on presidents, prime ministers and finance ministers. Who better to open Lehman's new London building than Gordon Brown? On 5 April 2004 he was ferried to 25 Bank Street, Canary Wharf, to pull the cord and unveil a memorial plaque in front of the media. Brown lavished praise on his hosts. He wanted, he said, to pay tribute to the contribution the firm made to the prosperity of Britain. It had never been afraid to experiment, he noted. 'During its one hundred and fifty year history, Lehman Brothers has always been an innovator, financing new ideas and inventions before many others even began to realise their potential. And it is part of the greatness not just of Lehman Brothers but of the City of London, that as the world economy has opened up, you have succeeded not by sheltering your share of a small protected national market but always by striving for a greater and greater share of the growing global market.' Lehman Brothers was certainly an innovator, although to what extent would not become fully apparent for another four and a half years. After Lehman went bust in the financial crisis, the plaque from Canary Wharf bearing Brown's name would become a collector's item, selling at auction in 2010 for £28,500 to a buyer with a presumably dark sense of humour.

For now, in 2004, it was possible to believe Brown's vision was being realised. Under Thatcher the City and the UK economy had been opened up. Under Brown, stable conditions had been created in which growth was strong, interest rates were low, inflation was marginal and financial services flourished. Canary Wharf had sprung from the decaying docklands and wharves of crumbling East London in the 1980s. Now firms such as Lehman and Barclays, and others, were opening enormous offices there. Under a Labour Chancellor the City of the Square Mile was modernising and breaking out of its old geographical constraints, pushing voraciously eastwards.

The global banks keen to be based in a lightly regulated and modernised City employed new staff, who would pay taxes and generate bigger and bigger profits that in turn boosted the government's coffers. A son of the manse, a Presbyterian Scot still unafraid to use the S-word (socialism) when he was in like-minded company, Brown could then have the piquant pleasure of using the proceeds from this banking boom to help increase public spending dramatically and do what he saw as good works, repairing the damage he felt had been done to the civic fabric in the 1980s. The arrangement struck his Labour advisers, including Ed Balls, as beautiful. Brown had fused a quasi-Thatcherite belief in the power of liberalised markets with New Labour modernisation, enabling an expansion of the state and public services. They were sure that the situation would continue being benign, which is why Brown's speeches were peppered with the phrase 'no return to boom and bust'.

In confidently declaring a new paradigm Brown was hardly operating in isolation. In America, his friend Alan Greenspan, the chairman of the Federal Reserve, was seen as the sagacious progenitor of never-ending global stability. Greenspan made occasional mild warnings about irrational exuberance in the markets, but generally the rise of the emerging economies such as China was thought to have combined with the rise of information technology and new trade patterns to create a second industrial revolution that could power growth for decades. The authorities had also proved they were capable of mitigating the worst effects of potential reverses. Whenever there was a problem, policymakers led by Greenspan managed to handle it and restore order. Only recently there had been another example of a mad bubble bursting in the United States. The emergence of the internet and associated technology had fuelled a stock-buying mania in the late 1990s as investors clamoured to buy anything associated with the 'e-economy'. For a time it seemed that any young, chino-clad technology geek with half an idea could secure millions or tens of millions in funding from venture capitalists keen to surf the wave of the future. On 10 March 2000 the boom peaked when the NASDAQ, the technology index on Wall Street, burst through the 5000 mark. Shortly afterwards firms with names such as WorldCom and Pets.com, which had rocketed in value, came crashing down. At the height of the madness, Yahoo had thought it sensible to pay $5.7bn for Broadcast.com, a website that was soon defunct. There had even been a widely tipped business called Startups.com, dealing in internet start-ups, which failed.

But the US authorities dealt calmly with the after-effects. Greenspan brought down interest rates and flooded the markets with liquidity to prevent panic. His view was that it was almost pointless trying to spot and prick bubbles in advance. It was much better to be on hand to mop up the mess afterwards, and to help get growth back on track as soon as possible with emergency action. The dot-com comedown was just the latest instance in which he had employed this technique. After October 1987's stock market crash he had also used liquidity, standing by to provide cash from the US central bank's reserves to help distressed financial institutions. This was judged widely to have turned a potential repeat of the Great Depression into a manageable event.

In the early 2000s the cult of Greenspan was attracting ever more followers. He was treated by politicians, central bankers and other experts as though he was the economic equivalent of Master Yoda in *Star Wars*. From his bathtub (he did his best thinking in the bath, he told interviewers), he would emerge to issue Delphic pronouncements about the condition of the global economy. He received an honorary knighthood from the Queen for his 'outstanding contribution to global economic stability'.

'If risk is properly dispersed, shocks to the overall economic system will be better absorbed and less likely to create cascading failures that could threaten financial stability,' he said in 2002.[15] The financial innovation of recent years was, he declared, on the whole an immensely positive development because it diluted risks so that they were much more widely dispersed. This was exactly what some banks, growing in size, wanted to hear. Goodness, the complex new products they were experimenting with to expand their activities might actually make the world a safer place. It was a beneficent analysis that also suited politicians who had to fight elections. On 18 May 2004, President George Bush gave Greenspan a fifth term as governor of the Federal Reserve, which meant that he had been appointed to that role by Presidents Reagan, George Bush, Bill Clinton and now George W. Bush. Greenspan, it was claimed, was presiding over a 'great moderation' or 'the great stability', a period of unprecedented equilibrium and prosperity. His nickname was maestro.

Senator John McCain, never noted for the quality of his economic insights, commented when asked if Greenspan should be asked to stay on at the Fed indefinitely: 'I would not only reappoint Mr Greenspan. If Mr Greenspan should happen to die – God forbid – I would prop him up and put a pair of dark glasses on him and keep him as long as we could.' In Britain, Gordon Brown was an equally big Greenspan fan. The pair shared an interest in ideas and academia and on the fringes of various international summits the friendship grew ever stronger.

Greenspan was the perfect figure around which the Brown operation could build a 'coronation' event, for his planned ascension to the premiership. By early 2005 the Brown team expected Blair to be gone, and their man installed in Number 10 ahead of a general election. A programme of activities was arranged around Greenspan being awarded an honorary degree at Brown's old university, Edinburgh. With the arrangements already made, the coronation had to go ahead with Blair still on the throne.

On Sunday 6 February 2005, Greenspan gave the annual Adam Smith lecture in St Bryce's, formerly St Brycedale, in Kirkcaldy, with Brown in the front pew. This was where his father had preached his sermons from 1954, when Gordon was aged three, until 1967. The strongest themes of the Chancellor's life and career – his father's preaching, notions of Scottish financial expertise and being reconciled to markets thanks to Adam Smith – all came together that evening in an atmosphere of mutual admiration, self-congratulation and hubris. From the pulpit, Greenspan acknowledged the extraordinary symmetry of the occasion in his opening remarks. 'Kirkcaldy, the birthplace, in 1723, of Adam Smith and, by extension, of modern economics, is also, of course, where your Chancellor of the Exchequer was reared. I am led to ponder to what extent the Chancellor's renowned economic and financial skills are the result of exposure to the subliminal intellect-enhancing emanations of this area.' Concluding a scholarly speech, Greenspan referred to the phrase 'the invisible hand' which Smith used to describe the workings of markets: 'One could hardly imagine that today's awesome array of international transactions would produce the relative economic stability that we experience daily if they were not led by some international version of Smith's invisible hand.' That night Brown hailed his friend Greenspan as 'the greatest economist of his generation'.

The next day, Monday 7 February, Greenspan got his honorary degree at Edinburgh with Brown in attendance. Brown even wore a white tie for the occasion, something he had hitherto been reluctant to do, choosing to turn up for dinners in the City of London in a lounge suit instead. Mervyn King, who had succeeded Eddie George as Governor of the Bank of England, got an honorary degree that day too. After the ceremony the trio of King, Brown and Greenspan posed for pictures.

History, it seemed, was running the way of all three men. There was a virtuous circle of seemingly unstoppable growth and intoxicating innovation, and the banks, including the Royal Bank of Scotland, were at the heart of it. What could possibly go wrong?

7

Fred the Shred

'They had a shared aspiration to make RBS not just a leading bank, but also one of the most widely admired companies in the world.'

Harvard Business Review, 2003

George Mathewson was drained. The Royal Bank chief executive had found the fight for NatWest highly exhilarating but by the spring of 2000 he was fatigued and badly in need of a rest. Having been the driving force at the Royal Bank for more than a decade, first leading the struggle to save it and then launching a quest to make it the world's best bank, he was now looking forward to standing back a little.

Lord Younger and Mathewson told the board it made sense to accelerate the planned elevation of Goodwin, so that he could implement his integration plan for NatWest which had impressed them so much. Mathewson told friends that winning the takeover battle wouldn't have been possible without Fred. On 6 March 2000, the Royal Bank announced that Goodwin would become chief executive with immediate effect, with Mathewson becoming executive deputy chairman. Younger would stay on as chairman only until January 2001, although he died shortly afterwards, in January 2003, following a battle with cancer.[1] In the spring of 2000, an exhausted Sir George Mathewson promptly took himself off travelling for several months, to look at various parts of the business and recuperate. Only five years since first going into banking, and aged forty-two, Goodwin was now a bank CEO with control of the Royal Bank train set. It had been a remarkable ascent.

Just as he had at the Clydesdale when he was asked for a plan, and during the preparation of the bid document in the NatWest battle, Goodwin snapped into action deploying precisely the same techniques, to forge one large bank out of the constituent parts of the Royal Bank and the much bigger NatWest. For some of those who worked most closely with him, this was his peak. 'Fred was born to do that integration because he was probably the world's greatest project manager,' says one of his team. A 'traffic-light' system was established so that Goodwin could see at any moment whether any given initiative was stalled, almost ready or completed. Working with Mark Fisher, he commanded the teams in charge of human resources, IT, retail banking, corporate banking and the rest, setting them their tasks and hourly keeping on top of the responses. Of course he started with an advantage, which was that he was building on the foundations of the Columbus Project from the mid-1990s. The Royal Bank – which had been transformed from a relatively sleepy institution into a more thrusting operation in just a decade – was used to rapid change.

Many NatWest staff responded enthusiastically after years spent working for a struggling organisation. To counter the 'Fred the Shred' name-tag, Goodwin decreed that tea and coffee dispensed from machines in NatWest offices should be free, where previously staff had been used to paying for it. 'It was a little thing, but it made a difference to how people saw us internally,' says an adviser. The new chief executive also moved to assure

NatWest staff that they shouldn't see the integration in terms of cuts. They should view it as an opportunity to be part of a bigger and expanding enterprise. That was gilding the lily somewhat. There was still a lot of 'shredding' to be done. As many as 18,000 staff in the combined group lost their jobs when positions were scrapped and back-room and head-office functions were merged, to create the 'synergies' Goodwin had promised investors in the bid document. The senior executives in both banks were also put through assessments, to establish who would stay, who would depart and who would take the top positions. Some senior NatWest people stayed on, such as Gordon Pell, a retail banker who had previously spent a long time at Lloyds, where he was one of the early advocates of something called payment protection insurance (PPI). Just days after the takeover of NatWest, Goodwin took Pell to lunch at Rhodes, in the City, and the pair discovered they got on well and had similar ideas on what to do with NatWest.[2] Pell joined the Royal Bank board, holding a number of senior executive positions while managing to avoid gaining a public profile.

Larry Fish ran Citizens, the US institution owned by the Royal Bank. Fish had taken over from Charles Grayboys in 1992 and was on the board of the Royal Bank, along with Norman McLuskie, who oversaw Retail Direct, the credit, charge and debit card end of the business. The finance director was Fred Watt and Iain Robertson – the old friend of Mathewson's from Scottish Development Agency days who was known affectionately as 'the bald eagle' – was now the director overseeing of Corporate Banking and Financial Markets (CBFM).

The guiding philosophy of the NatWest integration was that with a merged back room the bank could create and market financial products which could then be sold under the banner of the different brands in the group. So a NatWest customer would remain with the bank, but everything would be run on Royal Bank systems. This posed an enormous challenge for John

White, head of IT. White was a veteran of IBM's plant in Greenock, from which Mathewson had drawn senior staff and inspiration in his days at the Scottish Development Agency. There were suggestions that parts of the NatWest computer set-up might be superior to those in the Royal Bank. To maximise the cost-savings they pressed ahead with the original plan, Goodwin ordering that the systems for managing accounts of NatWest and its subsidiary Ulster Bank be bolted on to those of the Royal Bank in Edinburgh.[3] This process was declared an unqualified success by Goodwin in November 2002 and the press was informed it had been completed ahead of schedule. It meant that Ulster Bank, the smallest of the three in retail terms, would go last in the queue, with its customers' transactions processed each day after those of its sister banks.

IT, based in Edinburgh's Fettes Row, was part of the vast, centralised 'machine' being built by Goodwin and Fisher, his wingman on integration who oversaw 'manufacturing'. After the integration it had almost 20,000 staff, operated 400 IT systems, managed thousands of ATMs, processed and counted hundreds of billions in cash and handled the procurement of £3bn in services and goods in the UK and beyond. The theory was that with standardised back-room procedures and IT, the Royal Bank could purchase other banks or insurance firms and integrate them on the model of the NatWest takeover.

In other respects the reorganisation from the spring of 2000 went as planned too. Gartmore, the fund management business that came with NatWest, was sold off speedily for a little over £1bn. One of the casualties was Gartmore chief executive Paul Myners. The ambitious former journalist and investment banker had been on the board of the old NatWest and it was said that Goodwin found him arrogant, although they only met for two minutes. Myners went. He had the consolation of an absolutely enormous pension pot and he went on to hold a string of other lucrative city posts. Eight years later, the newly ennobled Lord

Myners – by then a Treasury minister appointed by Gordon Brown – would be handed the job of dealing with Goodwin's severance arrangements and pension during the crisis of October 2008.

Throughout the rest of 2000, with the integration running ahead of schedule, Goodwin's management team got the first proper chance to see what he would be like as a day-to-day boss. The early signs were troubling. They were used to Mathewson's freewheeling and unorthodox style, and an atmosphere in which those involved saw themselves in the words of one as 'a happy band of brothers'. Goodwin started to introduce tension. He seemed to want to interfere in everyone's business. That obsession with small details – which had been apparent at the Clydesdale Bank – was particularly noticeable again. 'He was instantly very different from George,' says a member of the management team. 'If there was an issue or a problem Fred was more interested in finding a victim and having them crucified. The bollockings were pretty much daily.' The new chief executive didn't favour shouting, or at least not very often. His preferred approach once again was the remorseless application of logic, to expose the complete ineptitude of his victim. The assault then culminated in withering sarcasm or laconic asides about their endless capacity for incompetence. 'Fill in the complaints book on your way out of the door,' he told a senior executive who was leaving his office after a particularly bruising encounter.

The morning meetings in Edinburgh were the main forum where he introduced his team to his management style. The gatherings were known as 'morning prayers', an epithet with austere Presbyterian overtones, or 'morning beatings'. Some thought that Goodwin was just trying to impose himself, and to establish that he was going to be more rigorous than the restless Mathewson, who sometimes rambled and had trouble concentrating. There were also moments when Goodwin's dry wit came through. After flaying the management team for their alleged failures in the first section of one meeting he then had to deal with the results of the staff survey, which included feedback on how those around the table were perceived by those who worked for them. 'Ah, a game of two halves,' he said, as he ran through findings which gave his executives high marks.

But it was the way he relished catching them out with sudden barbed questions that grated most. Remembers one senior executive: 'He would ask you things in a meeting that anyone well-balanced couldn't possibly know the answer to. How many mortgages did you sell last week in a particular branch? So you either said you didn't know and got eviscerated or if you were sensible you made up an answer.' When a problem was mentioned in the morning meeting Goodwin would often declare, with a shake of the head, 'Right, drains up', meaning that it was time to get down and dirty and examine the plumbing. He also hinted that he had a network of informants telling him what was really going on in the bank. The implication was that his management team could not be trusted and that its members could not trust each other. Says one of his lieutenants, loyal to him for many years: 'When he found something out he used to say to us in the morning meeting "a little birdie tells me …" and I used to think, Fred, you know what you should do with all those little birdies? You should fucking shoot them.'

Larry Fish, boss of Citizens, was appalled by Goodwin's sarcasm and behaviour towards other subordinates when he flew to Scotland for a visit. At the end of one meeting of the management team in Edinburgh he whispered excitedly to fellow executives as they spilled out for a cup of coffee after a session with Goodwin. He had not seen anything like this in American banking. 'This is simply outrageous. Is Fred always like that?' 'This is nothing,' one of the Scots told him, 'you should see him on a bad day.'

Fish's presence at some of these meetings in Edinburgh was a reminder that the enlarged Royal Bank wasn't simply a UK bank and that it had considerable scope to expand overseas. Goodwin had ambitions to build on the existing Citizens network, then still a relatively small retail bank with branches clustered in New England. Mathewson loved Fish, seeing his folksy demeanour as key to helping unlock retail banking business in north-east America. He was good at wooing big customers, schmoozing the locals and singing the company song in places such as Boston. Others were less convinced. Members of the Royal Bank management team had watched, astonished, as Fish sucked up to his bosses blatantly. One observed: 'Larry would say to George Mathewson in meetings, completely shamelessly in front of people, "George it's been your vision that has driven Citizens and leaders like you are rare."' Another thought he was 'the worst kind of American corporate guy': 'Larry Fish was the consummate American executive. All smiles and there were never any problems.' 'Larry', adds a colleague, 'was full of shit.'

Fish certainly had a well-practised routine. How did he explain Citizens' success? It was all about the 'credo', he told those who asked. 'It's about people,' he added. 'It's nice,' he observed, 'to be nice.' Fish developed the credo further when he took time off in 2002, to visit Japan, to read and to study flower-arranging, finally distilling his approach to what he termed 'the three Cs': 'customers, colleagues and community'.

In a lecture at MIT Sloan School of Management[4] Fish told students that it came down to 'saying thank you, and having a smile'. The audience was regaled with a story about the difficulty he had buying three screws from his local hardware store and problems he encountered at the dry-cleaners when he turned up to collect his shirts, encountering staff who were less than joyful. In contrast, he said, he wanted Citizens to be the best place in the world to work. To that end, he claimed he began each day by writing a thank-you letter to a member of staff: 'Dear Betty, I heard you got that new account. Well done, proud to have you on the team. Yours, Larry.' To spread the joy further, Fish explained that the bank prided itself on subsidising pet insurance for staff. 'I met a lady in Detroit recently. She could not say enough about pet insurance. She has 13 canaries. They're very fragile.' It was a little like watching Woody Allen do an impersonation of a caricature corporate charmer. 'And then,' says a colleague in Edinburgh, 'he had a story he always used about a cat. We heard so often about that bloody cat.'

An elderly lady whose feline friend has gone missing walks into a branch of the bank somewhere in New England. Fish takes up the story: 'She's got a notebook-sized piece of paper with a picture of her cat, Fluffy. Would it be OK if I put this up on the wall?' In other banks she would have been turned away, intoned Fish gravely. But not at Citizens. The notice was put up. 'We do the right thing. Nice is good.'

The cat anecdote was also deployed on trips to the UK in an attempt to impress investors and analysts, although several of his more cynical British colleagues, tongue in cheek, asked after one such presentation what had happened to the cat. 'Did they ever find Fluffy?' Fish ignored the question.

But the mockery of their American colleague by those in Edinburgh and London was tinged with resentment. Fish was a controversial figure when he visited. For a start he earned so much. Consistently he had proven himself to be good at retail banking. And he was far from stupid when it came to negotiating his own pay and conditions, earning him renown in the Royal Bank HR department for the sharp-eyed nature of his demands. When Goodwin took over, he told colleagues that he would fly to the United States to 'sort out Larry' and what was perceived to be his overly high pay, although in the event it turned out to be bluster and Fish's pay went up. For all Goodwin's 'Fred the Shred' moniker, he could be extremely uncomfortable with certain elements of one-to-one confrontation. If there was an awkward move to be made or a firing to be done – which at the senior executive level was only very rarely – Goodwin got others to do it. Sorting out Larry came to nothing, for now. Fish's compensation soared. In 2002 his pay packet was up 50 per cent on the previous year to £3.35m, including £2.66m in 'performance bonus'.[5] This package was much bigger than that enjoyed by Goodwin, who was on a total of £2.58m. Fish had also negotiated several performance-related arrangements. The unfortunately named 'Phantom 2000 plan' and the Citizens Long-Term incentive plan netted him many millions. 'Larry roped and doped Mathewson and then he did the same to Fred for many years,' says a colleague of both.

Fish's timing was perfect. The faster Citizens grew its income and the bigger it became the more money he had a chance of making. As Goodwin stormed through the integration of NatWest, the Royal Bank chief executive was eager to do more deals that would fuel expansion. With American property and mortgage lending on the up, the United States seemed to be the perfect place to look. Since the early 1990s, Citizens had been buying up tiny regional banks in its own neighbourhood. Now, if Fish, or friendly investment bankers such as those at Merrill Lynch, could help spot opportunities to snap up other bigger regional banks in the north-east of America, Goodwin was delighted to sanction such takeovers and bring the Royal Bank's newly acquired expertise in integration to bear. Citizens, and its owner RBS, might then increase its footprint in New England and beyond. In time it might even be able to push into the American Midwest, where borrowers of all incomes (and none) were particularly keen to get in on the housing boom.

The next opportunity to expand Citizens came in 2001. The Royal Bank lost out in the race to buy Dime Bancorp, which was sold to Washington Mutual, the Seattle firm which gorged on sub-prime lending and had to be seized by the American authorities in late September 2008 following the biggest bank failure in American history. In May 2001, during the holiday weekend, Fish took a call from Mellon Financial. Would the Royal Bank be interested in buying its retail banking arm? Fish phoned Scotland and Goodwin agreed in principle straight away. By July the deal was done, for $2.1bn, again with the assistance of Matthew Greenburgh at Merrill Lynch, and the money was raised in a day in the City of London.

The purchase would more than double the number of Citizens branches – to just shy of 700 – and gave the bank a strong presence in Philadelphia. The following year the Royal Bank picked up Medford Bancorp, with branches in the Boston suburbs, for $273m. Fish was even busier in 2003 when in January the Royal Bank completed the purchase of Commonwealth Bancorp for $450m, and in July buying Port Financial Corporation in Massachusetts for $285m. From the purchase of a relatively small Rhode Island outfit in 1988, the Royal Bank and Larry 'it's nice to be nice' Fish were growing a formidable American retail operation.

It wasn't only in America that Goodwin wanted to grow. Robertson's newly expanded part of the Royal Bank was the most intriguing prospect. In some ways it was a straightforward corporate bank, now the largest in the UK, serving the borrowing needs of businesses. It looked after 75,000 corporate customers and served 200 of the companies in the FTSE 250. But it was much more than that. An integral part of the operation – alongside the corporate units of the old NatWest and the Royal Bank – were the various trading operations in financial markets. The Mathewson mantra had been that the Royal Bank didn't do classic investment banking. Conventional banks, he warned, should be wary of trying to ape the fancy footwork of institutions such as Goldman Sachs or Merrill Lynch which indulged in huge amounts of proprietary trading in currency, derivatives and securities to make profits, alongside their work advising clients on deals.

This soothing claim was at odds with the expansion that had started under Mathewson himself – who made it clear to Johnny Cameron when he hired him to work under Robertson that he was to expand the Royal Bank's investment banking-type activities in London and beyond. It was also decided by Goodwin, Mathewson, Robertson and Johnny Cameron within weeks of closing the NatWest deal that after all they would not sell the Greenwich Capital business in Connecticut, which came with NatWest. Greenwich was expert in mortgage securitisation, was a dealer in US Treasury securities (the debt the US government issues), and was an underwriter, trader and provider of investment services to governments and big corporations. It would be hard to maintain the fiction that the prudent old Royal Bank didn't indulge in investment banking activities, when it owned an outfit such as Greenwich in America and was expanding so fast in this field in London. An unspoken compromise emerged. The Royal Bank would do some of what investment banks did, but other names were used for it.

In Robertson's division, Enron was a particular problem. One of NatWest's best corporate clients was the company that had emerged to dominate the American energy market. After the Royal Bank took over NatWest, Robertson and others did not want to lose Enron and marvelled at their confusing business model in which it was never entirely clear where the money was coming from. An energy company need no longer worry too much about producing energy or selling it, it seemed. They focused more on selling on, sliced and diced, their energy contracts and futures contracts. Then they booked vast paper profits with the aid of accountants. 'It's a kind of alchemy,' Robertson told his colleagues.[6] When Andy Fastow, the financial chief of Enron, who was close to the firm's boss Jeffrey Skilling, was in London he dropped into the Royal Bank. Robertson called several colleagues and told them to get up to his office quickly: 'You've got to meet this guy Andy Fastow.'

It turned out that Enron was a huge fraud and the business collapsed in late 2001, subsequently taking down Enron's auditor Arthur Andersen. Trials followed. One of the most controversial aspects of the scandal was the extradition of the

'NatWest Three', British executives from NatWest who had done a deal with Fastow that made them and him millions in weeks. The whole Enron experience contributed to Robertson's disillusionment and he agonised over why he did not spot it. 'Iain was an old-fashioned honest kind of guy, and this just underlined for him that the financial world was now full of people prepared to do terrible things that he didn't understand. It saddened him,' says a colleague. Another colleague of Robertson's says that the Enron scandal was a warning that should have been heeded, across the banking industry. Look at what Enron had been doing. They had taken contracts, parcelled them up and traded them on in such a complicated way that the whole business became entirely disconnected from any notion of worth or underlying value: 'The roots of what happened later with sub-prime mortgages were there in an extreme form in the financial engineering in Enron, and we didn't see it.'

Goodwin's concentration though was on growth. If it was unfair at that stage to call him a 'deal junkie', someone obsessed with the thrill of doing the next big transaction, he did revel in the process of making a purchase and then applying his project-management skills to incorporate it into the group of Royal Bank businesses. Although his colleagues thought he had a quixotic taste in targets and a highly unconventional take on what a bank should be buying, some of the purchases worked. International Aviation Management was bought in August 2001 for just £16m. If leasing aircraft did not seem like a natural fit with a Scottish-based bank, the expanded division was worth $7.3bn by the time it was sold in 2010. And it gave Goodwin a way of getting access, for the first time, to a private jet.

Other experiments were costly and time-consuming failures. Should a bank with bold ambitions really be in the second-hand car business, beyond offering simple loans to customers? The motoring-obsessed Goodwin believed it should be and that there was an opportunity in selling cars and then providing the finance deals to customers, which might complement the Lombard car and van leasing business that they already owned. In buying car dealership Dixon Motors in April 2002 for £118m, Goodwin made Paul Dixon and his son Simon Dixon very rich, as they pocketed more than £4m each,[7] but it turned out to be a very poor deal for the Royal Bank. Senior bankers couldn't quite believe that so much attention was being lavished on a mere car dealership. An appalled Johnny Cameron was given the job of agreeing to the deal, having to confirm it was partly his decision so that the board didn't think the Dixon Motors deal was a manifestation of Goodwin's mania for cars. Alan Dickinson was eventually dispatched to review the situation once the first concerns emerged and he did not like the balance of the deal one bit. 'It smells', he told Cameron, 'as though we are being ripped off.' 'Oh Christ,' Cameron responded, not enjoying the thought of having to tell Goodwin.

The chief executive responded to the news that his investment was looking like a dud by digging ever deeper into the micro detail. 'As it got worse we wasted hundreds of valuable hours talking about this thing at the morning meetings. We were discussing a bloody car dealership. It went on for ever,' says another member of the management team. In the end, Dixon Motors was sold back in a management buyout in 2005. The Royal Bank was down tens of millions and the car dealership later went into administration under new ownership. While the slowly unfolding farce contributed to a sense amongst his team that Goodwin was inexperienced, it was accepted that a chief executive might make mistakes. What was more worrying to Cameron, Dickinson and others was that it also suggested he had trouble admitting error. They felt that they were blamed for the car dealership imbroglio when they had not been enthusiastic about the deal in the first place and it had been Goodwin's baby. A pattern was established, where those with doubts about a transaction didn't feel it was worth speaking up sufficiently robustly because in doing so they would be taking on a chief executive with a bound-less capacity for grinding down opponents.

The danger was that Goodwin's approach might leave too little room for senior executives to admit to a hunch – perhaps based on years of experience spent observing a particular market. In a well-run organisation, sometimes the best question ahead of a potential disaster comes from someone who doesn't necessarily know the answer, but who senses that their colleagues might have got carried away with a daft idea. The culture developing under Fred Goodwin, in which he seemed to see persistent questioning as dissent, could militate against open-minded discussion.

'Fred was your classic bully,' says one of his most senior executives. Some executives gossiped that this was because he had been bullied at school in Paisley and was a naturally introverted type who had learned that the best way to defend himself was to keep others on their guard: 'I thought he did it because he always had to make himself safe, safe from attack,' says a colleague. 'I think he had no capacity for compassion. I really mean that,' says another member of his team. Another colleague thought it was all about an inability to realise the human cost of his actions: 'He had no understanding of the impact he had on others. I used to challenge him on it after he had had a go at someone and he was baffled. What's the problem? It's fine, we'll have a beer at some point, he'll be fine.'

The nature of Goodwin's relationship with Mathewson complicated matters. They had achieved a lot together. They had even been vindicated over the Bank of Scotland. As predicted it disappeared as a stand-alone entity after losing the race to buy NatWest. In theory the combination with the Halifax, a former building society based in Yorkshire, was a merger. In practice, both of the two top posts were filled by Halifax people, with Lord Stevenson of Coddenham[8] becoming chairman and James Crosby chief executive. Under Crosby, real power shifted south and the

Bank of Scotland's headquarters on the Mound in Edinburgh came to be seen by critics, including the Royal Bank team, as a mere shell adorned with a brass plate. Gratifyingly for Mathewson, the battle between the two banks, which had raged for almost three centuries, had been won conclusively by the Royal Bank.

Meanwhile, Mathewson was wrestling with how to police Goodwin. He tried at first to take a relatively indulgent view of the chief executive's approach. 'Fred was George's creation,' says a friend of Mathewson. 'George picked him, he promoted Fred and he made him so he had to back him.' Goodwin was learning on the job and Lord Younger – who knew little about the complexities of banking but who after a career in politics was a shrewd observer of human behaviour – had allowed Mathewson plenty of room to breathe and been on hand with advice when needed. The new chairman would try to give Goodwin some space. On the other hand Mathewson found it impossible to avoid having periodic blazing rows with his protégé. Alone the pair could get into heated discussions about the way Goodwin dealt with subordinates and his refusal to take advice.

In 2003 Mathewson moved to punish Goodwin, for the way the retail banking side of the business did not seem to be making as much progress as other parts of the Royal Bank. It was run by Benny Higgins, a colourful charmer. A schoolboy maths prodigy, fanatical Celtic supporter and poetry aficionado with a string of ex-wives, he had been tipped for the top at Standard Life, the Edinburgh savings and investment firm, before he left as a result of personal problems. He landed at the Royal Bank. Even then Higgins thought that the mortgages that banks such as HBOS and Northern Rock were issuing were 'insane' and likely to lead to losses, so he ran things conservatively. It meant that Goodwin's performance bonus in 2003 was hacked to £990,000, from £1.7m in 2002. This was a huge pay cut, with his total remuneration going from £2.58m in 2002[9] down to £1.9m in 2003. Goodwin set out to encourage Higgins to leave, which eventually he did. Ironically, he then went to HBOS, where he discovered that the lending policies were even more aggressive than they appeared and he moved on again, only to be vindicated in the financial crisis.

Cameron McPhail, who had managed the Columbus Project for Mathewson, was also forced out. After Columbus he had been put in charge of Wealth Management, which comprised the private banks Coutts, Adam & Company, Drummond Bank and the offshore operations of Royal Bank International. This was banking of a very rarefied and exclusive kind reserved for the super-affluent and extremely rich. McPhail detested Goodwin's management style and the atmosphere of ill feeling that it generated. He left in 2002. McPhail's long spell on gardening leave gave him time to reflect and he resolved to sell the shares he had accumulated, getting his money out of the Royal Bank at a good price.

These interruptions aside, Mathewson was generally extremely pleased. His vision of a Scottish banking colossus was being realised astonishingly quickly. True, by necessity more of what the bank did was based in London – with all those NatWest customers to serve and corporate clients to service – but the heart of the bank remained in Edinburgh, where the board met and many of the most senior executives lived. Vindication was piled upon vindication when the NatWest integration was completed early and the 'synergies' of combining the two banks turned out to be £2.03bn rather than the £1.73bn expected. All the NatWest back offices had been emptied of staff and the workings of the new group put on the Royal Bank platform. Those staff who remained shared in the good fortune. A 5 per cent of salary bonus was handed to 75,000 employees whose units had been directly involved in the integration. In addition, staff across the entirety of the new group were also given 10 per cent of basic salary as a profit share. Unsurprisingly, after this Goodwin was popular with staff when he spoke at conferences or went on visits to outposts of his empire.

Profits were continuing a seemingly relentless climb. In 2000 the Royal Bank had made £4.4bn before tax, in 2001 it was £5.8bn and in 2002 £6.45bn. The transformation was striking. Just ten years earlier, in 1992, the bank had come close to making a loss. In that year, before the full impact of the Mathewson revolution and with Project Columbus just getting under way, the comparatively small Royal Bank, with only 23,457 employees, scraped a measly profit of only £21m. Now it looked as though the next stop might be 8, 9 or even 10bn pounds.

Goodwin basked in the acclaim as the accolades and awards started to flow. At the end of 2002, a leading American business publication, *Forbes* magazine, announced that because of the successful integration of NatWest, it was making Goodwin its 'Global Businessman of the Year' and putting him on the cover. There was considerable excitement at the Royal Bank head office in Edinburgh, where there were signs that a 'cult of Fred' was developing. *Your Magazine*, the bank's own staff publication, had already become increasingly confident in tone and each month featured an inordinate number of pictures of Goodwin in various poses, meeting staff, opening offices and generally grinning a great deal. He was visibly growing in confidence, shedding some of his geekiness, losing the glasses and projecting an assured image.

The *Forbes* article meant that the Royal Bank was really on the map and being taken seriously in America and beyond. Goodwin relished the praise: 'He loved recognition and he loved awards. Unfortunately he took them seriously, which can be dangerous,' says a member of his team. *Forbes* dispatched a correspondent to interview the 44-year-old chief executive. The resulting piece[10] contained fulsome praise: 'The Royal Bank of Scotland now has a market cap of $70 billion, making it the world's fifth-biggest bank. Few realise that this 275-year-old Scottish bank, a nonentity on the world stage just a few years ago, is now bigger by [market capitalisation] than such household names as J. P. Morgan, Chase, UBS and Deutsche Bank.'

Profits were up, the cost-income had been reduced to make the Royal Bank one of the most efficient around and customer satisfaction and staff morale were on the rise.

Goodwin, said *Forbes*, was 'an original thinker' noted for his 'analytic rigour'. His friends queued up to pay tribute, led by his old mentor John Connolly. 'Fred never just accepts advice,' said the boss of accountants Deloitte & Touche. 'When we've all got a lot to do, it's very easy to say, "I've had the advice. That's the thing to do." He always makes time to satisfy himself that he has the right answer.' *Forbes*, possibly due to a lack of space, did not point out that Connolly's firm was by then the auditor of the Royal Bank, having won the contract shortly after Goodwin took over as chief executive. It wasn't all sweetness and light, however. 'When you meet Goodwin, he comes across as cool and witty. But there's acid just below the surface,' acknowledged the interviewer. Goodwin could be caustic, and due to a certain 'tartness' of manner he was not universally liked by those who worked immediately below him. Those extraordinary Royal Bank results had been achieved by making 'almost inhuman demands on his executives', one of whom described his boss as a 'prowling fox'. Goodwin talked openly of 'mercy-killing' competitors.

The real growth area, noted *Forbes*, would be America. There were more targets that Goodwin and Fish had for Citizens, although the chief executive stressed he was not interested in anything too risky on the other side of the Atlantic. There were, acknowledged the man from *Forbes*, a few sceptical mutterings. An analyst from Lehman Brothers in London had noted that the Royal Bank had the highest exposure to UK corporate risk, meaning loans might go bad if the economy turned down in the years ahead. In particular the bank was number one in Europe in 'leveraged finance', the provision of vast loans which allow companies to take on large amounts of debt to make acquisitions or to fund a management buyout. At the start of 2003, there were a few clouds on the immediate economic horizon, although they soon dissipated as the long boom resumed with full intensity.

After the *Forbes* accolade, an endorsement arrived from an even more illustrious source. The Harvard Business School – the pre-eminent institution providing MBAs and schooling trainee corporate titans in the latest management thinking – gave its blessing in a 2003 paper describing the aftermath of the NatWest deal.[11] Echoing the infamous 'Masters of the Universe' phrase, an epithet coined by Tom Wolfe to describe greedy young investment bankers on Wall Street in the 1980s, the Harvard study on Goodwin was headlined: 'The Royal Bank of Scotland: Masters of Integration'. Immediately underneath was a quote that Goodwin had given in an interview conducted for a corporate video with the BBC journalist Kirsty Wark. 'Hard work, focus, discipline and concentrating on what our customers want. It's quite a simple formula, but we've just been very, very consistent with it.'

The tone of the Harvard paper was solemnly respectful. After detailing the successes of the NatWest deal, the authors mused on the management style of Goodwin and pondered his aspirations. Could the Royal Bank – which had expanded so rapidly – carry on growing? There was no way would Goodwin rest on his laurels, it seemed: 'As he looked to the future he was confident that RBS would again prove the sceptics wrong.' Goodwin told the authors from Harvard that he was confident his entire organisation was ready to meet the challenge. 'They [the team at the Royal Bank] had a shared aspiration to make RBS not just a leading bank, but also one of the most widely admired companies in the world.' A small bank, which had started with just eight staff in Edinburgh's Ship Close, had weathered the centuries and reinvented itself so successfully that it was now the object of admiration and adulation by the high priests of global capitalism.

8

Sir Fred

'There's a perception among some investors that Fred Goodwin is a megalomaniac.'

James Eden, analyst, Dresdner Kleinwort
Wasserstein, 4 August 2005

Ever since taking over at the Royal Bank, Fred Goodwin had wanted a bigger headquarters. The Royal Bank's Georgian-fronted main office on St Andrew Square in Edinburgh had been home to the institution since the 1820s and although its elegant facade projected an image of genteel reliability, and the corridors of its management floor were hung with paintings evoking the bank's history, the building seemed too stuffy, small and imprac-tical. Even though next door there were bigger offices adjoining, it was concluded that the entire complex was a rabbit warren and architectural hotchpotch. This was not at all what one of Europe's biggest banks needed. George Mathewson had con-cluded as much in his final days as chief executive. Along with his friend Angus Grossart, Edinburgh financier and vice chair-man of the Royal Bank, Mathewson had cooked up a scheme that would involve the bank flattening a particularly ugly office block it had bought from the government, behind St Andrew Square. Leading retailers in the neighbouring shopping centre would get a pleasant new home, the Royal Bank would have a proper modern office attached to its elegant old home and the city's populace would be rid of a concrete monstrosity dubbed 'Scotland's biggest eyesore'.

Goodwin had doubts. The project was Mathewson's project, and the chairman needed to be indulged. But didn't the Royal Bank need to make a much bigger statement of intent by building a headquarters away from the confines of Edinburgh's New Town with its cobbled streets and space constraints? For a while there was speculation in Edinburgh that Goodwin was considering moving the headquarters to London, something he denied firmly when asked by his staff. A migration to England would have been a betrayal of the Royal Bank's heritage. What he had in mind instead was the construction from scratch of a giant head office on the outskirts of Edinburgh, somewhere near enough to the airport to make it easy to jet around the world to visit other parts of the bank's operations. It could be a symphony in glass and steel, with wide open spaces and state-of-the-art facilities for several thousand staff.

The talks with retailers in central Edinburgh were scuppered quite suddenly in the autumn of 2000 by the Royal Bank.[1] Mathewson, who was personally identified with the city centre scheme, was initially unhappy over the loss of face, although along with Grossart he became excited by the possibilities of moving out of the town centre. Thanks in part to the Royal Bank, Edinburgh was booming, with house prices rising at more than 10 per cent a year and property speculators looking for opportunities. If the Scottish capital was really about to enjoy a new golden age then it would eventually need to expand beyond its existing boundaries. In opting for building a daring new headquarters out near the airport, the Royal Bank was innovating and trying to show the way to other local businesses and developers. Eighty acres were purchased at Gogarburn, to the west of the Scottish capital. After RBS hit the wall in 2008, it was noted that its vast new headquarters had been built, appropriately it seemed, on the site of a former lunatic asylum. This was not strictly true. Gogarburn had been home to a hospital which enabled mentally disabled patients to be treated outside the asylum system, yet in the light of what went wrong at Goodwin's RBS this important distinction was deemed not to matter.

The chief executive's office was soon full of architects' drawings as Goodwin pored over proposals and examined the options. The old adage is that shareholders should be worried about the CEO becoming a megalomaniac when a company builds a grand new headquarters, and doubly worried when he puts a fountain in front of it. Goodwin liked the idea of Gogarburn featuring a large fountain. The architects – a Scottish firm, Michael Laird – drafted in the craftsmen of the Fountain Workshop, who were based in the Royal Dockyard in Chatham, Kent. They came up with 'a large external reflection pool with a 40m long overspilling weir edge' that framed the main entrance to the development, 'providing a crisp reflection of the architectural form'. The exterior of the main building was to be cast in dark glass and sandstone, with seven 'business houses' arranged around what was the spine of the development: an internal street lined with coffee shops, a hairdresser, a Royal Bank branch for staff to use, a chemist and other shops, giving the place the characteristics of a real town, 'Fredtown'.

The architects trumpeted 'a landscaped campus' with a conference centre and nursery. With a total floor area of over 800,000 square feet there would be room for as many as 3,500 staff. Next door, on adjacent parkland, was to be a Royal Bank business school in which executives would be tutored. It would be developed jointly with Harvard Business School, which, by a remarkable coincidence, was working on its academic paper hailing Goodwin and the Royal Bank as 'Masters of Integration' for the NatWest deal. The designs for Gogarburn were completed in early 2002, planning permission was granted that autumn and work began almost immediately. At the peak of the project as many as 2,000 workmen toiled on the site, constructing a monument to corporate ambition and racing to get it ready in time for a grand opening scheduled for 2006.

When the planned move to Gogarburn was discussed in public, the emphasis was often on the 'global' dimensions of the project. The word international was used a lot. Gogarburn was the right location, the chief executive said, because: 'There are a very limited number of sites in Scotland which would allow the expanded Royal Bank of Scotland Group to achieve the operational efficiencies that are necessary for a large international organisation.'[2]

Someone who seemed perturbed about notions of hubris at RBS was Lord Younger. Late in 2002, he was in a hospice stricken with cancer. At what would later turn out to be his death bed, Mathewson and Goodwin paid a visit, bringing artists impressions of what Gogarburn would look like and a picture of the RBS private jet. Joanna Davidson, Lord Younger's daughter was there with her father. After he had looked at the drawings and pictures, and his former colleagues had gone, he turned to her and said: 'When you see things like that you wonder if it's time to sell your shares in RBS'. Joanna told family members about it and, later on, her work colleagues. She also died of cancer in 2008, aged just 50. Some members of the Younger family think that Lord Younger may have in part been joking, while others are convinced that he knew the growth of RBS was getting out of hand.

Under Goodwin, the bank's focus was shifting markedly. While Mathewson's ambition for the Royal Bank had always been intertwined with his Scottish nationalist views, Goodwin's colleagues were clear that he saw it differently, although not aggressively so. A patriot, who shared Mathewson's pride that a small Scottish institution had grown to be the second-biggest bank in the UK, Goodwin also considered himself to be resolutely British at a time when the Scots were putting ever more emphasis on endlessly expressing their national identity. Indeed, his colleagues were convinced that he even voted Conservative, making him unusual north of the border. Even though he wanted to live in Scotland and raise his two children in Edinburgh, he was reluctant to make as much of a fetish out of his Scottishness as 'wee George' did. With the Royal Bank getting bigger, and with more of its activities in London and overseas, it would naturally have to become a little less Scottish in its outlook and behaviour. Some of the traditional details Goodwin was disinclined to change. When the board was meeting in Edinburgh and broke for lunch – perhaps inviting in some of the bank's senior executives to join them – it was a cast-iron custom that Scottish mince and potatoes (or mince'n'tatties) were always served. This was perhaps a little unsophisticated, and certainly not in keeping with the spirit of the ongoing financial revolution and the emergence of the Royal Bank as a global bank. 'It was great mince though,' says a member of the executive team.

In other ways, the emphasis was evolving in a manner that prefigured a significant change in outlook. From 2003 the term RBS, as opposed to the full name, Royal Bank of Scotland, gradually started to be used more often to describe the company under which myriad brands went about their business. The more frequent deployment of those initials, on the front of the annual report, in branding and in conversation, mattered. Many of the world's leading corporations – alongside which Goodwin now aimed to be measured – relied on using initials by which they could be instantly identified. In the coming age of globalisation, the biggest corporations and banks would need a readily identifiable brand in countries where language might be a barrier.

One of the ways in which large corporations or banks like to 'build their brand' across borders is sport sponsorship. The theory is that backing events which customers and potential clients enjoy watching will, sometimes in an ill-defined way, bring in business. In plastering its logo on the shirt of a sports star a bank is associating itself with athletic endeavour and success. It helps too that chief executives who approve the multi-million-pound deals for their companies to sponsor a particular sport often like watching from the best seats after partaking of corporate hospitality. So it was with Goodwin. Under his leadership, RBS set out to top the league in sponsorship of golf, rugby, tennis and Formula 1 motor-racing. For decades the Royal Bank had been a sponsor of the annual Open championship, the premier UK golf competition. It was a natural fit. Although the championship is played at courses around the UK, the Open is administered by the Royal and Ancient Golf Club in St Andrews, the home of golf. Among the R&A's members have been many Royal Bank customers and directors, and the two institutions are similarly proud of their Scottish roots.

Goodwin wanted to use golf to push RBS into America. To help he signed up one of his boyhood heroes, the golfer Jack Nicklaus, to be a 'brand ambassador' around whom a marketing campaign could be built. Goodwin loved the association with a global superstar who ranks as history's most successful golfer. He won the Masters six times, the US Open four times and the British Open three times. Nicklaus was particularly effective at impressing the clients, staff and journalis~~~ ~~ was dispatched to woo over dinner in the dining room~~~~~~~~~~ ~~S-owned private bank Drummonds, or at corpo~~~~~~~~~~~ events. His gentlemanly style – and willing~~~~~~~~~ dotes and tales of triumph that he must ~~~~~~~ times – endeared him to audiences. In ~~~~~~~~ put Nicklaus's portrait on two m~~~~~~~~ non-British, non-royal living ~~~~~~~~~ honour.[3] He was paid han~~~~~~~~ Nicklaus was put on £1m~~~~~~~

Somewhat trickier was another of Goodwin's boyhood heroes, Jackie Stewart. The successes of the 'Flying Scot' on the motor-racing track are unarguable. Three times world champion, in an age when drivers faced much more danger and safety failures regularly produced fatalities, the Dumbarton-born Stewart was a genuine sporting hero. From tax exile in Switzerland he had become wealthy by turning himself into a business based on sponsorship deals with companies such as Rolex (slogan: 'If you were racing here tomorrow you'd wear a Rolex'), Ford, Goodyear and Elf. Sir Martin Sorrell, the advertising mogul, noted how Stewart had been one of the first global sports stars to spot the opportunity: 'Jackie always had very, very strong commercial relationships. If a sponsor wanted to get Jackie to work for them they knew they were going to be getting value for money.'[4] Stewart was also put on £1m a year.

While it is clear why tyre, fuel and car companies might want the endorsement of Stewart, it is less obvious that a bank needs a racing driver on board. Goodwin – a car fanatic – saw it differently and Stewart became a brand ambassador. The pair had formed an extremely close friendship. Colleagues told how Goodwin loved to listen to Stewart's stories of Formula 1 derring-do, with the racing driver recounting how his heightened senses could detect danger around the corner in a microsecond. They also liked to shoot together, a pursuit to which Goodwin had taken like a duck to water.

According to Stewart, Formula 1 was relatively classless, extremely aspirational, transcontinental and the perfect sponsorship opportunity. In 2005, with Goodwin in the driving seat taking an extremely close interest in the details, RBS became the sponsor of the F1 Williams team. The bank's logo was stencilled on Williams's cars and whizzed around the track at high speed on the F1 circuit. Goodwin's executives quickly got exotic demands from Stewart's team. The high-rolling wanting to watch the Monaco Grand Prix could not possibly be expected to arrive by car. They would need helicopters, it was explained. For his part, Goodwin was thrilled to be trackside, pottering about in the pits with Stewart, meeting motor-racing luminaries and hearing the roar of the engines. It was an expensive business. RBS sponsorship of F1 cost £25m. In addition, each year for the Monaco Grand Prix, RBS spent £250,000 of shareholders money on renting a well-positioned, vast apartment that could be converted into a hospitality suite for guests for the day of the race.

There were many other deals. Rugby's six nations championship became the RBS 6 Nations in 2003. Before and after games at Murrayfield, several hundred guests drank champagne and listened to the star players give their take on that day's game. The sponsorship department grew remorselessly; entertaining became steadily more lavish and was conducted on an ever-grander scale. Peter Phillips, son of the Princess Royal and grandson of the Queen, was also hired to work in global sponsorship and tasked with finding new global ambassadors. Later, in 2007, his sister Zara Phillips, the equestrian star, was signed up on £90,000 a year.

Was it all worth the more than £200m spent on sport sponsorship under Goodwin? Banks certainly need to advertise themselves and entertain clients. Those who work in sport sponsorship say that when compared with other forms of marketing it is a relatively cheap way of catching the attention of tens of millions of viewers. But then they would say that. There was good done, certainly. From the age of thirteen the Scottish tennis player Andy Murray was backed by Royal Bank financial support, which helped him become the first British man in seven decades to win the men's singles title at Wimbledon in 2013. There were initiatives to support golf and tennis at the grass-roots level. Even so, it is impossible to avoid the conclusion that a bank which had only a few years before been relatively modest in its tastes – with a bit of golf sponsorship – was now, at Goodwin's instigation, spending hundreds of millions showing off. The risk was that this global self-aggrandisement might distort the thinking of those at the top of RBS.

'George was trying to build something for Scotland. Fred was trying to build something big and global,' says an adviser. 'There was GE, BP, HSBC and IBM. Fred saw RBS joining those big multinational companies.' The firm which Goodwin seemed to be most interested in was an American giant. GE, or General Electric, had been run for almost twenty years by Jack Welch, the pugnacious CEO and chairman who was born in humble circumstances and rose to end up lauded as the king of American business. Afterwards he had a career as a motivational speaker on management matters and was the author of highly successful books on succeeding in business with titles such as *Winning*. Goodwin initiated a few Welch-style 'work-outs' in which he challenged his team to examine their consciences and ask themselves if they had really done everything possible to make themselves as efficient as they might be. Welch also decreed that corporate life should be fun: 'Have a ball! Why would you want to come to a place as a stuffed shirt and hang around a corporation? It's dumb, unless you had a ball at it!'

Although Goodwin looked rather buttoned up, dour even, he could certainly enjoy himself, as he demonstrated in the bar at the annual management awaydays. In late March or early April each year the top 500 or so RBS executives gathered for their annual conference. It was a highlight of Goodwin's year and until Gogarburn opened the bank took over Gleneagles for several days. At the famous five-star hotel nestling in the Perthshire hills there would be strategising, bonding and drinking. Every year it was a big production, with speeches from Goodwin and the other senior members of the management. While the daytime sessions involved presentations on business, the fun was in the evening. There would be a dinner and then infamously epic drinking sessions stretching into the early hours. On these occasions

Goodwin's capacity for consuming large amounts of whisky and beer while not showing any ill effects was formidable. These were boom years, with RBS flying and spirits high. For the senior managers from far-flung parts of the business who might not often see Goodwin in a social setting these evenings offered a chance to have a chat with a boss who was widely admired because of the bank's success. Some were notably nervous and hung back, others jostled for a word and the opportunity to drink as part of his circle. This was what he really loved, Goodwin told colleagues. A senior executive remembers: 'Fred could be great over a beer, telling very funny stories. He just didn't do it enough with us.'

But Goodwin had a decent stab at it. Each year in late January or early February the dozen-strong executive team would also have its own wine-fuelled 'boys outing' to St Andrews, staying in the Old Course Hotel, which overlooks the hallowed home of golf. 'Fred loved it. And he introduced the idea of presents being handed out to us,' says a regular attendee. 'I still have all the cashmere jerseys.' Weather permitting, the executive team would play a round on the Old Course. The Christmas lunches in the 'mess' in Edinburgh, starting at noon and finishing very late, were also infamous. One of the executive team recalls a game involving assorted bankers dipping a finger in sambuca, one lighting it and then passing around the flame, with the first person to opt out declared a sissy.

The boss who could take part in carousing and enjoy bonhomie was again, as he had been at the Clydesdale Bank, difficult to square with the character at the morning meetings. Some on his senior team found it baffling and bizarre that Goodwin could transform himself so dramatically from jovial drinking companion to demonic corporate robot. The driving imperative spurring him on, everyone was clear, was growth. After the wonders of the NatWest deal, the City wanted to know what the Royal Bank and its boss would do next to maintain the momentum. The answer was do more deals.

RBS's insurance business was expanded again. Churchill – with its nodding bulldog character and 'Oh yes' catchphrase from the popular television adverts – was purchased in June 2003 for £1.1bn[5] and then run alongside Direct Line, the groundbreaking business that Peter Wood had started in 1985 as the first telephone-based insurer. Ireland also seemed to offer opportunities, with Ulster Bank keen to get into the booming property market south of the border in the Republic. It snaffled First Active, an Irish savings institution that in the 1980s had bought up modest building societies with names such as the Guinness Permanent Building Society and then turned itself into a bank.[6] It was said to be particularly innovative in property lending. Indeed, First Active was the first outfit in Ireland to issue 100 per cent mortgages, requiring no deposit from those taking out a loan to buy a house.

Larry Fish's Citizens empire in America maintained a cracking pace too, adding Community Bancorp in October 2003 for $116m and Roxborough Manayunk Bank in January 2004 for $136m. 'Fred liked doing acquisitions. That got him out of bed in the morning,' says a member of the management team. With the praise pouring in, it was perhaps unsurprising that Goodwin sought to replicate earlier success by buying so many other businesses. The model that had been designed in the NatWest takeover was applied repeatedly: buy something, set the management on the ground clear targets, put everything on the RBS IT and 'manufacturing' platform, remorselessly interrogate any problems along the way and then look for the next opportunity. There were some warning signs that as RBS increased in size it was becoming more difficult to repeat the original trick. At Churchill there were staff complaints when elements of the integration and sackings were botched. John O'Roarke, the chief operating officer of RBS Insurance, gave his own staff three out of ten for the way it was handled. He acknowledged afterwards: 'What people are saying is: "Give me some certainty as to when we can go." That's the bit we have failed to deliver on. There is an argument that we opened the kimono too soon.'[7]

'Opening the kimono too soon' seems to have involved implying to Churchill staff after the takeover that they were for the chop, when actually they were needed to keep the business going for a while during the integration, before some of them would be sacked. 'We said it was all doom and gloom and you are all going to lose your jobs when it might have been more appropriate to say, for IT people, there will be a long business-as-usual period.'

The use of a term such as 'manufacturing' to describe the back-room part of the RBS business that dealt with processing, procurement, managing the bank's property portfolio and IT, also jarred with some. 'No real banker talks about the basics of banking as manufacturing, as though it is tins of baked beans being produced,' says a senior retail banker. 'But then it should never be forgotten that Fred wasn't a banker.' Some of the older hands noticed that Goodwin seemed to have little interest in the basics of banking and concepts such as credit and risk. Instead, just as during his days at the Clydesdale Bank he often became most exercised when it came to footling matters. Following the death of her father, Lord Younger, Joanna Davidson joined the Royal Bank as head of corporate social responsibility. She confided in family and friends about how difficult she found it working for Goodwin, with his temper and tendency to meddle. When she took him a selection of designs for the company Christmas card he blew his top and said they were all terrible. That's it, he declared. I'm taking over direct control of the production of the Christmas card. Untidy filing cabinets, with documents piled on top, were another source of annoyance. An edict went out across the bank that storage cabinets must be procured which featured a rounded top, making it impossible for staff to leave anything on the surface: 'Somewhere in a warehouse are thousands of old flat-top RBS filing cabinets that were not Fred-compliant,' says an RBS manager.

Carpets bothered him too. The old building at Waterhouse Square in Holborn was no longer big enough to accommodate all the executives and the growing army of traders in the expanding investment banking side of the business. Several new London offices were opened in Bishopsgate on the edge of the City in 2003. On the twelfth floor of number 280, with views out across the East End and north London, Goodwin was installed in an office so vast that it would have been possible to play a game of five-a-side football. Next door was a 'war room', where management meetings could be held, and next to that another large office for the chairman, Mathewson. On the floors below there was room for thousands of London-based employees. But before the move could go ahead, Goodwin made a visit and decided that he hated the carpets that had been laid on the executive floors. They were the wrong shade and had to be replaced. Goodwin could take a joke on the subject, just about. Howard Moody announced to that year's awayday gathering at Gleneagles that Fred should be given an award for services to the British carpet industry. In comparison to Gogarburn, 280 Bishopsgate counted as mere tinkering. The new international headquarters in Edinburgh got the full force of his attention as he tuned in to discussions about workflow, finishes, paint, catering – and fountains – all to create the perfect building. The joke, behind his back, was that the boss was an architect manqué who was relishing constructing a monument to the bank and perhaps even to himself.

Then there was the executive car fleet, which he took an exceptionally close interest in. These were the chauffeur-driven cars, twelve in total, that were on standby to ferry about Goodwin, other top executives and directors who needed to travel on RBS business in London, Edinburgh, Belfast and Dublin. They were leased through the bank's Lombard vehicle fleet management and when it was time to order a new fleet of Mercedes S-Class, the chief executive became very hands-on. Mercedes asked what shade of blue RBS would like. It must,

Goodwin stipulated, be Pantone 281, to match precisely RBS's corporate blue. Similarly the leather interior must be exactly the correct shade of beige matching the carpets in the management suite of offices. The cars would have to be spray-painted to order. Mark Fisher was dispatched to Germany to supervise the order. Fisher was a fellow petrol-head renowned among staff for his ability to perform an impression of a Ferrari accelerating. It was said, rather cruelly, by his colleagues that he was so keen to copy the boss that he bought the same cars and adopted his friend's latest hobbies too, taking up shooting when Fred was introduced to guns.

Goodwin loved cars. His highly logical and keenly analytical brain was attuned to taking apart an engine and putting it back together again.[8] Vintage cars remained his main hobby and a conversation about this had long been a way to get his attention. In Edinburgh a friend of Goodwin's recalls mentioning in passing that he was thinking about buying an old and expensive car, whereupon he received a good-natured lecture for the next twenty minutes about the workings of its engine and in particular the wonders of its beautifully designed carburettor.

The fixation on details could lead him into bizarre confrontations with members of his senior team. Alan Dickinson found himself called out of a meeting by an agitated secretary. Fred was on the phone and didn't sound at all happy. Dickinson thought that some terrible and sudden calamity must have befallen either the UK economy or RBS, and he rushed to take the call. 'Alan, what on earth are you doing? I've just discovered you've got an events team.' Dickinson explained that, yes, of course he did. The part of the bank he was involved in managing employed tens of thousands of people and it made sense to have a small group which could organise the functions, roadshow events and dinners required to entertain customers and reward staff. Goodwin was appalled, and a ten-minute argument ensued. Events were 'his' bailiwick, Goodwin said, and they were supposed to be run centrally, out of RBS headquarters. As Dickinson finished the call and went back into his meeting to continue where he had broken off, he wondered if Goodwin, chief executive of a large 'international' bank, really shouldn't have much better things to worry about. A compromise was later brokered by Howard Moody, by which Dickinson's events team would be based in Edinburgh – notionally under Goodwin's control but with everyone else knowing they really reported elsewhere. Even then it seemed like an energy-sapping waste of time and a distraction from the real business at hand, although a pattern was well established in which the highly remunerated executives usually found a way of accommodating Goodwin's demands and not making a fuss.

After mid-2004, there were early signs that the gloss might already be coming off the Goodwin model. The acquisition of Charter One in the United States, bought to add to Larry Fish's empire, was RBS's biggest deal since NatWest and the largest purchase Goodwin made in America. It made Citizens one of the top fifteen banks by size in the United States and gave it added reach in the Midwestern states, where a property boom was under way. Goodwin told the City that it would mean that 25 per cent of RBS group profits would now be generated on the other side of the Atlantic. The immediate problem was that the price Goodwin agreed to pay – £5.9bn – seemed steep.[9] Fish, who had benefited personally so much from RBS growth in the United States, was not keen and by this point did not like the relentless pressure from Goodwin to always do more and get bigger. Shareholders, who had to stump up £2.5bn of the purchase price, also grew restless. Fred Watt, the then finance director, tried to reassure investors that RBS wasn't pursuing 'growth for growth's sake'. Ominously, Charter One added to the sense that Goodwin was an empire builder with only one trick, namely buying businesses with shareholders' money and then looking to do it again for the sake of increased scale. Certainly the emphasis, in communications with staff, was on how huge RBS was becoming. Says a staff member of the period: 'It was always look at us and see how massive we are. We're the fifth-largest bank in the world and aren't we great.'

Goodwin and Mathewson had also entered the rarefied world of executives who fly by private jet. The Falcon 900EX, which its French manufacturers Dassault boasted was designed to 'bring the world within your reach', had the private registration number G-RBSG. The first 'G' is the standard way of denoting UK registration but the rest looked as though it stood for 'Royal Bank of Scotland Goodwin'. Passengers enjoyed 'soft, deep pile carpeting', relaxing on 'supple leathers'. And 'two dozen panoramic windows drench the cabin with natural light . . . while the galley houses all the essentials for a fine dining experience 45,000ft in the air.' When the *Sunday Telegraph*[10] discovered the existence of the jet there was a bizarre exchange in which RBS initially denied it and then fell back on the defence that the plane was owned by Lombard Aviation management, the RBS-owned firm. The plane travelled widely, criss-crossing the Atlantic and popping down to Spain (where coincidentally Sir George was on the board of Santander). It could fly to Beijing, although it needed refuelling on the way.

Just as the first serious concerns were surfacing that the Royal Bank might have got itself lost up in the stratosphere, the British establishment completed its embrace of the RBS chief executive. When, on 12 June 2004, it was announced that Goodwin was to be knighted for services to banking he displayed a boyish delight. From Paisley he had risen rapidly to be feted as one of the best bankers of his generation. Now he was being accorded a great honour by the British state, a reward for hard work in which his wife Joyce could share. She became Lady Goodwin. 'Fred was very puffed up. He really, really, enjoyed it,' says a friend. 'He was very proud of everything receiving the knighthood represented for himself and RBS.'

Contrary to what was reported later, it was not offered at the instigation of either Gordon Brown or Tony Blair. Even though they honoured and ennobled a long list of bankers, Goodwin actually became Sir Fred thanks to the intervention of the then First Minister of Scotland,[11] Jack McConnell and the Scottish government's honours nomination committee. McConnell, one of that rare breed, a Blairite in the Scottish Labour Party, became convinced that Goodwin deserved proper recognition for what he had done at RBS. Even though the chief executive was a long-standing, if mute, devo-sceptic, his achievements fitted neatly with Labour's post-devolution claims north of the border. The success of RBS seemingly validated the argument that a home-grown international firm could create jobs and do well under a Scottish Parliament. The Scottish Labour leadership was also keen to rebut the charge that the party was excessively statist and unfriendly towards enterprise.

The case for a Goodwin knighthood was bolstered by his being a convinced unionist. Mathewson had accepted a knight-hood under Donald Dewar,[12] one of McConnell's predecessors as First Minister, but Mathewson's sympathies lay with the SNP and his close friend Alex Salmond, the leading nationalist and then future First Minister. Salmond was an RBS man through and through. Before he became an SNP MP he had been an econ-omist working at the Royal Bank, and after entering Parliament in 1987 he maintained a keen interest in hearing gossip about the progress of RBS and its main characters. Goodwin recognised the importance of getting on well with both sides, and was un-failingly courteous to McConnell, whose administration then recommended him for a knighthood. In London this request from Edinburgh was perfectly in keeping with the mores of the moment. Didn't Tony Blair and Gordon Brown fete bank chief executives – Goodwin included – and invite them to Downing Street for cosy chats? More than twenty senior bankers received knighthoods, peerages or other honours from New

Labour. As well as Goodwin, at HBOS there was his counterpart Sir James Crosby, who was knighted in 2006. It does not seem to have occurred to anyone involved that it might be better to hold off giving knighthoods to these bankers until well after they had retired and it was clear, once a decent interval had elapsed, that their periods in charge had not resulted in damage to the company concerned or the country's economy. At the time the possibility of a disastrous outcome seemed inconceivable.

The Goodwins were now breathing the rarefied air at the summit of the British establishment. On Saturday 11 December 2004, Tony and Cherie Blair invited them to dine at Chequers, the weekend residence of the British Prime Minister. It was an eclectic gathering.[13] Among the fourteen guests sitting down for dinner that night was Charles Clarke, who four days later would be appointed Home Secretary following the first resignation of David Blunkett. There was also the football commentator John Motson and his wife.

Otherwise, it was the contact with Gordon Brown, in regular phone calls and meetings, that Goodwin seemed to relish most. 'Gordon and Fred are actually quite similar,' says someone who knows them both. 'Both are quite introverted individuals and that expresses itself in sometimes extremely awkward dealings with others.' The pair had first met when Goodwin was at the Clydesdale Bank in the mid-1990s and had kept in touch. Says a senior journalist, who for several years had conversations with Goodwin: 'Fred was a pretty plugged-in individual who loved gossiping about Gordon. Come on, here was a boy from an ordinary background who had landed in the big time and he revelled in it.'

If a knighthood and contact with Brown and Blair risked making Goodwin prematurely grand, Gogarburn compounded matters. The £350m RBS headquarters was at that point approaching completion under the watchful eye of the chief executive, who visited the site regularly to check on progress. Gossip about

how pernickety and demanding he was being circulated in
rival banks and among City reporters. Goodwin's relationship
with much of the financial press in London had been generally frosty, outside a select group of journalists who received
the occasional invitation to lunch or the odd call. He was
not a chief executive generally at ease mixing with the media,
unless it was a high-profile and glamorous TV presenter such as
Kirsty Wark, who was hired to interview him for a corporate
video. His dislike of personality profiles or being interviewed
about himself was well entrenched. In 2004 RBS invited City
editors to its hospitality marquee at the Chelsea Flower Show.
Goodwin was elsewhere that night, a few doors down in the
hospitality suite of another bank. Anything to avoid the press.
Other senior executives were actively discouraged from having
dealings with the media. Having a low opinion of those who
work for newspapers does not make Fred Goodwin unusual,
but it became problematic when some journalists who were
not being wooed noticed that he struggled to hide his distaste.
Says an RBS executive: 'Some journalists were saying Fred was
a complete dick. They decided to start yanking his chain.'

One of the roles traditionally enjoyed by those who work on
British newspapers is tweaking the tail of powerful public figures,
particularly those who are deemed to have become too self-
important for their own good. One of the main outlets for this
journalistic sport is the newspaper diary column, where waspish
items about leading personalities can appear under a pen name. In
the autumn of 2004, the *Sunday Times* City diary, Prufrock, which
is published in the paper's business section, started running
unflattering and amusing items about Gogarburn and Sir Fred.
Louise Armitstead, a City reporter, struck a rich seam and Will
Lewis, then business editor of the *Sunday Times*, was happy to
publish the results several weeks in a row. Gogarburn, the paper
reported, would have its own bridge ('A Bridge Too Far')[14]
designed to make it easier to get to the nearby airport, thus sparing

Sir Fred from being stuck in any traffic jams with the hoi polloi. There would be a 'scallop kitchen', to prepare Scottish seafood just as Sir Fred liked it.

The sensible response of a chief executive taking such incoming fire is to try to laugh it off. Instead, Goodwin hit the roof, called in the lawyers and demanded that a writ be issued against the *Sunday Times*. The bridge, he raged, was stipulated by the local council as a condition of planning consent, to ensure that the thousands of RBS staff driving to work would not cause gridlock when they tried to get into Gogarburn. On the other hand, the giant sculpted version of the RBS logo pinned in hubristic fashion to the bridge – which would be seen by anyone driving in or out of Edinburgh – was certainly not a condition of planning permission.

It was intimated that because of the diary stories RBS would withdraw its advertising from Rupert Murdoch's News International titles, which included *The Times*, *Sunday Times* and the *Sun*. It was a nerve-racking moment for Will Lewis, but Les Hinton, then chief executive of News International, declared that Goodwin could 'get stuffed'. He wouldn't bow to a big advertiser issuing threats to journalists.

At RBS, the attempt to sue the *Sunday Times* was becoming deeply embarrassing. The writ issued in November accused the paper of running a campaign designed to expose Sir Fred to ridicule. Yet by losing his temper and suing over diary stories about a bridge and a kitchen, he was making himself look ridiculous. Goodwin finally acknowledged that a deal had to be brokered. Lewis and a colleague at the *Sunday Times*, John Waples, travelled to St Andrew Square in Edinburgh for peace talks with Goodwin and Howard Moody in early January 2005. Drink was taken in considerable quantities and it was agreed that Goodwin would withdraw the writ while the *Sunday Times* would publish an interview with him in which he dealt with some of the myths about Gogarburn and extolled its virtues as a first-class location for staff to work. The scallop kitchen was not just for scallops. It would also prepare other varieties of seafood.

A spell had been broken though. Boosterism and baubles had accompanied almost everything RBS had done since it took over NatWest. Now the mood changed. Several analysts, those who work for other banks, writing notes which help shape market sentiment, started to give voice to the concerns of investors.[15] In June 2005, James Eden of Dresdner Kleinwort Wasserstein, on a routine call in which analysts get a chance to dial in and question the chief executive, told Goodwin: 'What's hurting your share price is the view that you're acquisition-crazy.'

That same month, a secret internal report, which examined how Goodwin was perceived outside the Royal Bank, was delivered to members of the board at an awayday at Gleneagles, during a joint strategy session. The study was particularly scathing about his treatment of bank analysts. He treated them, it was said, as though they were idiots, which hardly helped RBS make its case. Non-executive director Peter Sutherland, the London-based chairman of Goldman Sachs International, tackled Goodwin and asked him what he was going to do about the perceptions of arrogance. Sutherland, who had no time for Goodwin socially, thought he had taken it well. One of Goodwin's management team, more familiar with reading his moods, thought differently: 'Sutherland went for him and the back of Fred's neck went red, which was a giveaway that he was furious. I have to say it was the first time I ever felt sorry for him.'

John-Paul Crutchley's paper 'What Went Wrong with RBS' from the same period also examined why the share price had lagged for two years. Earnings per share were lower than other banks', partly because Goodwin kept making acquisitions that shareholders had to pay for, although Crutchley, then of Merrill Lynch, argued shortly afterwards in July 2005, that RBS shares were again a 'buy' because Goodwin's appetite for takeovers seemed to have waned, for now. On 4 August 2005, at the presentation of the RBS interim results, analyst James Eden came back for another go and again Goodwin could not hide his irritation. There was a 'management discount' in the RBS share price, Eden said. Even though the analyst thought it was unwarranted, he intimated that the share price was low because investors didn't like Goodwin's approach. Finance director Fred Watt tried to push back against Eden, but Goodwin wanted to take this one. There were 'lurid rumours going about' on what RBS might do next in terms of expansion, he said, and he wanted to 'close that industry down'. Watt, rather unwisely, asked Eden to define the term 'management discount'. 'Well,' came back the answer, 'I think there's a perception among some investors that Fred Goodwin is a megalomaniac who pursues size over shareholder value.'

Unused to direct public criticism, Goodwin sounded stung. 'I think I remember reading that even in your own note, James, so it's not the first time I've heard that and I'm sure there are people who think that, if only because you wrote it. So last year it was one person who thinks it. I really don't think it stands a lot of scrutiny.' He wanted, he said, an open dialogue. He wanted, he said, to move on.

9

Canny Scottish Bankers

'This building is a fine tribute to the many generations of "canny" Scottish bankers, who have made – and are still making – such a valuable contribution to the national economy.'

Queen Elizabeth II, 14 September 2005

Having knighted Goodwin – or having been told to – would the Queen do the honours when it was time for Gogarburn to open? Of course. Negotiations with the Palace were not going to be difficult. The Royal Bank chief executive's links to the royal family went beyond receiving a knighthood. The Queen was a long-standing customer at Coutts. And between 1999 and 2003 Goodwin oversaw the Scottish branch of the Prince's Trust, before being promoted to the chairmanship of the entire Trust from 2003. Some of the senior RBS executives felt that their boss was far too fawning in the presence of Prince Charles. Says one: 'It was a bit embarrassing how much he loved hobnobbing with the royals.' But the Prince found the banker very useful indeed. The Prince's Trust had been founded in 1976 to offer support, training and inspiration to young people, with the aim of getting them into work and improving their lives. Goodwin brought a much-needed accountant's eye for detail and introduced more rigour to the financial management of the charity. It was whispered that the royals credited him with 'saving' the Prince's Trust. Goodwin's charitable work certainly earned him the loyalty of Prince Charles. In 2004 he was invited to become a trustee of the Queen's own Silver Jubilee Trust, another charity established to help young Britons.

The word came from Buckingham Palace that the Queen would open Gogarburn and Goodwin got to work making plans. The building was ready early, of course, and staff began moving in to the new headquarters from the spring of 2005. The official opening was fixed for September of that year, when the Queen would be in residence at Balmoral, her estate in the Scottish Highlands. When a working group was established by Goodwin to plot the day down to the last detail it became clear that these preparations would be implemented in his customary style. He explained to the various executives and marketing types that he had arranged a fly-past on the day by four Tornados stationed at RAF Leuchers, near St Andrews, in Fife. It was rumoured that Goodwin knew the commanders at the base and had called in a favour. A member of the communications team asked bravely whether this jet-propelled flourish was an entirely good idea. Might a fly-past at the opening ceremony not suggest of RBS that 'we're a bit up ourselves'? Goodwin's ire was such that he demanded the individual not be in his line of sight for the next few months.

It had actually been a very pertinent question, even if Goodwin didn't want to hear it. Was RBS in danger of getting 'a bit up itself'? It looked to be well on the way. When the company prepared a corporate video celebrating the triumphs of Mathewson and Goodwin, Howard Moody, the communications chief, even secured the rights to use the music from the film *Gladiator*.[1] Where once they had channelled the spirit of *Braveheart*, William Wallace and Mel Gibson, now they were going up a gear, and associating themselves with Ancient Rome, the Emperor Marcus Aurelius and a sword-wielding Russell Crowe.

While the immense pride of those at the top of RBS, and those further down the bank too, was certainly understandable, considering the growth of the company and the new exalted status that Gogarburn embodied, a fly-past in the presence of the Queen was usually reserved for great state occasions. It wasn't normally sanctioned for the opening of a glorified office block, even if it sat at the centre of a 'landscaped campus'. Perhaps the critics had been on to something when they mocked the puffed-up pretensions, flummery and fanfare that went with the Gogarburn development.

On 14 September 2005, hundreds of guests – the Scottish great and good and the not so great and good of the corporate, social and media worlds – gathered to marvel at 'Fredtown'.[2] Mathewson thought that Goodwin simply loved the occasion, although he appeared slightly uncomfortable or nervous at certain points, perhaps understandably. In the event, the official opening of Gogarburn went off as smoothly as Goodwin had planned. The Queen and Duke of Edinburgh were welcomed at the door at 11 a.m. by a receiving party whose members included the Secretary of State for Scotland Alistair Darling, the First Minister Jack McConnell, Mathewson, Goodwin and Mark Fisher. The pipes of the Highland Band of the Scottish Division provided the accompaniment as four Tornado jets from 56(R) squadron crossed the River Forth and screeched overhead. The royal couple met the architects and then groups of staff members presented by Gordon Pell, Johnny Cameron, company secretary Miller McLean and HR director Neil Roden, before mingling with guests who were consuming canapés and sipping champagne. It was soon time to move through to the

A bust of William Paterson in the Bank of England, the institution he helped found before devising Scotland's disastrous Darien scheme which led to the creation of The Royal Bank of Scotland in 1727.

Above: Archibald Campbell, Earl of Ilay and the 3rd Duke of Argyll. The old Etonian aristocrat involved in the Treaty of Union became the Whig political master of Scotland and a founder of the Royal Bank.

Right: The wily John Campbell, long-serving cashier of the Royal Bank who handed over the money Bonnie Prince Charlie needed to fund his invasion of England during the 1745 Jacobite rebellion.

The headquarters in the heart of Edinburgh's Georgian New Town, from 1828 until the construction of Gogarburn.

Sir Michael Herries, chairman of The Royal Bank of Scotland Group when the bank was the target of failed attempted takeovers by Standard Chartered and what became HSBC.

George Mathewson, George Younger and Fred Goodwin ahead of launching their audacious bid for the much bigger NatWest in 1999.

'Fred the Shred' being chauffeured in a car from the executive fleet in which he took such an interest.

The newly arrived Deputy Chief Executive and heir apparent to Mathewson in his office at St Andrew Square.

Riding shot gun. The boss of RBS added shooting to his other hobbies, which are repairing cars and playing golf.

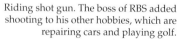

Two knights, Mathewson and Goodwin, show the Queen and the Duke of Edinburgh around Gogarburn on 14 September 2005 when the monarch opened RBS's new headquarters on the outskirts of Edinburgh.

Gogarburn: a landscaped campus for 3,500 staff, a symphony in glass, steel and sandstone built to Goodwin's specifications as a home for a global financial giant.

Gordon Brown opening the London office of the US investment bank Lehman Brothers at Canary Wharf on 5 April 2004. Here he is chatting to the company's chief executive, Dick Fuld.

Alan Greenspan receiving his honorary degree at Edinburgh University in 2005, accompanied by Brown and the then Governor of the Bank of England Mervyn King. The night before, the Governor of the US Federal Reserve had given the Adam Smith memorial lecture in Brown's home town of Kirkcaldy, Fife.

Larry Fish, boss of Citizens, the American retail arm of RBS.

Johnny Cameron, who oversaw investment banking. Bafflingly, in the aftermath of the financial crisis he was the only RBS banker to be singled out for investigation by the authorities.

'The Three Amigos', Fortis boss Jean-Paul Votron, Fred Goodwin and Emilio Botin of Santander announce their disastrous three way bid for Dutch bank ABN Amro.

Accountant John Connolly. The Deloitte boss was a mentor to Goodwin. The firm he ran signed off on RBS's accounts as it headed for disaster.

The regulators: (top left) John Tiner, the chief executive of the Financial Services Authority (FSA) from 2003 to 2007, an advocate of 'principles based' light touch regulation of the banks. (top right) Investment banker Hector Sants, who succeeded Tiner and tried to overhaul the organisation, but let RBS run its capital low when it was taking over ABN Amro in the autum of 2007. (Bottom left) Sir Callum McCarthy, civil servant, banker, chairman of the FSA from 2003 and keeper of bees. (Bottom right) Lord Turner, who followed as chairman of the FSA in September 2008 just as the Royal Bank and the financial system were about to blow up.

The end of boom and bust. Prime Minister Gordon Brown and Chancellor Alistair Darling announce the massive bailout of the banks by taxpayers. Downing Street, October 2008.

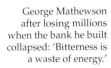

Goodwin and McKillop arrive on 20 November 2008 for the RBS shareholders meeting held to rubber stamp the humiliating government rescue. McKillop and Goodwin apologised to shareholders and staff.

George Mathewson after losing millions when the bank he built collapsed: 'Bitterness is a waste of energy.'

Fred and Joyce Goodwin arrive back in Britain following a spell in exile.

Goodwin alone, after his marriage collapsed.

Clean-up operation: RBS chairman Sir Philip Hampton and Goodwin's successor as chief executive, Stephen Hester, face MPs at Westminster.

'internal street' at the heart of the building where the formal opening ceremony would take place.

Mathewson introduced Her Majesty. With the Duke of Edinburgh, the RBS chairman and Goodwin seated behind the Queen on a stage constructed for the occasion, she addressed the assembled grandees and RBS staff filling the hall and peering over balconies. It was, she noted, 278 years since RBS had been granted a royal charter by one of her predecessors, King George II. She paid tribute to those who had ordered the building of Gogarburn: 'Even a prudent bank needs to build a new head-quarters once in a while.'

The Queen does not write her own speeches. They are scripted by officials trying to capture the mood of the moment, who have to give the monarch something encouraging and fitting to say in front of an expectant audience.[3] This short speech praised the prudence and good husbandry of Scottish bankers down the ages. Viewed from the other side of the financial crisis – in which RBS and the old Bank of Scotland in HBOS had starring roles – this is unfortunate. 'For many years, Scotland has had an enviable reputation for efficient financial management in a highly competitive international market,' the Queen went on. 'This building is a fine tribute to the many generations of "canny" Scottish bankers, who have made – and are still making – such a valuable contribution to the national economy.'

That tribute and the day at Gogarburn should have been the crowning glory for Scotland's canniest banker, yet by the autumn of 2005 all was not well. The golden boy, the master of integra-tion, was being criticised. Even when RBS bought a 5 per cent share in Bank of China for £900m that August it was seen in the City through the prism of Goodwin's alleged deal mania. Ironically, he had been doubtful about the wisdom of the transac-tion. It was members of the board who were much more keen and who had wanted to buy a bigger stake, 10 per cent, if possible. In the end it turned out to be a good investment, as RBS almost doubled its money when it sold the stake after the financial crisis. In 2005 it was presented as more evidence that Goodwin was on an ego trip, particularly because it came with a seat on the board of the Bank of China. In one sense the complaints from analysts such as James Eden, grumbling from shareholders and sniping from some journalists were merely irritating distractions. But some of the critics were also asking a perfectly valid question to which RBS didn't seem to have an answer. What would Goodwin and his team do now? Growth had been so rapid since the pre-NatWest period that it was difficult to see how it could be sustained without another huge and risky purchase, perhaps of a bank in Europe or the United States, for which investors had no appetite.

Consider the balance sheet – total assets – of RBS by the end of 2005. It had ballooned since the takeover of NatWest. At the end of 2001 it stood at £369bn. By 2005 that figure was £776.8bn. Profits before tax were up dramatically in the same period, from £4.25bn to £7.9bn. That growth at the top of a long boom was coming from aggressive expansion. In 2005, the contribution to profits by Corporate Markets – the division under Johnny Cameron, which included investment banking activities – was £5.2bn, up 24 per cent on the previous year. Ulster Bank's contribution to profits was up 15 per cent to £530m. And after swallowing Charter One, and pressing the accelerator on property loans in the United States, Larry Fish's Citizens' contribution was £1.57bn, a blistering increase of 47 per cent. How sustainable or sensible can it be to carry on trying to grow at anything like these rates year after year? Eventually, history suggests, the boom slows, pauses or even goes bust. In the early years of the twenty-first century this seemed to have been forgotten. Generally there was no belief that the bubble would burst.

There was also a little jiggery-pokery in the RBS figures – or

'spin and bullshit', as one of Goodwin's team calls it. The manufacturing costs – of the vast centralised machine that Goodwin
and Fisher had built to service RBS – were never properly
broken down or adequately explained. The suspicion was that it
obscured empire-building and costs that should be lower.

In late 2005 the simple question being asked of Goodwin was
how he could maintain such a thundering rate of progress.
Adding to the sense of dislocation, change was coming to the
boardroom of RBS. Mathewson wanted to retire and the two
vice chairmen, Sir Angus Grossart and former BT chairman
Lord Vallance, stood down in April. After eighteen years, the
Mathewson era was drawing to a close and a replacement was
readying himself to take over.

Sir Tom McKillop didn't want to become chairman of a bank.
In fact it was just about the last thing he fancied doing. Six years
spent on the board of Lloyds – wading through pile upon pile of
board papers and dealing with bankers – had convinced him
that chairing the board of a financial services company wasn't
how he wanted to top a successful career. But Peter Sutherland,
the chairman of BP, suggested to Mathewson that he had identified just the man to be his successor. McKillop, a research
chemist by training who had risen to become chief executive of
the pharmaceutical firm AstraZeneca, sat on Sutherland's board
at BP. Sutherland sat on Mathewson's board at RBS. He might
get a discreet call from George about RBS, Sutherland told
McKillop.

This was a slightly unorthodox way for a large company
to choose a chairman, but typical of Mathewson's RBS.
Standard procedure in most large companies is that several
non-executives will make approaches to a potential chairman,
then there will be formal interviews, due diligence completed
and an appointment made. Here the outgoing chairman was
doing the picking, just as Mathewson had when he personally
sought out Goodwin in 1998. Mathewson had been the main

moving force in the organisation since 1987, an extraordinarily long period in modern corporate life. 'In getting Tom, George was seeking to protect his legacy rather than risking the arrival of someone who might not like what they found and tear it up,' says a colleague.

Dublin-born Sutherland is Ireland's most impeccably connected international panjandrum and transcontinental schmoozer. A barrister and former politician, this jowly, Jesuitical, self-confessed Europhile has been Attorney General of Ireland, EU commissioner, head of the World Trade Organisation, chair of the court of governors of the London School of Economics and chair of Goldman Sachs International. As an apostle of the global establishment who helped liberalise international trade during his time at the WTO, he is sometimes referred to as the architect of globalisation, the process whereby tariffs and trading barriers are lowered to aid trade between emerging economies and the older, established economies. Sutherland is extremely well connected politically. He lobbied to become president of the EU Commission, only being blocked by President Chirac because of his association with Goldman Sachs and BP. In 2007, as chairman of BP, he was on hand, although just out of shot, when Tony Blair was filmed shaking hands with the despotic Muammar Gaddafi in a tent in the desert, a gesture which completed the process of bringing the dictator in from the cold. BP then signed a £545m oil exploration deal with the ill-fated Libyan leader's government.

In 2005, the rapidly growing RBS had global aspirations but to a transcontinental mover and shaker such as Sutherland it still lacked a certain international sophistication. Appointing McKillop as chairman of RBS would deal with two problems at once. Even though much of its core activity took place outside Scotland, there were political sensitivities. Throughout the history of RBS the chairman had always been a Scot, and Mathewson was insistent that this should remain the case.

McKillop, a high-flying Scotsman who had made his name in an industry that was genuinely global, thus ticked two boxes: home and international. A third box went unticked, of course. He wasn't actually a banker – as his critics pointed out after the financial crisis – but he had sat on the board of Lloyds. Anyway, RBS had no tradition of appointing a banker as chairman.[4] What seemed more important now was that he – and incidentally the chairman had always been a *he* – should be a strong character capable of understanding the unique history of the Royal Bank and the need for it to behave more in keeping with its status as an emerging global corporate giant.

Like Goodwin, McKillop had risen from a humble west of Scotland background. Born in 1943 in Dreghorn, Ayrshire, he was made the 'dux' of his school, the award handed out to the pupil judged most academically gifted. A first-class degree in chemistry at Glasgow and then a PhD followed. He had always envisaged spending his career in academia, until a job offer from ICI in 1975 made him reconsider. After running teams engaged in drug research he found he had a skill for management and by 1999 he was leading the merger that created AstraZeneca. He remained as chief executive of the firm until 2005.

Becoming chairman of RBS did not appeal, he told Mathewson when the pair had dinner in McKillop's flat in Chelsea. Mathewson persisted and played the Scottish card. After such a long time away, wasn't it time to give something back? Do it for Scotland. The call of his homeland began to tempt McKillop and his wife agreed that they should 'reconnect, go back'. There would be a nice symmetry in him returning to his roots to chair the biggest company in the land of his birth. The appointment also came with the use of a flat in a town house in Heriot Row, in the heart of Edinburgh's New Town, thrown in for when the chairman needed to be in the Scottish capital. McKillop set about doing some due diligence of his own, taking soundings from friends in the City, seeing John Connolly, the boss at

RBS's auditor Deloitte (who was very positive) and talking to Miller McLean, the RBS group secretary, to satisfy himself that the company's governance was as it should be. It seemed that although Goodwin was a very strong character, his dealings with the board were open and transparent.

McKillop asked to see the FSA's 'Arrow' reports, the regulator's assessments of its dealings with RBS and Fred Goodwin, and he was encouraged by what he found. Similar reports on Lloyds, that he had seen in his time on the board, struck him as having been much more scathing in their criticism than those he read on 'Fred the Shred'. Goodwin also visited McKillop at his flat in Chelsea and the pair got on well. They talked about the remarkable evolution of RBS and the challenge of finding ways to continue growing. Right, he would do it, McKillop decided. He informed Mathewson and joined the board as deputy chairman on 1 September 2005, a fortnight before the Queen opened Gogarburn. The understanding was that he would take over as chairman the following April.

As he familiarised himself with the company he would soon chair, McKillop concluded that there was a slight whiff of parochialism about some of RBS's dealings. For a bank that was now the fifth-biggest in the world it still seemed a little homespun and naive in certain regards. Some of the Scottish touches immediately struck McKillop as gauche. Should an international bank really serve mince and potatoes at every board meeting? And shouldn't the board be more international and diverse in its membership? Mathewson had made some efforts to broaden its composition to include more non-Scots, bringing in Sutherland and Colin Buchan, whose name made him sound Scottish when he hailed from South Africa, as well as Steve Robson, the former Treasury mandarin. Still, the board seemed very British with a strong Scottish tinge. This was basically a British bank with what seemed to be a strong US retail business attached. But Citizens was run almost separately by Larry Fish.

Goodwin's management style was rather dysfunctional, McKillop observed. In front of the chairman the chief executive always took care to be calm and professional to the extent that McKillop never once saw Goodwin 'shred' anyone. Scrupulous politeness characterised his dealings with the board too and sometimes he said very little at its meetings. Board members found that requests they made, to visit parts of RBS or get a briefing on a particular part of the business, were fulfilled. 'If you want that then you must have it,' Goodwin, with his hands outstretched, told Archie Hunter, the retired senior accountant from KPMG who had recently joined the RBS board to chair the audit committee. The idea that surfaced later, that a stupefied board was somehow terrified into silence by a maniacal Goodwin, was bogus.

The obvious problem, McKillop concluded after touring the bank and interviewing RBS's most senior people, came underneath board level, when Goodwin was dealing with his own executive team. His approach appeared to rely on an odd combination of styles. It was a weird blend, McKillop noted, of an 'empowerment culture' with daily control. The concentration was on milestones, targets, projects and goals, with numbers attached. Goodwin's executives were given considerable autonomy to run and develop the parts of the business for which they were responsible, if they met their targets for rapid growth. 'If he trusted you and you met your numbers you were generally OK,' said one. But if there was even a flicker of a problem, or a hint that someone was off track, or a tiny detail he didn't like the look of caught his eye, Goodwin was likely to interrogate the person responsible remorselessly in the manner familiar to all who had worked for him down the years. This helped explain why the morning meeting – 'morning prayers' or the 'morning beatings', as some called it – could become a wearing litany of problems, game-playing and blame-dodging. The smart executive had an incentive not to mention real difficulties, concerns, or even new ideas, for fear of being embroiled in a seemingly endless inquisition. When Johnny Cameron referred in passing at a morning meeting to something Alan Dickinson had done to reduce the amount of paperwork in the corporate banking division, Goodwin snapped: 'What's Alan done? What's he done?' Dickinson sighed – silently cursing Cameron for mentioning it because he would now have to explain every aspect of a relatively minor piece of administrative reorganisation. This wasn't an environment in which asking an open-ended question was going to be a sensible course of action.

'McKillop saw it straight away. He got it,' says a colleague. 'When he joined the board he saw the problems with Fred and realised that the governance wasn't yet up to the standard an international company needed. The question is why he decided when he became chairman not to take the first of his three chances to move Fred on.' Part of the answer was that when he visited the twenty largest institutional investors who owned a lot of RBS stock, McKillop felt the message he received was that Goodwin was someone he should hang on to. This ran contrary to some of the adverse comment which had appeared in newspapers, with Goodwin warned off pursuing more major acquisitions by the litany of criticisms since 2004. Yet with no obvious successor in place, it was deemed better that he stay and deal with the challenges facing the bank. Investors pointed to charts and research suggesting RBS had peaked. One said to McKillop: 'You're big in the UK, which is a mature market, and you're big in the US. What about the emerging markets and the rest of the world? Where's your growth?' Other than the shareholding taken in Bank of China, it seemed like a fair question. The share price, which not long before had lagged because investors feared that Goodwin might be a megalomaniac 'deal junkie' obsessed with big purchases, now traded below expectations because RBS seemed to have no convincing plan.

Goodwin was going through something of a slump himself at Christmas in 2005. Reports had surfaced late in the year that the chief executive was thinking of moving on and Mathewson, in his final months as chairman, denied the rumours.[5] The truth was that Goodwin was thinking about his future and had discussed it with Mathewson. With McKillop's appointment as chairman confirmed and announced to the press on 21 December, Goodwin took a month off and tried to decompress, staying away from the office. Some of his colleagues believed the criticism had got to him, others that he was tired but had no intention of leaving and merely wanted to feel needed ahead of the handover from Mathewson to McKillop. 'Fred was a bit bored with running RBS,' says an RBS director of the period. 'He wasn't a natural-born banker and was thinking about whether he should do something else.'

He and his wife had perhaps reached the pinnacle when they were invited to a dinner in Washington. On 2 November 2005 they were there when the Prince of Wales and the Duchess of Cornwall, on a tour of the United States, were George W. Bush and Laura Bush's guests of honour at the White House.[6] The Goodwins had really arrived, mingling with the Republican end of the Washington establishment. There that night were George and Barbara Bush, Nancy Reagan, the defence secretary Donald Rumsfeld, the financier Henry Kravis, the designer Oscar de la Renta and, somewhat incongruously, the actor Kelsey Grammer. Joyce Goodwin was not boastful, but she brimmed with pride when she told friends back in Edinburgh about the evening.

Whatever Goodwin's motivations, this period of uncertainty was a potential opportunity for McKillop to start preparing the chief executive's eventual departure. It was an opportunity McKillop did not at that point consider taking. A colleague of both men says: 'When he became chairman Tom's first conversation with Fred should have involved him saying thanks Fred, it's been great. You've been doing this for six years and it's time to think about your next challenge. All sorts of companies will be interested in talking to you and there's no rush, and no need for unpleasantness, but over the next six months to a year we're going to be getting ready. That should have been done straight away. There is a chance a new chief executive would then have looked differently at what was about to happen.'

McKillop and the board did subsequently undertake detailed succession planning, although in 2006 any handover of power was seen as being several years away. 'We always thought in terms of Fred not being there for any more than ten years in total,' says a director. The alternative approach, requiring an almost immediate search for a new CEO, could have been messy. By an accident of timing – with the organisation losing Mathewson, its leader for so long, and the incoming chairman not being an established banker – Goodwin had been deemed temporarily indispensable. Staying also involved the lure of vindication and proving his critics wrong. Hadn't RBS faced scepticism from the City at almost every stage of its development since Mathewson set out to make the Royal Bank the best? The critics had been wrong then and they were wrong now. McKillop's conclusion when he took over as chairman was that he needed to get fully behind the chief executive while he, Goodwin, tried to work out what RBS should do next.

Mathewson stood aside at the end of April 2006, with his achievements celebrated inside and outside RBS. A portrait was painted, with Mathewson in his kilt, so that it might be hung, like that of the great John Campbell of the eighteenth century, in a prominent position in the bank's headquarters. In one corner of Mathewson's portrait was a tiny detail, two small logos representing RBS and NatWest, the English bank it conquered.[7] Andrew McLaughlin, the chief economist, corralled groups of executives and staff for several sendoffs. In a speech to the Royal Economics Society McLaughlin took it all back to the Darien Scheme in the 1690s. Then, buccaneering Scots inspired by William Paterson had set out to conquer the New World but their planning had been poor. Their wild enthusiasm had run ahead of practical realities, said McLaughlin. In contrast, George had avoided Paterson's pitfalls and had done the meticulous, hard work at every stage of RBS's expansion. Generous profiles were also published in a variety of newspapers. When Mathewson moved from deputy chief executive to chief executive in 1992 the Royal Bank had made a profit of £21m. By the time of his final year as chairman that had risen to £8.3bn. Its market capitalisation – meaning the total value of its shares – had rocketed from £1.6bn to £60bn. 'Not bad; not bad at all,' wrote one commentator.[8] How would Goodwin, the successor he had anointed, possibly top his achievements?

Lacking an answer, Goodwin alighted on more 'organic growth'. That phrase, redolent of wholesome germination, has a reassuring ring, even though there is nothing intrinsically safe about growth that is organic. All it means is expanding existing parts of a business in search of profit rather than buying any-thing new. If a bank blows up because its growth was too quick, or it turns out to have been investing in existing activities that are even riskier than basic banking, it makes no difference that it came with the word 'organic' as a prefix. In 2006, the area which Goodwin thought offered the most scope was Johnny Cameron's investment banking division, already making such a large contri-bution to RBS. Cameron sat on top of Corporate Markets – which had been Corporate Banking and Financial Markets (CBFM) – a giant division which contained the UK Corporate Bank and Global Banking & Markets (GBM) where RBS, in common with many other banks, delved deeper into trading, derivatives, se-curitisation, foreign exchange and complex corporate loans. GBM had grown quickly and could grow a lot more.

Johnny Cameron was at heart an aristocratic and upmar-ket salesman, a motivator of staff who most enjoyed dealing with customers. His father, Cameron of Lochiel,[9] had been deputy chairman of the Royal Bank. Harrow, and then politics, philosophy and economics at Oxford, led to Johnny's first job in 1976 as a graduate trainee with Jardine Matheson, the old Scottish Far-East trading company, which sent him to Tokyo, selling cosmetics such as Dior perfume. He learned Japanese and played a lot of rugby. After a year studying at MIT Sloan in the United States, he looked around and considered going into banking in London, although in the early 1980s banks were regarded as a bit of a backwater. This was pre-Big Bang. On a trip to talk to the bankers Jonathan Agnew and Archie Cox about a possible job in the London office of Morgan Stanley, he was told that they had under a hundred employees and were never going to employ thousands of people in the UK. Today, Morgan Stanley employs more than 5000 staff in London. Instead of investment banking, the fashion in the early 1980s was for ambitious graduates to join one of the large consultancies that wrote reports for firms on how they might overhaul their business. Cameron signed up for McKinsey and was soon very bored. Work involved sitting in a cubicle all day, with the phone never ringing, writing a study on the National Australia Bank, profiling one of the UK's largest china manufacturers (advice: don't buy it) and for British Telecom counting how many switches it had. He was restless. Bond trading and investment banking looked much more exciting. He made the move.

After joining County NatWest, where he was their 'Japanese man' in London, Cameron prospered and rode the wave of the financial revolution rolling through the City, with a long spell at Kleinwort Benson, which was then sold to the German bank Dresdner in 1995. This was the flipside of the increasing internationalisation of the City that came with Big Bang. First the stockbrokers and then even the grand British merchant banks were steadily snapped up and subsumed by foreign buyers. More aggressive outfits, such as Goldman Sachs, J. P. Morgan and Merrill Lynch, were staffed with a new breed of young bankers prepared to work the punishing hours demanded in an era when large 'compensation' packages were becoming the dominant currency of the industry. The British firms, which tended to be sleepier, more conservative and sometimes down-right inept, were exposed to competition and struggled to adapt. Foreign rivals sought to snap up their customers and their assets. They also wanted to strengthen their presence in a resurgent and increasingly international City of London. The UK's Morgan Grenfell was consumed by Deutsche Bank in 1989; S. G. Warburg & Co. went to the Swiss Bank Corporation in 1995; and Hambros Bank was sold to Société Générale in 1997. In 2000, Robert Fleming & Co, a London-based investment bank and asset manager, was sold to the Americans. Flemings had been established and controlled by a Scottish family whose most famous member was Ian Fleming, the creator of James Bond. The bank had long been a leading outpost of the 'metrojocks', the Scots who made a lot of money in London. All that is left of the bank is a gallery in Mayfair, displaying the bank's excellent collection of paintings by Scottish artists.

In contrast, the Royal Bank of Scotland of the late 1990s was on the way up and determined to avoid extinction. George Mathewson asked to see Johnny Cameron in London and convinced him to come aboard. Cameron had been reluctant when he was approached a few years previously but in 1998 he pitched up at Waterhouse Square in London to run what was then RBS's Corporate Investment Bank. When Goodwin was hired soon afterwards as chief executive in-waiting Cameron was sore. Mathewson, he told friends, had led him to believe that he stood a chance of being a contender for the top post and then straight away he hired someone else.

There were numerous compensations. After the NatWest takeover Cameron was given the job of 'bashing together' the various bits of the two businesses that became CBFM, which was chaired by the widely respected Iain Robertson, Mathewson's old friend. NatWest was a good deal bigger than the Royal Bank in areas such as the capital markets, where the bonds that governments and companies issue to borrow money are originated and traded. The ignominy of being taken over by a smaller rival generated some resentment and a few of those in senior positions at NatWest's Global Financial Markets division were so unfriendly that their operation was christened 'Go Fuck Me' by Cameron and his team. When it was folded into the much smaller Royal Bank there were casualties and firings, although Cameron's team found that many of those from NatWest who stayed were pleased to be under ambitious new management.

Addressing staff at the time, Cameron warned that amidst all this change, the Royal Bank must not 'lose the magic'. His team should try to hold on to the idea that they were 'insurgents', in the spirit of cross-border raiders – or border reivers in the Scottish phrase – who remained hungry for fresh success. The 'Make It Happen' advertising slogan – and the idea that RBS had a 'making it happen' culture – came from Cameron's division in this period. 'Make It Happen' had been generated by an advertising agency working for CBFM and was snaffled for the whole bank by Goodwin when Howard Moody, the director of communications, and Goodwin heard it. Make It Happen encapsulated the image they were endeavouring to create, and it featured in adverts and leaflets. It appeared on posters plastered in airports across the world, in a campaign which was given the internal codename 'Paint it Blue'. The invocation to action emphasised that this was a company with a 'can-do' mentality. RBS was going to make it happen.

The campaign even resulted in Goodwin receiving yet another award, this time from an unlikely source, Dr Henry J. Heimlich, the inventor of the famous Heimlich manoeuvre. Staff at the Heimlich institute had seen an RBS advert airing in North America in which a diner chokes on his food, while four colleagues talk in a matter-of-fact way about how to intervene, without doing anything. A customer at a neighbouring table calmly steps in and performs the Heimlich manoeuvre, which removes the obstruction. The slogan flashed up at the end – 'Less Talk, Make It Happen, the Royal Bank of Scotland' – was spoken by the Paisley-born actor Tom Conti. Heimlich judged the advert a great humanitarian effort and announced that Goodwin would be handed his institute's prestigious 'Save A Life' Award. In September 2004 Goodwin travelled with Cameron to Cincinnati for a lunch held in his honour at the Queen City Club, where the hosts even laid on a piper.[10]

Goodwin had not always had faith in Cameron. Indeed, Cameron came under fire from some of his colleagues in other parts of the bank who whispered that they thought he simply wasn't the right person to run such a complex part of the Royal Bank. His critics said he was too much the bond trader at heart who loved selling rather than concentrating on strategic thinking. For a while, in 2002, it had even seemed as though Goodwin agreed and was prepared to fire Cameron. There was a sudden rash of provisions – the word bankers use when they are signalling expected losses, either because loans they made have gone bad or trading has been adversely affected in some unexpected way. Obviously, it lowers profits. Goodwin thought CBFM should have been able to predict the scale of it more accurately, while Cameron tried to convince him otherwise. Banking simply did not work in the neat way that an accountant might think. The situation could change quickly, with the unimaginable becoming reality. There were some unpleasant interviews, and Cameron was convinced that Goodwin went into a room for a meeting prepared to fire him and 'bottled it'. For all his Fred the Shred moniker, once again Goodwin had demonstrated a fear of sacking people himself. Larry Fish, at Citizens, thought that in this case it was the British class system at work, and that Goodwin found it difficult to manage the urbane, aristocratic Cameron. 'He is uncomfortable telling Johnny what to do,' Fish told colleagues.

The provisions that had concerned Goodwin stopped rising. By December 2002 at the CBFM annual staff conference, that year titled 'Ahead of the Wave', Cameron said the storm had passed. There was a motivational speech on teamwork and leadership from Humphrey Walters, the round-the-world yachtsman. Cameron told his staff not to be depressed by the setbacks that year and stressed that they should think like winners. It all went down very well. Then Goodwin spoke and was extremely supportive. Cameron felt Goodwin had decided that he was the right guy and worth supporting. Cameron's team knew that their boss had been under the cosh from Fred, and now it was onwards and upwards. CBFM certainly grew quickly. In 2004 its contribution was £4,265m, up 18 per cent on the previous year.

By 2005 when Iain Robertson decided that he wanted out (he had finally had enough of Goodwin's approach to running RBS, he told colleagues), Goodwin put Cameron in overall charge as chairman of the corporate banking and markets business. This had two elements. The UK Corporate Bank served large corporations and customers doing business in Britain. And while Global Banking & Markets (GBM) didn't call itself a pure investment bank, it was the international and more exotic element of the operation with trading outposts in North America and elsewhere.

In early 2006 Goodwin told Cameron and his team to find ways for Corporate Markets and the GBM part of it in particular to generate that 'organic growth'. The message to Cameron from Goodwin seemed simple: go for it, make it happen. Goodwin also arranged for Cameron to join the board in early 2006, just as McKillop was taking over as chairman. Cameron's elevation was not a universally popular move. Sutherland, who had brought on McKillop, was no fan. Sutherland's view was that to run GBM the Royal Bank instead needed someone from one of the bigger, established investment banks, probably from America.

Cameron wasn't sophisticated enough, he felt. The guy had never even been to Davos, the annual gathering in Switzerland where the global elite of political leaders, financiers, billionaires and investment bankers meet each January to ponder their supposed achievements, attended on by academics and select journalists. The truth was that Goodwin – who didn't attend Davos either, because he feared being eclipsed by bigger bankers, it was rumoured – had barred Cameron from going to Davos. Neither was in the same orbit as Sutherland, a Davos-devotee used to calling on world leaders such as Vladimir Putin.[11]

Steve Robson was uncomfortable too. The former Treasury mandarin and fellow non-executive director was unhappy with the way Goodwin ran the show. Was Cameron the right person to be in overall charge of such a complex and fast-growing part of the business with complicated activities on the other side of the Atlantic? Some of Sutherland and Robson's colleagues on the board were in no doubt that the pair wanted to get Cameron out, and perhaps even Goodwin too if they could manage it. This was all awkward for McKillop. He didn't rate Cameron highly and owed the chairmanship to Sutherland's intervention, but he had also resolved to support Goodwin, who seemed to want to back Cameron and his team strongly. A cocktail of confusion, miscommunication, rivalry and resentment was brewing. It would help fuel several calamitous decisions that were about to be taken.

10

Safe as Houses

*'US house prices are not going to fall by 30 per cent.
They just aren't.'*

Fred Goodwin

Thirty miles to the north-east of Manhattan, up the coast and overlooking Long Island Sound, lies Greenwich, Connecticut. Once the acme of New England affluence and privilege, by the late nineteenth century it was home and playground to some of America's grandest families. The arrival of the railroad signalled a new influx, turning it into the perfect commuter town for those working in New York and wanting to reside somewhere sedate, monied and respectable. This is the land of country clubs, yachting, refined 'preppy' living and good schools. The family of the elder President Bush, father of George W. Bush, lived here when he was a young child. But by the late 1980s the blue bloods and WASPs, the White Anglo-Saxon Protestant ruling class that sat at the pinnacle of American society, started being elbowed aside in Greenwich by members of a new emerging elite. The place was flooded with vast amounts of wealth via the town's recently arrived moneymaking machine: the cluster of hedge funds and related firms in Connecticut that grew to feed off Wall Street and the markets in nearby New York City.

When *Vanity Fair*'s real estate section investigated in 2006, at five minutes to midnight in terms of the approaching financial crisis, it found that the average – average – price of a house sold in Greenwich the previous year was $2.5m.[1] And that wouldn't buy you much of a property. The biggest hedge-fund bosses competed to pay tens of millions of dollars for houses, tearing down properties built just a few years before and building monster mansions with every upscale feature conceivable. A lot of people in Greenwich were, and are, making a lot of money.

Hedge funds began as a way for wealthy investors to protect themselves against the risk of markets turning down or commodity prices rising. They evolved into mechanisms which could deliver returns superior to traditional banks or investment firms. The hedge involves buying shares, or options on shares, and other financial instruments. Essentially, those in charge of the fund are taking positions, making well-informed bets on which shares, commodities or currencies will go up and which will go down. These bets are placed using the vast sums that clients have entrusted to them in the expectation of a much better profit than is available with run-of-the-mill investment firms or banks. They can also leverage themselves massively, using borrowed money to do it. They operate across all sorts of markets, carry a lot of risk and when they get it right make much bigger returns than conventional financial firms. The pioneers were mathematicians and scientists who realised that with the application of serious brainpower, and computing, it was possible to beat the market far more effectively than testosterone-fuelled traders dealing on the basis of instinct or feel for the market ever could.[2] Hedge funds gradually expanded into so-called 'alternative investment' firms, making all sorts of trades and buying and selling anything that offered the prospect of a large return. The client pays a fat fee to be involved.

There are obviously considerable risks. Hedge funds do blow up if there are just a few misjudgements, and they are lightly regulated. In 1998 the implosion in the United States of the splendidly misnamed Long-Term Capital Management necessitated a $3.6bn rescue by Wall Street firms, at the instigation of the authorities, because the fear was that its failure would spread panic in the markets.[3] Long-Term Capital Management was a Greenwich-based firm. For a while its failure shook the prevailing confidence that complex computerised models and innovative new financial products offered stability and ever-bigger profits. The moment of reflection was fleeting. The hedge funds – in Greenwich, in New York, in London and elsewhere – rapidly continued their lucrative work into the booming first decade of the new century. And no wonder. Get the calculations right, with the assistance of those computer models and the brightest graduates, and the hedge fund, and the client, could make money when markets rose and when they dipped. Generally being private partnerships, there was no pool of shareholders demanding a large slice of a hedge fund's profits. Worker bees in successful firms could earn millions and those right at the top could make hundreds of millions of dollars – a year. In 2006, the average pay of the top twenty-five hedge fund managers was $363m according to the *Institutional Investor*'s Alpha report, and lower-paid managers on the list, those outside the top twenty-five, made $40m.[4] A good proportion of that money washed ashore in Greenwich or nearby.

It was here, on the waterfront, that RBS did its business in a four-storey concrete block set in a landscaped park on Steamboat Road. RBS's Greenwich Capital was not an exotic hedge fund. Its main business was more mundane, in the trading and underwriting of US Treasuries, government debt. Greenwich Capital also securitised mortgages, creating asset-backed securities (ABS), in effect bonds made up of pools of mortgages assembled from lenders who wanted to transfer the risk of their loans and in the process generate more money that they could then use to lend even more. Yet even though they were not running a hedge fund – they were part of a regulated bank headquartered more than 3000 miles away in Edinburgh – the top managers at RBS in Greenwich were based in a town where the prevailing ethos among their friends was predominantly 'hedgie'. Pay was soaring and property prices were rocketing on the back of financial innovation. Greenwich was an environment in which one might easily go a little crazy in an effort to make many millions and keep up with the neighbours.

'People were making so much money and you could see in the eyes of the guys at Greenwich that they were hungry for as much of it as possible,' says a once-frequent visitor to the building at Steamboat Road. RBS had originally intended to sell Greenwich Capital when it came as part of the purchase of NatWest in 2000. But after a quick inspection of the books, Iain Robertson, Johnny Cameron and Goodwin decided that it was a promising business worth keeping. The firm's boss, Konrad 'Chip' Kruger, left and made himself even richer at a nearby hedge fund, naturally.[5]

Day-to-day control at Greenwich was handed to Jay Levine and Ben Carpenter in 2000, although Levine was very much seen as the senior partner in the relationship. He lived in Greenwich with his wife Tammy, and a colleague describes him as 'smart and mathematical with a lot of friends who worked for hedge funds'. Another colleague says his gift with numbers was 'exceptional, really something'. Finance was in Levine's blood. His father, Howard, had been highly successful in the mortgage business and was best friends with Angelo Mozilo, the Bronx-born founder of Countrywide Financial credited later with a starring role in the sub-prime mortgage crisis.[6] After graduating in economics from the University of California, Davis, Levine spent a year at the University of Leeds in England and then moved into banking. His reputation was made at Salomon

Brothers, the investment bank. There his expertise was in devising innovative mortgage products of the kind that the financial newswire Bloomberg euphemistically described as extending 'housing finance to a broader range of borrowers'. In the 1990s this was a rapidly growing industry, with President Bill Clinton's administration looking for ways to increase home ownership to millions more Americans, a noble aim as long as borrowers can afford the payments.

In the excitement, checks on credit-worthiness were weakened and the amount the buyer needed to put down as a deposit was reduced to almost nothing. In any case, the mood of the era was for all kinds of financial deregulation. Lobbying from Wall Street and machinations by friendly politicians in Washington meant that the so-called Glass–Steagall Act had been chipped away at for years. It had been introduced in 1933, during the Great Depression, to keep retail, savings and mortgage institutions separate from investment banks, so that their risky trading on the markets did not again bring down the banks that consumers relied on. In the 1980s and 1990s the expanding finance industry had successfully eroded Glass–Steagall to the point that shortly before leaving office Bill Clinton signed its death warrant. Banks were extending into all manner of innovative activities, money was plentiful and credit was cheap. A long period of historically low interest rates spanned the presidencies of both Clinton and his successor George W. Bush. Cheap home loans were billed as an extension of the American dream. They also created an opportunity for profit – a lot of it – for those who ran hungry banks.

The RBS operation at Greenwich did not originate sub-prime mortgages. It did not directly offer loans to customers who wanted to buy a house and then wait while they paid it back in instalments over twenty-five years. However, it was moving beyond basic mortgage securitisation and into the market for collateralised debt obligations (CDOs), which had been developed on

Wall Street in the late 1980s and then refined by a team from J. P. Morgan in the late 1990s.[7] The architects of the CDO took existing mortgage securitisations (batches of Asset Backed Securities) and repackaged them into new structures. Investors liked CDOs because they provided a stream of income, based on the distant homebuyer making his or her repayments each month. At the top of the structure of a CDO sits a tranche that is labelled triple-A or even better, super-senior debt. This means that whoever holds such stuff is first in the queue for money. If there is a problem they get what income there is before those holding the lower-rated parts of the CDO. The idea was that this process helped spread risk, it being deemed highly unlikely that lots of homeowners would suddenly be unable to pay or that the value of their house would somehow collapse. A few might default, but the CDO was made up of so many loans that most of it was bound to be fine. It would require some sort of economic earthquake for it to really go bad. Meanwhile, investment bankers liked it because making and selling the CDOs created profit for the bank, a slice of which went into the pot for their bonuses. The banks could also buy, or put together themselves, products 'hedging' the risk of there being a problem in the future. And they could buy 'mono-line' insurance. Who could imagine such insurers failing?

At RBS it did not seem like that big a deal. After all, their CDOs were made up of other people's loans. CDOs were not even deemed worthy of much detailed attention when Goodwin, Johnny Cameron, Jay Levine and several others did a half-day of presentation to analysts in London on 3 October 2005. It just seemed to be taken for granted by the executives that the amount of work the bank did in that area would grow. Cameron wasn't entirely clear on the potential implications of the expansion into CDOs and Goodwin, say colleagues, certainly did not know how a CDO worked. That day an analyst asked near the end of the event why CDOs had only been mentioned once, briefly. Wasn't this odd, when they were obviously fast-growing and perhaps risky? Brian Crowe, Cameron's colleague, explained to the audience that it was complicated, and then didn't answer the question properly. RBS was issuing CDOs and it would be a growth area in the next two or three years, he said. Others asked about whether the bank was more broadly taking too many risks on that side of the business. Goodwin was a model of reassurance: 'Our appetite you would find pretty conservative if you were to define it – not wanting any undue excitement.'

There was about to be rather a lot of 'undue excitement'. The message from Goodwin to Cameron had been clear when the RBS executive team had its annual trip away in early February 2006. The chief executive wanted growth, and the bank's board concurred. GBM had grown its income by 30 per cent in 2005 with 24 per cent planned in 2006. For 2007 the target was another 25 per cent. The aim was for RBS to catch up quickly with its more established rivals, either banks such as Barclays that had big investment banking arms alongside their retail and commercial operations, or pure investment banks such as Goldman Sachs. 'I want us to be bigger than J. P. Morgan,' Goodwin told a fellow banker.

The board raised no objections, in fact quite the opposite. If the new RBS chairman had a concern it was about trying to get Goodwin to agree for the first time to undergo a proper annual appraisal and sign up to personal goals on how he ran the company. McKillop also wanted to bring a little order to the board and professionalise the working relationship between chief executive and chairman. Mathewson and Goodwin had actually had some stand-up rows when on their own, when Mathewson thought Goodwin was getting RBS a little too deep into investment banking or not listening to his advice, but it did not manifest itself in any concerted attempt to get Goodwin to change or ship out. 'George was a terrible, terrible chairman who didn't spot the danger in Fred's way of working,' says one of the longest-serving senior executives of that period. 'That's harsh,' says another of their colleagues when this is put to him. 'But George is quite emotional and scattergun.' McKillop offered the chief executive support while attempting to get him to work more collaboratively with his executive team. He thought he was running a programme of Goodwin improvement.

Otherwise, at the June 2006 'off-site', McKillop's first such strategy session with the board and other senior executives, the mood was highly optimistic. There was very little discussion of the detail of the expansion of GBM and what little there was involved terms that seemed reassuring. 'CDOs were never mentioned, it was much more general than that,' says a participant. A member of the board adds: 'Even the word securitisation sounded safe and reliable, as though it was something that you could trust, and the term structured credit sounds sensible too.' McKillop agreed that the priority was growth. The investors he had visited wanted to know what RBS would do next, and Goodwin's idea of building on parts of the business such as GBM that seemed to be doing well and recording healthy profits seemed perfectly reasonable. The instruction to GBM was unequivocal. On 21 June 2006, Brian Crowe emailed Cameron, Robertson and David Coleman, the group chief credit officer: 'The board has been very bullish in the last twenty-four hours across all the GBM business in wanting to avoid the defensiveness in approach that we tend to adopt, and to be more aggressive and ambitious.'

Levine and Greenwich were already ahead of them. The boss of Greenwich was increasingly upbeat, 'on a roll' says a colleague. He had hosted a dinner for key staff and handed out T-shirts emblazoned with the words 'Think Big'. They should be bold, they should not fear losses, the team was told. In March 2006, Levine moved to reorganise his team. Bob McGinnis, who ran the mortgage securitisation business, was stripped of his responsibilities. McGinnis and Levine were old colleagues. They had worked together at Salomon Brothers in the late 1980s, collaborating on what may even have been Wall Street's first ever securitisation of sub-prime mortgages. McGinnis had joined Greenwich in 1997 and experienced the Royal Bank takeover when it bought NatWest.[8] Greenwich had weathered the crisis in the markets when Long-Term Capital Management fell over in 1998. After the shock of 9/11 Greenwich had prospered, as most of its competition was based in lower Manhattan near the ruins of the World Trade Center and faced months of disruption. Now, after everything, Levine was effectively dumping him over lunch. 'Why do you carry on working, Bob? You should stop,' Levine told his colleague. 'What's it all for? Who are you going to leave all your money to?' McGinnis was furious. He was getting a lecture on life and effectively being dispensed with. Levine said they might be able to find something for him, which came in a troubling form.

Shortly afterwards Levine wanted McGinnis and several others to meet Rick Caplan from Citigroup. Levine said Caplan had contacted him with a proposition. He could bring his team of twenty-five people from Citigroup and do what they had done there with CDOs. Last year they had made a $600m profit for the bank. McGinnis was incredulous. Greenwich already had someone good running their CDO desk, Fred Matera. Why would they bring someone in over his head?

After dinner, McGinnis and Levine discussed it. You know how Rick and his team made $600m for them last year, McGinnis said. Easy, his colleagues had simply stuffed $25bn or maybe $30bn of AAA bits of structured credit directly onto the Citigroup balance sheet. The CDOs pumped out profit for now, but the bank had all the risk on its balance sheet. 'Come on, Jay, we don't have that kind of appetite for risk at Greenwich, do we?' Caplan had also given an unclear answer that unnerved McGinnis when he asked how much of that material on the Citigroup balance sheet was insured. Not a lot.

Bruce Jin, who had taken over as the head of risk at Greenwich, was also deeply concerned when he heard what was planned with the arrival of Caplan. He expressed his worries to colleagues at Greenwich, but Levine was determined. Caplan would move over to grow the CDO unit and be co-head with Matera, with the pair reporting to McGinnis. Caplan was hired in July and turned up in early September. Both Matera and McGinnis decided to make the best of it, if this was what was wanted. They would also do well financially if the arrangement worked out. A dozen, rather than twenty-five, new staff were hired. Going into the second half of 2006, the bonus-incentivised team was now twenty-five strong and working flat out. In 2005 RBS had issued eleven CDOs with a total value of $3.3bn, with Greenwich and London doing the work together. Now Greenwich had the appetite it could do a great deal more on its own. In less than a year, between July 2006 and May 2007, RBS Greenwich churned out fifteen CDOs worth $11.7bn on its own. The global CDO market doubled from 2004 to 2005 and then again from 2005 to 2006 and in a booming market for these products RBS was also doubling its market share.

It sometimes took months to put together CDOs as the various loans were assembled in what the traders termed the warehouse, a virtual storeroom where they sat ticking over on the books of RBS. The presumption in London on the part of Brian Crowe and his team was that the CDOs were supposed to be made and then sold on as quickly as possible: 'That's what you do in a markets business. You sell,' says one of Crowe's executives. 'On our behalf they had built a very good CDO origination machine but not a distribution machine.' In other words, Caplan and Matera's team retained bits of the CDOs and they started to build up on the bank's balance sheet.

'I really don't think Jay was a bad person,' reflects one of his colleagues in London. By the height of the boom Jay Levine was certainly becoming a very rich person. In three years – 2004, 2005 and 2006 – he was paid in the region of £40m. Visitors from London and Edinburgh to Steamboat Road found the atmosphere 'buzzy', 'entrepreneurial', 'non-stuffy' and 'go go go'. 'Jay and his people were very American and great at making you feel welcome. It was all smiles and "Hey, what's going on with you guys?"' On 29 June 2006, in another indication of how committed both Levine and his bosses back in London were to the growth of the North American operation, the turf was cut on a new $400m headquarters in Stamford, a few miles from Greenwich. This development wasn't on quite the same scale as the RBS mother ship opened in Scotland by Goodwin. Stamford was more a 'mini-Gogarburn'. Local dignitaries, including Governor Jodi Rell, a Republican, turned out for the ceremony to launch the development, which was being built just off the Connecticut Turnpike on a 500,000-square-foot plot a few miles from Steamboat Road. In the new building the 700 or so staff moving from the Greenwich facility just down the road would be joined by 550 relocating from New York. The plan was to hire another 600 staff by the time it opened for business as the RBS Americas head office in 2009.

Who was monitoring all of this? Levine and the business based in Greenwich reported to Crowe, as chief executive of GBM, and to Cameron – who was chairman of GBM. For all the terminology of investment and banking, the various parts of Cameron's division earned him and some of his staff such substantial rewards in several simple ways. They helped large companies or entrepreneurs borrow, either by loaning them money or arranging the financing of their debt through bond issues. In the case of leveraged finance, RBS might take a share in a company that was borrowing money to do a deal or embark on a major project. Other specialised teams traded currencies (foreign exchange); other groups sold derivatives and futures that allow companies to hedge against risks such as the price of a basic commodity shifting.

Cameron also oversaw Alan Dickinson, who reported to him as head of UK Corporate Banking with 50,000 staff in branches and regional headquarters. On its own it served 90,000 British business customers. At that time it was expanding fast too, like some other banks pushing to eat up more of the UK commercial property market and making large loans to developers and companies wanting to capitalise on the roaring British property boom. As well as growing Greenwich, GBM was trying to push into other markets in Tokyo, Singapore, Hong Kong and elsewhere. The combination was a remarkable construct, considering that at the beginning of the decade RBS had been a relatively small Scottish bank. Now it was in an entirely different league. For a large fee in 2006, RBS teams in Spain and London arranged the £15bn of funding needed for Ferrovial, the Spanish construction company, to load itself with debt and buy BAA, then the owner of the UK's main airports.[9] When the football club Arsenal wanted to sell £260m of bonds to refinance the construction loans it had taken out to build the Emirates Stadium in north London, it turned to RBS for help. In North America it raised a large part of the finance for a $35bn energy deal, when ConocoPhillips bought Burlington Resources.

It required armies of structured finance experts, analysts and teams of highly competitive traders who all swam in the giant bonus pool. In the highly competitive environment at the height of the boom, star investment bankers and traders could make millions by moving, or threatening to move, to rivals. The more they made for the bank the bigger their bonuses, although across the industry the profits, which the personal bonuses were based on, were sometimes opaque. Were they always real profits, or had they been booked as such when some of it might turn bad, or turn out not to have been a profit at all, if conditions changed? Those who made a cash bonus from selling a CDO one year did not have to give the money back a year later if what they sold turned toxic. Indeed by then they might have been poached and moved on. Few in London or Edinburgh stopped to consider the risky implications of this in 2006, or if they did they did precious little about it.

GBM did have a well-staffed 'risk function' in London tasked with monitoring all this activity. For this Cameron relied on Howard Burnside and Riccardo Rebonato and their teams. Rebonato, RBS's global head of market risk and quantitative research and analysis, reported to Crowe as well as Cameron and to the group risk managers David Coleman, and the ultimate boss of that part of the operation Peter Nathaniel. Rebonato was in the curious position of also being an academic and author who had written extensively on banks, risk and the financial crisis. Indeed, he even published a weighty book in September 2007, just as the crisis was beginning, in which he argued that the model of risk being used by banks was overly reliant on large numbers of staff taking measurements and ticking boxes and thinking that this somehow eliminated risk. Bankers needed to return to making commonsense judgements, he argued in *Plight of the Fortune Tellers: Why We Need to Manage Financial Risk Differently*. This important theory could have done with being applied more forcefully in 2006 and 2007 at RBS, where Rebonato was employed. 'Riccardo grimaced a few times and thought we should have been hedging a bit more,' says a colleague, 'but he certainly didn't put up a big red flag.'

On top of the meetings to discuss risk, the bank had numerous daily credit committees, where bankers looking to loan or make major decisions had to go to have their initiative approved. There was an internal audit function with a licence to tour the entire business, external auditors Deloitte and Archie Hunter's audit committee, on which sat Robson and other directors. That committee made visits to Greenwich and was generally happy with assurances received. There was no shortage of lookouts posted. Then again, everything seemed to be going so well.

For steering the ship Cameron earned less than Levine,

although the rewards were still titanic by most standards. In 2006 Cameron's basic salary was £889,000. A bonus of £2,340,000, plus other benefits, made for a combined total of £3,496,000. This was half a million less than Goodwin in the same year. He took home £1,190,000 in salary plus a bonus of £2,760,000, making a total of £3,996,000. The chief executive's renumeration was rocketing. Between 2005 and 2006 it rose by £1,103,000, an astounding increase in one year of 38%. Still, by the epic standards of Barclay's Bob Diamond, the American investment banker who had built Barclays Capital and who was despised by Goodwin, they were modestly paid.[10] That same year Diamond was paid a total of £10,692,000. Like their colleagues, all these people were also tied into various stock options potentially worth additional millions. And then there were their pensions, although Cameron did not have the preferential deal that Goodwin had secured for himself.

In 2006 and 2007 Goodwin was loyal to Johnny Cameron. To those who sometimes asked questions about him, such as the RBS chairman Sir Tom McKillop and board member Peter Sutherland, the chief executive would say they had to understand that RBS Global Banking & Markets was run by a three-man team with Crowe and Leith Robertson. Cameron, although the chairman of GBM, was only one third of the equation. 'If you wanted someone to get on a plane and go to Paris for lunch to charm a big client he was your man,' acknowledges a critic. There was no one better with clients than Johnny, Goodwin emphasised. Those who had concerns should not think for a moment that Cameron was running the investment banking division alone, which now accounted for such a large chunk of RBS profits. Cameron himself found that ever more of his time was spent on the road, visiting major clients in France, Germany, Italy, Spain, and New York, where he would look in on Jay Levine and his team in nearby Greenwich.

The GBM chief executive, Brian Crowe, was in daily contact with Levine at Greenwich as well as overseeing RBS's two trading floors in London. Crowe was regarded as the markets man, a brainbox, someone steady and cerebral seemingly immersed in the full complexities of investment banking. He was also an Anglican lay preacher, and since the financial crisis he has been ordained. 'If Brian said something was so then you believed it,' says a colleague. Cameron and Crowe had adjoining offices in 135 Bishopsgate on the ninth floor. It was a peaceful, calm and reassuringly charming environment in which to earn a lot of money. There was even a fish tank.[11] Crowe's deputy was Leith Robertson, a pugnacious Edinburgh banker and dealmaker who oversaw structured, leverage and project finance, lending to large corporates. Cameron was the chairman of this trio, who was now on the RBS board and the main presence in the morning meetings with Goodwin and his colleagues in other parts of RBS. 'Johnny very much liked the kudos that went with being on the board,' says a board member.

There were some in 280 Bishopsgate and at Gogarburn who thought the set-up in GBM was much too ramshackle and potentially confusing. 'Have you got clear written down lines of management responsibility from Fred?' a friend of Cameron's asked him. Cameron didn't answer. Neil Roden, the HR director, said to Goodwin that the structure in GBM was a mess and needed tighter control. It relied too much on Crowe, as the numbers man, knowing everything. 'It's all stored in Brian's head,' he told the RBS chief executive. Goodwin was initially not overly concerned, keeping faith with 'Johnny, Brian and Leith'. It was paradoxical. Goodwin normally thrived on the accumulation of precise detail, whether it related to the shape of filing cabinets, or to executives whose numbers were flawed, or to vintage cars he worked on at a weekend. Yet he had shown almost no interest in the workings of RBS's booming investment bank. Even though Cameron's office was only 100 metres down Bishopsgate in another building, Goodwin hardly ever visited. Cameron and others cringed when Goodwin made a rare foray and tried to show the GBM team that he understood how a derivative worked by explaining it in terms of the workings of a car engine.

Goodwin's main concentration was on the numbers, targets and goals that each divisional head would sign up. 'Meeting your numbers every year was what mattered to Fred,' says one of Goodwin's most senior executives. 'He didn't want to get too closely involved with anything he didn't know about. Fred was good at branding and giving RBS discipline and he functioned quite well in a traditional banking environment. But eventually nearly half our profits were coming from non-traditional banking, the part he didn't understand. If it feels like you are making too much money for it to be true you usually are.' It was as though, a member of the board says, he had fenced off GBM and was reluctant to engage. 'Fred is one of those guys who has to be 10 out of 10. He always has to come top in everything he does. When he's not in complete control and command of something he would rather avoid it, which means that he is uncomfortable in front of people who know more. He always likes to be on topics where he is an expert.'

There was some confidence on the part of the board that the arrival of a new finance director at RBS in February 2006 had strengthened the entire operation. With enviable timing, Fred Watt had opted to leave for family reasons. His replacement was Guy Whittaker, who had been group treasurer at Citigroup, one of America's largest banks.[12] Whittaker had been very much the board's own appointment to balance Goodwin. 'On paper,' says a member of the board, 'Guy looked the part. But I'm afraid it turned out he wasn't.' It was hoped that Whittaker's experience on the other side of the Atlantic would make him a strong finance director. He was obviously able, although there might be a question mark over the temperament of this mild-mannered soul. Would someone so diffident and eager to please be prepared to say no to a strong-willed chief executive, as finance directors sometimes have to?

There was much more than Cameron's divisions for Whittaker to get to grips with and try to understand. The rest of RBS – retail in the UK, Ulster Bank, insurance, wealth management and private banking brands such as Coutts and Adam & Company – had been expanding too, although at a less frenetic pace. In these businesses the vast majority of RBS staff worked for rewards that would not have bought them so much as a parking space in Greenwich Connecticut. Many of the staff had invested in the bank's shares when they were offered options each year, expecting to create a nest egg for themselves and their families. And why not when the tone of those at the top was so confident?

Goodwin and the other senior executives were particularly bullish on Thursday 9 November 2006, when they hosted an investors' day conference for analysts under a 'Drivers of Growth' banner. Jay Levine was beamed in on video. Cameron enthused about the prospects. Gordon Pell, now running the retail bank, noted that some of the air was 'coming out of the tyres' in terms of the UK consumer lending boom, but he also explained why the stirrings of a row about PPI (payment protection insurance) miss-selling by UK banks including RBS had been much overdone. As ever, Goodwin was optimistic: 'Whatever the economy, whatever the world throws at us I am very confident that we will deliver growth which when compared to our peers is superior and sustainable, as we have done historically. So, I do believe that and we will, I believe, make it happen.'

One of the most upbeat of all was Cormac McCarthy, the chief executive of Ulster Bank. The Irish property market had gone bananas in recent years and RBS, with Ulster Bank, was right in there. In private, McCarthy had expressed concerns to colleagues about what Goodwin was asking him to sign up to in terms of promising growth. The percentages struck him as aggressive and he had emerged upset from several meetings, needing to be calmed down by colleagues.

Today he told of prospects for growth in Ireland that were 'almost limitless'. With so many newly rich Irish people, McCarthy had set up a team to connect with 'high-net-worth individuals'. Ulster Bank was expanding on every front, in personal loans, mortgages, the youth market and business lending. The booming Irish economy meant a wave of infrastructure building by the government and an opportunity for RBS to profit by helping those bidding for the lucrative contracts. 'The Irish economic story is very, very good both North and South. In the South the demographic effect, interest rates, the State finances, low tax rates continue to provide a very confident outlook for the next three to four years as far as anyone out there can see.'

There was one speck on the horizon. Larry Fish referred that day to 'headwinds' in the US banking market, although he did not elaborate. 'Headwinds' was a polite way of pointing out what was not then widely appreciated: US house prices had peaked in the summer of 2006 and there were the first signs of a decline. Instead, Fish talked in a folksy way of business banking and the increasing use of debit cards by American customers. The reality was that the progress of Citizens had slowed almost to a halt, as the annual results for 2006 published a few months later demonstrated. It turned out that Citizens' profit had hardly increased on the previous year. At $2.9bn it was up just 2 per cent, nothing when compared to the rate at which GBM was ballooning. Goodwin had long looked for an opportunity to remove Fish from his highly remunerated post and this slowdown at Citizens was his chance. The £5.9bn acquisition of Charter One in the United States in 2004, which ironically Fish had only reluctantly gone along with pushed by Goodwin, had not been a success. Several fellow members of the board had complained privately about Fish. In particular Joe MacHale, the former J. P. Morgan investment banker, had twice come back from trips to America as part of the audit committee claiming that Fish, a fellow board member, appeared to be running the

Citizens business too much for short-term profit with bonuses, his own included, in mind. McKillop, apparently fearing ill feeling, would not put such concerns in front of the board. But Goodwin wanted to 'sort out Larry'. Now, finally, it seemed when viewed from London that Fish was about to get fired. He did not yet suspect it, but Goodwin was getting ready to remove Fish as head of Citizens, although yet again he would stop short of sacking him.

There was another possible explanation for those 'headwinds' and the recent poor performance of Citizens, of course. Fish's division was in the old-fashioned mortgage and personal lending business in the world's largest economy and if there were to be a serious problem in America, with falling house prices, negative equity and consumers facing problems paying, it might show up first as a flicker in the results of institutions such as Citizens. Goodwin – an 'optimist' as Cameron used to observe to his team – told Cameron and other colleagues that it was fine: 'US house prices are not going to fall by 30 per cent. They just aren't.' Goodwin was not for slowing down and as 2007 began he was ruminating on the possibility of even more growth. Anyway, RBS didn't do sub-prime, did it?

The American economy was wobbling; the machine Goodwin had built was spread across continents; reporting lines were confused; his management style had been questioned; the chairman was new; and the rate of expansion had been quite staggering since he and Mathewson masterminded the purchase of NatWest in 2000. The RBS balance sheet – its total assets – had ballooned. It was more than £800bn by early 2007. Imagine if, on top of all that, Goodwin and his colleagues purchased large parts of a Dutch bank and in the process doubled the size of their own balance sheet. That was precisely what they were about to do.

11

Light Touch

'Three of the four largest banks individually have assets
in excess of annual UK GDP'

Bank of England

When John Campbell and a handful of colleagues set up for business in the Royal Bank's offices in Ship Close in Edinburgh in 1727 banking was very simple. The activities of British bankers remained more or less straightforward for much of the following two centuries. A bank such as the Royal Bank of Scotland was merely an institution that took in deposits from customers – initially only a very small number of depositors – and then lent it out to others whom the bank judged capable of paying the money back. For this loan the bank charged interest and accrued a profit, some of which could be dispersed to its shareholders with the rest used to expand the bank's activities and make further loans. When it issued notes or made loans, it did not keep a matching amount in its vaults. That would be prohibitively expensive and would defeat the point of the exercise, which was to provide increasing amounts of capital to individuals and businesses with good ideas that could make a profit, which might flow back into the bank in deposits and be lent out to others with potentially profitable ideas, and so on.

Of course, successful banks also have to navigate around storms in the economy, trying to detect when a period of sustained economic improvement has become a bubble that might burst. Historically, this tended to mean that successful banks were naturally suspicious, particularly of their own customers. Human frailties such as a tendency to over-optimism and the propensity of some people to lie and commit fraud necessitated caution. Sensible bankers have always known that while they lubricate the economy, providing those who can turn a profit and create employment with capital, they can still be caught with their trousers around their ankles. In such circumstances a racy bank – its directors motivated by excitement, lust for bigger profits or a misguided belief that they are cleverer than their predecessors – can easily find itself in trouble. If there is then a sudden panic, caused by bad news in the wider world that knocks confidence or the emergence of fears about a specific bank, there might be a 'run' on one or more institutions. Panicked customers, the depositors with which the process began, then rush to take their money out and discover to their horror that the bank obviously does not have every penny immediately to hand.

Complicating the process, banks sometimes borrow from each other, in order to oil the wheels of credit and so that they can lay their hands on money if they need it in a hurry or want to smooth the transaction of daily business. In the onset of a sudden crisis this does create the possibility of a chain reaction, as a panic about one bank spreads to others that are connected to it by lending. That is what happened when the Ayr Bank (mentioned in Chapter 2 and cited by Adam Smith) went bust in the eighteenth century having overextended its line of credit in London. Good banks discovered early on that it should be possible to avoid such disasters if they prove over decades that they are sound and trustworthy organisations. A bank must have access to liquidity, in safe assets such as government bonds that it can sell quickly if it needs cash. And if it keeps sufficient capital itself then, in the event of some loans going bad, there will be enough to be able to write off the losses and assure other customers that, this blip aside, all is well with the underlying business. No bank can ever eliminate the possibility that it will have to take such a hit. After all, banking by its nature is rooted in risk and the decision to lend someone money involves the possibility that it might be lost. The question is how the risks might be minimised and the profits maximised. That is banking.

It was in this spirit that the Royal Bank of Scotland advanced for most of its history. In England too were bankers at Barclays,[1] founded by Quakers, and Lloyds,[2] who operated according to exactly the same set of assumptions, although they only became joint-stock banks, with a large pool of shareholders, much later than the Royal Bank and the Bank of Scotland which had operated on that model from their inception. It was an important distinction. A bank that issued shares could use those funds to increase its activities. There was limited liability too, meaning that investors and directors were not liable for the total debts of the bank. It helped increase the availability of capital, aiding those who wanted to expand their businesses. Only from 1826, after a series of Acts of Parliament, was the model widely adopted in England. The Scots could claim, and did, that they were innovators, running ahead of their neighbours. Across Britain, savings banks and building societies established as mutuals, which were owned by those who saved with them, also proliferated.

By the end of the twentieth century the expansion of global trade had led to a transformation in the scale and complexity of what banks could do. Leverage – the amount a bank is prepared to lend compared with the amount of capital its executives think sensible to keep to guard against disaster – had been steadily increasing as bankers grew more confident that they could manage the trade-off between risk and potential reward. More lending meant more international trade by companies; more trade meant more demand for lending, subject to periodic economic downturns. Other less straightforward types of banking were prospering as well, of course: well-established American investment banks such as Goldman Sachs and Lehman Brothers, who advised companies wanting to do deals and raised the money from the markets for them, also profited on their own account by trading shares, bonds and currencies. The arrival of the computer and the creation of vast trading floors increased enormously the potential for them, and others, to make money from the wave of money now washing across continents. There was also a huge demand from corporations for the new products being invented by investment banks that might hedge against risks.

London became the leader in foreign exchange, the trading of money. It might be done on behalf of companies moving money to pay a supplier in a different country or it could be one of millions of transactions carried out for its own sake. Repeatedly slice off a slither of profit as the money flows across borders and the cumulative result might be a vast return. By 2012 the UK had an estimated 38 per cent share of the global foreign exchange market, with an astonishing daily turnover in London of $2000bn.[3] In the region of 40 per cent of the global derivatives market – futures, options and contracts which derive from underlying assets – is also traded in London.[4] Customers are betting that the price of a particular share price or a commodity such as wheat or oil, or an interest rate, is going to go in a particular direction. At any one time there are $640 trillion in contracts out there being bought, sold and renewed, aided by computerised trading that can facilitate rapid decision-making based on tiny movements.[5]

While this might seem to have little to do with the activities of a conventional and supposedly 'boring' British bank, such as RBS, the high-street banks were not insulated from these innovations. In fact, such was the scale of the potential rewards that some wanted to take part, even if initially it was just on the fringes. The deposits that customers put into a bank provided cheap funds for aggressive trading desks to use. The bigger profits they made could then be recycled as loans to customers or the payment of dividends to shareholders. Anyway, trading in this fashion, while risky, is potentially more exciting than the unglamorous work on the other side of banking, of managing relations with a corporate customer who wants an overdraft. It was another virtuous circle, in theory. The traders benefited from association with a solid retail bank and made profits that the conventional bankers could use in part to make more loans to businesses and those seeking mortgages. The old banks were not, initially at least, much good at this. Barclays' early attempts to diversify in this direction were not a success, and it was arguably only with the arrival of Bob Diamond that it found a way of making proper money out of being a so-called 'universal bank', which does almost everything from ordinary retail banking through to complex investment banking.

Another trend was apparent in the UK. The number of banks decreased steadily after a period of marked consolidation, with takeovers and mergers undertaken in pursuit of scale and efficiencies.[6] In 1960 there were sixteen UK clearing banks – so described because they can clear cheques between two parties. That sixteen has since been reduced to five. Subsumed within RBS itself are eight of those fifteen others from 1960: National Provincial, Coutts, District, Westminster, Williams-Deacon's, Glyn Mills, National Commercial and National. Even though some of those had been minor banks, there is no doubt that by the turn of the century British banks were more concentrated, serving a far greater number of customers and engaging in a wider range of activities.

And banks grew dramatically in size. The Bank of England reported in 2010 that, collectively, the UK banks' balance sheets were now more than 500 per cent of annual UK GDP – gross domestic product being what the country produces each year. In 1960 the combined balance sheets of the sixteen clearing banks amounted to £8bn, representing just 32 per cent of GDP. By 1990 it was 75 per cent of GDP and by 2000 143 per cent. The BoE noted in 2010: 'Three of the four largest banks individually have assets in excess of annual UK GDP. Relative to the size of the national economy, the UK banking system is second only to Switzerland among G20 economies, and is an order of magnitude larger than the US system.'

At root, this is why George Mathewson at the Royal Bank of Scotland and his rival Peter Burt at the Bank of Scotland fought so hard for the chance to buy NatWest in early 2000. The consensus was that with banks enlarging themselves, smaller banks had to catch up or face obliteration in a financial revolution. The idea that one or other might choose to carry on at roughly the size they were – making a healthy profit sensibly and employing people – went unmentioned as shareholders cashed in, selling their shares when a decent offer came along.

It was recognised internationally that the expansion of finance in countries such as the US and the UK brought dangers for the banks, the bedrock of the financial system, and for the rest of us who depended on them. How might these increasingly intricate and enormous institutions be regulated to ensure they were not going to blow up with potentially catastrophic consequences? This dilemma exercised regulators and central bankers when various scares in the 1970s demonstrated how internationally interconnected banks had become. In the 1980s, in the unprepossessing Swiss city of Basel, bankers and regulators had a first proper attempt at regulation. They understood that the risks apparent in a bank run were magnified many times when one factored in the size of banks and the potential for a cross-border emergency. A run at an important institution, one with operations in other countries and a web of links with other international banks, might destroy confidence and damage the global economy. What they agreed eventually – although they were actually bounced by the authorities in New York and London – sounded plausibly as though it would deal with the problem. In Basel I, in 1988, and then in Basel II, published in 2004 although never fully implemented, minimum standards were laid down for how much capital banks must keep.

Big banks are often reluctant to keep more capital than the bare minimum. They are under pressure from some shareholders to hold as little of it as necessary because they would rather that as much of the profits as possible go to them. The Royal Bank under George Mathewson and Fred Goodwin adopted a policy known as 'efficient capital', which meant running capital a little lower than might be ideal on the basis that their business was historically sound and they knew what they were doing. When Tom McKillop asked about this he was told by Goodwin: 'Our investors like it.'

Under Basel a bank's assets were rated, in five categories, according to how risky they were. Banks had to hold roughly 8 per cent of the total value in capital, and a lower number for what was termed 'core tier 1' capital, of ultra-safe assets. It was appreciated that the value of the bank's assets could deteriorate unexpectedly and rapidly. But how might a bank keep track of this? The stock market crash of October 1987, when markets in London, New York, Hong Kong and elsewhere fell dramatically, concentrated minds. If banks had enormous portfolios of all kinds of assets on their books – loans, bonds, securities, stocks, derivatives – they needed a way of being able to measure at close of business each day how it was looking. Increasingly complex risk management systems were evolved in banks to monitor the extent of the exposure and flag warnings, particularly in trading. A lot rested on the adoption of something called VaR, Value at Risk, which teams of risk managers and risk committees inside the banks used to assess, according to various formulae, how much a bank might lose on a particular asset in an emergency.[7] It was supposed to be an early warning system. It had been developed by a team at J. P. Morgan in the early 1990s and computer-assisted modelling was integral to the process. VaR was pivotal to the expansion of banks, and what was to follow, because it created a sense of reassurance and confidence. The teams of risk professionals that managed the process checked that the traders were acting within the VaR guidelines set for the bank, and if they were then all was probably fine. Risk was being measured, modelled, every day, constantly.

The increased complexity of banking did not make life easy for national regulators, who still had oversight of their country's banks even though it was hoped that international agreements had made the system safer. After the Big Bang of 1986, Margaret Thatcher's government had relied on a network of committees to try to police the City, in a system of self-regulation, with bank supervision overseen by the Bank of England.[8] When Gordon Brown became Chancellor in 1997 he wanted a much simpler system and a beefed-up single body modern enough to cope. In the event, after his row with the Governor of the Bank of England, a messy compromise was agreed. Instead of the Bank of England losing its traditional oversight of bank regulation entirely, the 'tripartite' system was established in which the Financial Services Authority (FSA) handled the day-to-day monitoring, the Bank of England was supposed to consider the stability of the overall financial system and the government, in the shape of the Treasury, kept in touch with both. Howard Davies, a technocrat who had worked for the Treasury and the Foreign Office, ran the CBI and would go on to the top job at the London School of Economics. He set up the FSA as executive chairman then left in 2002. Later the organisation was criticised for its performance in that period in the run-up to the collapse of Equitable Life, England's oldest insurance provider.

The successor to Davies as chief executive in September 2002 was John Tiner, a high-flying accountant who had been hired the year before to oversee the insurance side of the FSA's activities. Tiner had a gift for timing his exits. He had left the auditor Arthur Andersen in 2001, only months before it collapsed in 2002 over its involvement in the Enron scandal, and he later departed the FSA in July 2007, hailed at the time for the good job he had done regulating financial services. Arriving at the FSA's offices in the North Colonnade of Canary Wharf, Tiner was no greenhorn when it came to banks. He had led the team at Arthur Andersen hired by the Bank of England to investigate the collapse of Barings Bank when it was brought down by the activities of the trader Nick Leeson in 1995. Tiner knew about bank runs and how quickly a piece of exotic trading could go wrong.

The FSA boss, supported by the organisation's new chairman Callum McCarthy, subscribed to a then fashionable theory. If the banks had become so intricate, with vast risk-management teams and access to the cleverest thinking and computing, then no state regulator or state employee could hope to outsmart them. There was no point in the regulator tying up bankers in complicated sets of specific rules, when they already had to comply with Basel and the laws governing accounting. Better to set broad principles on conduct to which the banks could sign up. Eventually, he and his colleagues hit upon the idea of rewarding those who cooperated by granting a 'regulatory dividend' of lighter scrutiny. This was termed 'principles-based regulation'. Much of the rest of the FSA's work was in consumer protection, examining the products that banks or other financial services providers sold, while the teams dedicated to monitoring the conduct of the individual banks were small.[9]

Says one of his colleagues from the FSA: 'John is a very nice man who just happened to get it completely wrong.' Tiner's thinking was certainly very much in line with the mood of the age. The bankers, in charge of such large organisations, now had an extraordinary degree of privileged access to senior politicians who shared the prevailing view that regulation should be 'light touch'. Chancellors had long invited in groups of bank chief executives for conversations, to get a sense of what was happening on the ground in the economy. Now bankers were treated more like dignitaries and ushered into private un-minuted individual meetings in Number 10 and Number 11, and invited to sit as experts on government 'taskforces'. It was hoped that the innovative, expansive spirit of banking would imbue other areas of economic and national life.

The Conservative opposition, having initially issued some warnings about the dangers of the tripartite system, generally came to accept the situation. After all, in regard to the City, Blair and Brown were continuing the work started by Margaret Thatcher and Nigel Lawson, which had been designed to make London once again a world financial capital. By 2007 the financial services sector in the UK was paying the Exchequer £67.8bn in taxes, which accounted for 13.9 per cent of the overall tax collected by the government that year.[10] In such a climate, bankers who complained to the Prime Minister and Chancellor about regulation found that their concerns were taken seriously. Even the much heralded 'light touch' was deemed too heavy. On 26 May 2005 Tony Blair made a speech in which he attacked excessive regulation: 'Something is seriously awry', he told the Institute of Public Policy Research, 'when the Financial Services Authority that was established to provide clear guidelines and rules for the financial services sector and to protect the consumer against the fraudulent, is seen as hugely inhibiting of efficient business by perfectly respectable companies that have never defrauded anyone.' Callum McCarthy, the chairman, was so stung by the criticism that he wrote to Blair, assuring him that regulation was proportionate. Brown in particular found that Fred Goodwin was particularly persistent in complaining about the FSA. Much later Brown started to wonder if this, the chance to lobby him on regulation, had been the main reason that Goodwin was prepared to spend so much time with him in meetings and at dinners. At the time Brown was clear what he wanted, however. On 24 May 2005, at the launch of his Better Regulation Action Plan, he said: 'The new model we propose is quite different. In a risk-based approach there is no inspection without justification, no form-filling without justification, and no information requirements without justification. Not just a light touch but a limited touch.'

Even without such pressure, the Royal Bank itself was not an easy bank for the FSA to regulate when Tiner took over. Goodwin's personality saw to that. According to his colleagues, the RBS chief executive initially had difficulty taking the FSA seriously, seeing it as an unsophisticated, bureaucratic organisation that caused unnecessary problems without really understanding what modern global banking was about. Its focus was certainly more on consumer protection and less on the scrutiny of high finance and the stability of large banks. Indeed, the deputy chair from 2004 to 2007 was Dame Deirdre Hutton, known by some newspapers as the 'Queen of the Quangos', because she made a career out of serving on public bodies. After a spell at the Glasgow Chamber of Commerce, she sat on ten quangos in three decades. She had run or chaired, variously, the National Consumer Council, the Scottish Consumer Council and the Personal Investment Authority Ombudsman Bureau. Until June 2005 she was also a member of the government's 'Better Regulation Task Force', which Gordon Brown had established with the aim of limiting burdens on business.

If the extent of Hutton's banking expertise was questionable, there were others on the FSA's board who did have more relevant experience. McCarthy, the beekeeping chairman, had worked in senior positions at Barclays, and before that at Kleinwort Benson, as well as spending time as an official in government. Fellow board member Hector Sants was a career investment banker who had switched to regulation. He became head of the unit in the FSA that monitored wholesale activities, which included investment banks. Astonishingly, one serving board member of the FSA actually still ran a bank, a retail bank. James Crosby was the chief executive of HBOS when he was appointed to the FSA board in January 2004. The bank Crosby presided over had a particularly aggressive attitude to lending, as would later become apparent at the height of the financial crisis. When a whistleblower, Paul Moore, attempted to warn his colleagues at HBOS that the bank was taking excessive risks on property and commercial lending he was fired, by Crosby.[11]

Throughout Tiner's tenure there was concern in the FSA about Goodwin's assertive behaviour and the management of RBS. The FSA's requests for individual meetings with the members of the Royal Bank board were rebuffed when the regulators wanted to test claims that Goodwin bullied the board. Goodwin, says a colleague, didn't want board members 'telling tales out of school' about his behaviour, so the FSA could meet the board only as a group. The regulator complained to George Mathewson on several occasions, who responded that the board he chaired put up sufficient challenge to the chief executive. Such was the extent of the supervisors' concerns that in October 2004 the FSA management considered ordering a '166 review', in which it would hire an outside firm to conduct an independent investigation into RBS. In the event, assurances from several board members that they were not dragooned by Goodwin were enough to satisfy the FSA, which stopped short of launching a formal investigation. Goodwin, it seemed, also realised he had gone too far and urged on by Mathewson he undertook to be more helpful to the regulator after a 'clear the air' meeting that he held with the FSA in late 2004. After this the FSA even allowed Goodwin to soften a letter it planned to send to the Royal Bank board, which dealt with concerns the regulator had that the bank's 'stress testing' was inadequate. The draft was sent to Goodwin and he amended it.

If the FSA still had concerns, by the autumn of 2006 the regulators hoped that the arrival of a new chairman, McKillop, would mean Goodwin came under greater internal scrutiny than perhaps had been the case with Mathewson. It was also thought that Guy Whittaker, the new finance director who had come from Citigroup in the United States, was sufficiently worldly-wise to take on Goodwin if necessary. The FSA management was reassured.

The supervision team in the FSA dedicated specifically to overseeing the Royal Bank was, anyway, very small. In 2005 only one manager and six officials were charged with scrutinising this rapidly expanding bank. A curious decision was taken in April 2006 – to keep separate the teams that looked at retail banks and those that supervised mainly wholesale financial activities. Hector Sants ran the latter while Clive Briault ran the former. There was certainly some cooperation between the two teams: 'Clive's lot would ask Hector's team for advice and support when they were coming to see us, so they talked,' says an RBS executive in GBM. Not enough, perhaps.[12]

'What I really think they didn't understand at the FSA,' says a board member at RBS, 'is that the Royal Bank was a retail bank that now had a mini, or not so mini, Goldman Sachs lodged inside it.' Trips were made by FSA teams to Greenwich, in Connecticut, to interview Jay Levine's staff, and there was some scrutiny of GBM's credit and risk processes in London and elsewhere. Nothing substantial showed up, although there were recommendations that GBM improve its governance procedures, to keep track of its activities in the United States and fifty-three other countries. The FSA was then satisfied this had been done. In February 2007 the decision was taken to have 'fewer but better' staff looking at RBS and other banks. This left the team badly stretched. At one point there was just one staff member focused on GBM, who was also responsible for scrutinising Barclays Capital, Bob Diamond's giant investment banking arm at Barclays.

The main focus in the supervisory teams under Briault – including the group looking at RBS – principally involved checking that RBS's procedures in areas such as credit and risk were in line with what was laid down in the regulations. The bigger question of liquidity – was it certain that a bank with such a large balance sheet could safely lay its hands on enough money – was not regarded by the FSA as a central concern. It was referred to at points in speeches by officials and reports, but never pounced on as a potentially fatal weakness. Anyway, there was no expectation that there would suddenly be a shortage of money. Supposedly the Value at Risk (VaR) system also meant that the banks had clearer sight than ever before of what was at risk as their balance sheets expanded. At Tiner's management meetings participants remember almost no discussion about the safety of the banks, for good reason: it was hardly mentioned. 'Prudential' matters were a low priority barely touched on there or at the board. Between January 2006 and July 2007, only one topic out of sixty-one discussed at the FSA board dealt with the risks that banks were taking. In the same period, the FSA director responsible for regulating RBS and other retail banks reported 229 items to the board. Only five of them related to 'bank prudential issues'. In Tiner's annual report in that period, the chief executive reported on 110 items. One of them related to bank safety.

If the FSA was not robust, might the Bank of England – which still had responsibility for the overall stability of the financial system – take a lead? No. Shortly after Tiner took over at the FSA, there was a change of the guard at the Bank of England too. Sir Eddie George, the chain-smoking governor who had been its bulwark, retired at the end of June 2003 to be replaced by Mervyn King, until then his deputy. King came with a formidable academic record and a clear view of what the Bank of England should be doing. As deputy governor he had been the architect of an innovative new approach to economic policy in the UK, after the pound fell out of the ERM, the European Exchange Rate Mechanism, on 16 September 1992. That had represented the end of the government's doomed attempt to create economic stability and control inflation by pegging the pound to the then all-powerful Deutschmark. When that failed, spectacularly, King suggested instead that the central bank, the Bank of England, should concentrate remorselessly on targeting inflation by adjusting interest rates up or down according to what the Monetary Policy Committee, which he chaired, voted for. John Major's government bought the idea, and Gordon Brown continued the policy, even giving the bank and the MPC independence. Brown boasted that it had helped deliver an unprecedentedly long period of low inflation.

Broader financial stability, the responsibility that had been left with the bank after the establishment of the tripartite system seemed hardly to interest King at all, compared with an obsession with perfecting his policy on tackling inflation and meeting the target set by the government. He did not present the bank's reports on financial stability, although he did preside at the press conferences when it was time for the news on inflation. He rarely attended meetings of the Financial Stability Committee and it became, as Chris Giles the economics editor of the *Financial Times* later reported, 'a talking shop'.[13] In 2006, a senior civil servant, Sir John Gieve, was appointed as deputy governor responsible for financial stability, as well as being given a seat on the MPC. He was an odd choice. Gieve had had a notably torrid time in his previous post, as Permanent Secretary at the Home Office in the scandal-hit period immediately before Labour

Home Secretary John Reid infamously described the department as 'not fit for purpose'. Yet rather than him being retired, he was moved to a role that might be pivotal in the event of a financial crisis. Regarded as a decent man, it was difficult to see his appointment as anything other than him being 'parked' in the Bank of England after a bruising few years in Whitehall. There were suggestions that he lacked contacts in the City, and in banking, but his division was anyway looked down on in King's Bank of England.

Gieve made several confusing speeches in 2006, in which he touched on systemic risk. In July 2007 he seemed to sense that something potentially serious was up, as a result of the slump in sub-prime housing in the United States, although he could not quite articulate it in terms that made any impact. He concluded by being on message with the governor. The US housing market was on a downswing and there might be difficulties resulting in the boom having been combined with massive expansion in the new derivative markets. The picture, he noted, was cloudy. 'It is our job on the MPC to work through these issues and reach a judgement on them. Our target is to reduce inflation to 2 per cent and keep it there. I can assure you that we will do whatever is needed to achieve that.'[14] By then Gieve was being frozen out, anyway. Paul Tucker, the deputy governor charged with responsibility for markets, was certainly growing more concerned about the impact of the decline in US housing. But this was tricky territory. The governor's model – concentrate on the business of managing inflation and all else will follow – was malfunctioning, and King was not known for his ability to admit mistakes.

The accountants were supposed to be another line of defence. A bank must be audited, in effect to confirm to shareholders and customers that its accounts and valuations add up and are in keeping with the law. By the eve of the financial crisis these firms themselves had been transformed too. If there had been consolidation and complexity in banking, with fewer and much bigger banks, in accountancy the trend had been even more marked. There are now only four such firms – the 'Big Four' – operating in the UK (Deloitte, PWC, KPMG and Ernst & Young). It is said that smaller firms do not have the resources to audit a large bank properly.

Just as bankers and regulators had Basel, auditors in the UK from 2005 put faith in their version of the International Financial Reporting Standards (IFRS) which allowed a generous way of calculating what provisions banks should make to cover potential losses on loans. This had the effect, argue critics, of making bank profits bigger, or look bigger, and of increasing the bonuses linked to profits. It contributed to banks being able to take on greater leverage and lend more. And then the auditors would sign their accounts off, and enjoy higher fees as they had to audit banks that were getting larger. This put the auditors in a highly profitable and ethically questionable bind.

RBS was not entirely straightforward to audit. Goodwin was instrumental in removing the old auditors, PWC, and in the spring of 2000 Deloitte won the contract. Goodwin, it is said by former RBS executives, wanted an auditor which would be much more cooperative, and Deloitte was Goodwin's alma mater. Touche Ross, where Goodwin had risen so fast, had become part of the firm in the UK. The senior partner in Deloitte was his old mentor John Connolly, who had talent-spotted Goodwin as a rising star at Touche Ross, and then helped make him the firm's youngest partner. As a result Goodwin and Connolly were often bracketed as friends, although it was more complicated than that. Goodwin as RBS chief executive was intensely demanding of Deloitte staff and as a result the Royal Bank was regarded by Connolly's team as a 'pain in the arse' client that paid well. Connolly himself was a blunt, sharp-elbowed, racehorse-owning boss, a fanatical Manchester United fan and friend of Sir Alex Ferguson, who ran his firm extremely hard, for the maximum profit. The relationship with RBS was a valuable global contract for the firm and Goodwin, a tricky customer, had to be attended to.

Initially, Deloitte moved a senior partner to its Edinburgh office, in the city's George Street, who reported to headquarters in London. Albert Hazard (appropriately named for an accountant) was installed so that RBS could have a senior man on hand to minister to Goodwin. It was a worthwhile investment for Deloitte. The Royal Bank's growth was good business. When the audit contract began in 2000 it was worth £5.5m in fees to Deloitte, but as the Royal Bank expanded and its structure became more complicated, the auditor could earn much more. By 2006 the contract was worth £9.9m and in 2008 £38.6m. On top of the audit fees, Deloitte was also awarded other work for advice on tax or corporate finance. In 2008 it amounted to £20.1m. In the year of the financial crisis alone Deloitte's connection with Goodwin paid off to the tune of almost £59m.

Surely the auditors in this period were at least maintaining a proper dialogue with the regulator, the FSA, to flag up any concerns they might have? Again, not really, no. Auditors have protection in law, allowing them to raise privately with a regulator anything they discover that they do not like the look of. When the Bank of England ran regulation there was such contact. Once the tripartite system was established after 1997 it seems that it dwindled to almost nothing. As the FSA later admitted: 'The regular practice of auditor-supervisor meetings fell away gradually following the transition from the Bank of England to the FSA as banking supervisor.' In 2011 the House of Lords Economic Affairs Committee inquiry into the power of the big four[15] found that: 'In 2006 there was not a single meeting between the FSA and the external auditors of either Northern Rock (PwC) or HBoS (KPMG), and only one meeting between the auditor of RBS (Deloitte) and the FSA; and that in the whole of 2007 there was only one FSA/auditors meeting with each bank auditor.' In 2008, with the financial world ablaze, there were no meetings between the FSA and Connolly's firm Deloitte about RBS. The auditors and regulators were not communicating. Another line of possible defence against disaster was full of holes.

None of this seemed apparent in 2007. In July of that year, Tiner left the FSA and said: 'This seems to me to be the right time to pass on the baton, with the FSA set firmly on the road to more principles-based regulation.' Next, he was appointed to write a report for the government on the corporate governance of the National Audit Office. It was as though there was an establishment 'revolving door'. Ed Balls, then the Economic Secretary to the Treasury, Brown's friend and most trusted adviser, also praised the FSA in generous terms. When the National Audit Office published its review of the regulator, Balls welcomed the findings: 'The report shows that the FSA is working well, and is a world leader in a number of areas – which can only be good for the competitiveness of the UK financial services sector.' At a meeting with Gordon Brown on 30 April 2007, the chairman of the National Audit Office said that the FSA was 'an institution that the UK can be proud of'.[16]

Two months after Tiner left the FSA and handed over to Sants in the summer of 2007, the FSA was then blindsided by the run on Northern Rock, when credit markets froze. Deirdre Hutton also left the FSA as deputy chair in 2007, and was soon appointed by the government to chair the Civil Aviation Authority. She remarked shortly afterwards: 'I don't know anything about aeroplanes.'[17] She had thought about this, however, and concluded that she had skills, developed in many quangos such as the FSA, that were transferable: 'My main interest, I realise after quite a long time working, is making organisations work properly.' Hutton was replaced at the FSA by Crosby, the former boss of HBOS who had been on the board since 2004. He had left HBOS in January 2006 on 'a high-note' recorded the *Financial Times*. A knighthood followed. Later, only months before the banking system failed, and Crosby's old bank HBOS had to be bailed out, he was appointed by the government to lead a taskforce looking at the workings of the mortgage industry.

When it came to HBOS and more importantly the much bigger RBS, a bank that had grown from minnow to mammoth in just seven years, there was little in the way of searching scrutiny. The regulatory authority was pursuing light-touch, 'principles-based' oversight. In the case of RBS, the auditor Deloitte was doing well out of a difficult client. The Governor of the Bank of England was focused narrowly on managing interest rates and had little regard to what was going on in RBS or any of the other banks, whose balance sheets now dwarfed the rest of the UK economy. And the Chancellor who had presided over an extraordinary boom – marked by an explosion in levels of personal indebtedness – was getting ready to move next door and become Prime Minister.

On the evening of 20 June 2007, Gordon Brown turned up to make his last speech as Chancellor at the Mansion House. This annual address is when a Chancellor gives the grandees of the City, assembled for dinner, his assessment of the prospects of the UK economy. That night an excited Brown was only a week away from realising his ambition of making it to Number 10. He fizzed with the possibilities of what lay ahead and spoke of 'a new world order' unleashed by global trade. He was, he said, 'more optimistic than ever about the future of our islands, just one per cent of the world's population, in this new era of globalisation'. The City had shown the way to the rest of the country, Brown claimed. Together, as Chancellor and City, he told his audience, they had been involved in creating what he considered an 'era that history will record as the beginning of a new golden age for the City of London'. Britain was, Brown said, ideally placed to capitalise: 'While never the biggest in size, nor the mightiest in military hardware, I believe we are –

as the City's success shows – capable of being one of the greatest success stories in the new global economy. Already strong in this young century, but greater days are ahead of us.' Stability must remain the watchword, he observed. After all, Britain was a 'world leader in stability', and Brown promised to 'entrench that stability, by ensuring Britain's macroeconomic framework remains a world benchmark'. This would very soon be proved to be Panglossian propaganda for a doomed experiment. It was delusional drivel.

That same month, Mervyn King's pivotal role was also being celebrated, in a fitting location. The Society of Business Economists hosted a private dinner to mark the tenth anniversary of Gordon Brown granting independence to the Bank of England, with King as the guest of honour. Economists and various dignitaries, including former Governor Eddie George, who was now Lord George, gathered in the City for drinks and then a convivial discussion over dinner. It was a chance for King to relax among friends and reflect on the achievements of recent years. The Governor was a little worried, belatedly, about the exuberance of the markets. He had mentioned it in his speech the evening of Brown's last address at the Mansion House as Chancellor. But inflation was low and growth had been strong, with only minor deviations, for almost a decade and a half. The venue for this private dinner had been booked by RBS's chief economist. It was held at 280 Bishopsgate, on the twelfth floor, in the dining room just along the corridor from Sir Fred Goodwin's office. Goodwin sent his apologies. He would very much have liked to be there, but he was too busy in meetings about RBS's attempted takeover of the Dutch bank ABN Amro.

12

Double Dutch

'We face 2007 with confidence'

Fred Goodwin presenting the
annual results on 1 March.

Tom McKillop wanted Fred Goodwin to tell him about ABN
Amro. The RBS chairman broached the subject in a phone
call one evening early in January 2007, from his flat in Chelsea.
Was there any substance in these rumours circulating in the City
that they – RBS – might be interested in buying the Dutch bank?
It was being said that Goodwin had even had discussions with
the ABN Amro chief executive Rijkman Groenink. Goodwin
was supremely relaxed: 'Groenink? Oh, I've been talking to him
for ages and keeping the door open in case we can do something.' Parts of the bank he ran are a perfect fit with us, he told
McKillop.

The chairman wasn't sure. Not only had the board recently
committed the bank to pursuing 'organic growth' in their existing businesses rather than launching expensive takeovers,
McKillop thought that the organisation lacked the international

experience and talent to swallow a large foreign bank such as ABN Amro on its own. If other banks might be persuaded to join in and divide the spoils, that was another matter. Still, it was good to keep talking; you never knew what might emerge from such discussions. Even though RBS had been put in the 'sin-bin', as investors and journalists called it, as the result of Goodwin being deemed to be 'acquisition crazy', any bank with ambitions keeps an eye out for takeover or merger opportunities.

In January 2005 there had been a few rumours that the Royal Bank might be interested. On that occasion, Groenink had dismissed the speculation, telling guests gathered at a New Year reception[1] that 'the only Scotch on offer is at the bar'. Despite this rebuff, the name ABN Amro sat discreetly for years on RBS's long list of potential options for review, in case something changed. Says a board member: 'It wasn't an idea that was plucked out of the air, and everyone thought, God that's a weird one. It had been bandied around internally and externally as an obvious fit for us, or indeed for Barclays.' Banks on the prowl keep an eye on each other. Rival chief executives might meet for lunch or drinks several times a year in order to maintain a channel of communication, in case a deal with a rival that was once unthinkable should suddenly become feasible. There can be an added piquancy to these ostensibly polite encounters in that it is sometimes unclear which of the two lunching partners will eventually be the eater and which one the eaten. On 31 October 2006, Goodwin had contacted Groenink to suggest they meet. It was obvious that the whole or parts of the Dutch bank – which was flabby and in poor shape with unhappy shareholders – might soon be on the menu, and he did not want Barclays or another rival getting in first. They fixed on a meeting in early January.

In the interim, in December 2006, Matthew Greenburgh and a small team from Merrill Lynch had a meeting with Goodwin, Guy Whittaker and Iain Allan, Goodwin's head of strategy, to brief them on the possibilities. ABN Amro was a huge group with interests well beyond the Netherlands. Greenburgh, who had been there for the NatWest takeover and many deals in between, told Goodwin and his colleagues that they should start to think more seriously about what RBS might be able to acquire if, as anticipated, discontented shareholders seeking a profit forced a break-up or sale of ABN Amro. Of particular interest to Guy Whittaker, the finance director, was the Dutch bank's Global Transaction Services division: 'If you want to move one hundred million euros anywhere in the world quickly they've got a great system for doing it,' Goodwin was told. The business in America, LaSalle, a bank based in Chicago, looked promising too. Both were worth acquiring, in Iain Allan's view, although the rest of the Dutch bank was not. Like many other European banks, it was just a conglomeration of various inefficient units patched together. Goodwin especially wanted LaSalle. It would fit in neatly with what he was preparing to do next in the United States. He was aiming to bring together the various businesses RBS owned there under the 'RBS Americas' brand. That would involve moving against the highly paid Larry Fish at Citizens.

Goodwin was far from gung-ho at the Greenburgh briefing: 'Fred was cautious, intrigued, interested in LaSalle,' says one of those present. He said he thought the possibilities were interesting and he would keep open that line of communication with Groenink. If ABN Amro decided to sell its American operations, he wanted to be called first. On 9 January, Goodwin flew to Amsterdam for talks with Groenink. The ABN Amro boss was suspicious. Hedge funds which owned shares in ABN Amro had been agitating for months, sensing weakness and an opportunity to cash in. A takeover battle would probably drive up the share price for the benefit of said hedge funds. Was Goodwin collaborating with one hedge fund in particular? The non-executive chairman of Tosca, the London-based fund which had been making noises, was George Mathewson, wasn't it? Goodwin assured him that he was not plotting with Mathewson. RBS simply wanted the chance to buy ABN Amro's American arm if it became available, or maybe a bit more if they could come to an accommodation. They agreed to keep in touch. Groenink told colleagues that he was convinced he was being lied to, and that Goodwin and Mathewson were collaborating to break up the bank he ran. Hadn't Mathewson suggested to him a few months ago, when the pair met, that the Dutch should explore a merger with RBS?

Like the Royal Bank, ABN Amro was proud of its roots. The Dutch in Amsterdam had been important financial innovators long before the Scots thought of the Darien Scheme or of establishing their own banks.[2] Groenink and his colleagues were desperate to avoid the indignity of being the bankers who sold out one of the Netherlands' longest-established companies to foreigners.[3] When he had taken over as boss he had promised growth and down the years he had discussed the possibility of mergers or of taking over various rivals. Those efforts to find a partner had come to little and now he and the bank he ran were being hunted. On 22 February, a hedge fund, TCI (The Children's Investment Fund management), wrote to Groenink lamenting the 'terrible shareholder returns' under his stewardship. It urged the board to pursue a 'break up, spin-off, sale or merger of its various businesses, or as a whole'.[4]

That month, more members of the RBS board were introduced to the idea that Goodwin was interested if ABN Amro or parts of it became available. No major objections were raised, although there were questions from Steve Robson and others about how it might possibly work. Goodwin was businesslike and unemotional. It was not a deal they absolutely had to do. He advocated proceeding one step at a time.

While Groenink was determined to avoid being stitched up by Scots he suspected of double dealing, he was prepared to talk to another British bank. For months, John Varley at Barclays and the

ABN Amro boss had been discussing a merger that would mean a combined group's headquarters being in Amsterdam. By early March, the rumours had reached Matthew Greenburgh's Merrill Lynch team that a deal with Barclays was likely. Goodwin rang Groenink and was assured there was nothing afoot imminently. 'Groenink's lying,' the RBS chief executive claimed to his colleagues. Indeed, on 19 March, McKillop's birthday, it was confirmed to investors that Barclays and ABN Amro were now in formal and exclusive talks. In the light of this, Goodwin wrote to the RBS board with a clear message: 'This is not a must do deal', although he would continue to look at the options. Nonetheless, the pace was being upped. On 28 March at a board meeting in London, head of strategy Iain Allan gave a presentation to the board on the possibilities. It was explained that 'the execution risk would be high' and Allan stressed the need to get partners who could help. There were mixed views around the table once he had concluded and departed, although there was general agreement that the whole of ABN Amro would be much too tough to digest. The cost – upwards of 60bn euros – was obviously prohibitive. The consensus was that Barclays had stolen a march and that it was frustrating.

Then Goodwin coolly produced his response. Says a member of the board: 'It was a rabbit from a hat. Guess what, guys, we can do it. I've got a consortium and if we do it as a consortium, we can beat Barclays. And the board looked at him just as they look at Derren Brown (the illusionist). They looked at his left hand and they looked at his right hand, metaphorically, and the whole conversation was are you sure, can we, can we really, has this ever been done before, can we do it, will it work?' Fatefully, the tone was set for all of the subsequent discussions involving Goodwin, McKillop, Sutherland, Robson, MacHale, Cameron, Pell and the others: 'From that day on, literally from that day on, every board meeting was dominated by "can we do this?". Insufficient attention was paid to "should we do it?".'

Goodwin was already well advanced on constructing a consortium. Matthew Greenburgh and his colleague at Merrill Lynch, Andrea Orcel,[5] had revealed to him that Fortis, the Belgian bank, might be interested in a tie-up. Santander, run by Emilio Botín, the former board member of RBS and good friend of Goodwin and George Mathewson, was enthusiastic. If the three banks could agree how the spoils might be divided, they could bid and possibly beat Barclays. 'Fred wanted to be bigger than Barclays. Had to be bigger than Barclays and here was a chance to do it,' says one of his management team. First, Greenburgh and Orcel knew, Goodwin had to 'click' with the chairman of Fortis, Maurice Lippens. Lippens had read about 'Fred the Shred', and while admiring what he had done in banking, the Belgian thought that he sounded rather abrasive. In the event, Goodwin and Lippens got on extremely well. Two days after the RBS board meeting, on 30 March, they met in Brussels for lunch at the offices of Fortis and Goodwin did what he could do when he wanted to clinch a deal. He turned on the charm. It helped that Lippens had a long-standing animosity to Groenink, on the grounds that he felt he had been misled in the past on various proposed deals. In contrast, Lippens was impressed with the RBS chief executive and agreed to proceed. The Belgians wanted the domestic Dutch retail banking business of ABN Amro, the Spanish would take Brazil and Italy and the Scots would get LaSalle in the United States and the investment banking operations.

A summit was arranged in great secrecy. On 12 April the RBS, Santander and Fortis private jets touched down in Geneva, and Goodwin, Botín, Lippens and their teams took over an entire floor of the city's Four Seasons Hotel. Greenburgh and Orcel facilitated the meetings, and worked at smoothing the way in an atmosphere that was, initially at least, tense. Goodwin was accompanied again by Whittaker and Iain Allan, although it was Goodwin and Whittaker who went into the meetings, with

Allan left outside. Goodwin knew that Allan had doubts about buying all of ABN Amro. He argued that LaSalle was worth getting because it would fit with Citizens. And Global Transaction Services was worth securing. But for the first time on a major acquisition Allan was sidelined in the talks and instead left to write the letter that would go to ABN Amro announcing a bid. Whittaker, who had no experience of such deals, now found himself at the chief executive's side. He was made integral to the process. By 8 p.m. the three banks had the outline of an agreement and it was time for a glass of champagne, before everyone headed for the airport and their private jets waiting on the tarmac. There still remained much to resolve, such as how exactly they would pay for the takeover. Would it be paid mainly in cash, or with shares? And how would Groenink and John Varley respond? Still, the bid was on.

An amazing rise was being completed. Ten years earlier Goodwin had merely been running the tiny Clydesdale Bank, and a couple of years before that he was not even a banker. Now this accountant was the emerging kingpin of European banking. There had long been talk that there would be enormous cross-border takeovers similar to the consolidation of banks that had taken place within countries, leading to a smaller number of dominant big banks and the creation of a European rather than a purely national banking industry.[6] And here was RBS playing a leading role in making it happen. Botín and Lippens agreed that Goodwin would be chairman of the consortium. In recognition of Goodwin's feted skill at handling integrations, all of ABN Amro would go onto RBS's books before the constituent parts were then dispensed to the Royal Bank, Santander and Fortis.

As well as the concerns of Iain Allan, when the deal was discussed in April there was some nervousness in the RBS management team, with the senior executives gossiping and whispering to each other out of earshot of Goodwin. Cameron, noted several of his closest colleagues, did not seem wildly enthusiastic, although the expansion of the investment bank was supposedly part of the rationale for the takeover. Brian Crowe, the chief executive of GBM, was privately wary: 'Brian looked despairing and he was leery of ABN Amro,' says a colleague. Others say he hid it well. Alan Dickinson, running the UK bank, did not like the idea and Gordon Pell, chairing the retail bank, grimaced when the subject of ABN Amro was mentioned. But no one made a stand in a meeting or confronted the chief executive. No one resigned.

The board asked questions, although they tended to be about logistical practicalities rather than the wisdom of embarking on the voyage in the first place. In only a few months, almost without its members realising, the board had been swept along from a position in which RBS was supposedly pursuing "organic growth" and not in the market for any more major takeovers to one in which it was in a race with Barclays for a slice of one of the biggest takeovers in European corporate history. In part it was because Goodwin handled the board skilfully by endeavouring not to look too keen and progressing calmly until the assumption was that they would do it. There are many to blame for the way they became caught up in the moment, although one of McKillop's colleagues thinks this was the second chance the chairman missed to stop Goodwin. 'When ABN Amro came up Tom's response to Fred should have been thank you but no, forget it sunshine, start planning your next career move.' McKillop was under no such pressure from his colleagues at the time. Sutherland wanted the next CEO to be someone more versed in running an institution with a large investment banking, although moving Goodwin along wasn't felt to be an urgent necessity. There were other potential prizes that might flow from ABN Amro some of them felt. It was not a reason to do the deal, says a member of the board, but it would facilitate an eventual shake-up of the management in GBM: 'The creation of a bigger investment bank after we got ABN Amro would allow us to get rid of Johnny [Cameron] and get in someone with more experience of running a big investment bank.'

The RBS board was becoming steadily more enthusiastic about ABN Amro. The full board and the smaller chairman's committee discussed the deal in eighteen meetings and at no point did anyone oppose it. Sutherland was very much in favour, as was Bob Scott, the senior non-executive. 'The board looked to Peter Sutherland for a sanity check,' says an investment banker. 'And Goldman Sachs' (whose international arm Sutherland chaired) 'had no skin in the game.' Goldman was not advising any of the parties in the consortium or the rival bid. Joe MacHale, also a strong-minded character with considerable experience of investment banking, thought that the biggest prize was getting the global transaction service, which would give RBS global heft. Steve Robson had concerns about the risks but these did not cohere into anything like a consistent critique of the bid. The former senior civil servant had a mandarin's gift for asking arch questions. 'Steve was always the one with snippy points to make, trying to trip up Fred in small ways,' says another board member. It just never became an all-out assault on the idea of the deal, even though he was deeply troubled by it privately and did not trust Goodwin. 'It is tragic. It is obvious Steve should have resigned then,' says a friend. But he didn't.

There were fresh obstacles. The consortium's original plan – toasted with champagne in the Four Seasons Hotel in Geneva back on 12 April – had unravelled. Formally notified of the Goodwin-led consortium's intention to bid, Groenink had agreed to sell LaSalle, the supposed prize that RBS wanted, to Bank of America. It was a move designed to make Goodwin desist, give in and let Barclays and Groenink do their deal. Goodwin was furious on being told the news. Further inflaming his anger, he discovered that John Cryan, a senior investment banker at UBS who had worked on deals with Goodwin in the past, had helped facilitate the LaSalle sale for Groenink. By phone Goodwin gave

Cryan both barrels. Cryan's friends say he told Goodwin he thought that RBS should not be buying the other parts of ABN Amro, which seemed to be full of all sorts of toxic material, bad loans and exotic investment banking products on which the UBS team had struggled to put an accurate value. Goodwin would not hear it, and brimming with confidence he told Cryan not to be such a 'bean-counter'. The accountant from Paisley was upbraiding the career investment banker for being a 'bean-counter'.

Perhaps the due diligence process would give RBS a clear picture. Companies examine the books of the firm they are buying to satisfy themselves and their shareholders that it is what it appears. This time only limited checks could be made, because the consortium's bid was hostile. Barclays and John Varley – aiming for an agreed merger – had much better access to ABN Amro's books and staff. This so reassured Goodwin that he said 'due diligence light' would be sufficient for the consortium. If Barclays had done a thorough run-through and were pressing ahead then it must be fine, he told colleagues and analysts. The presumption was also that the Dutch regulator which oversaw ABN Amro had a decent reputation and had not expressed serious concerns about the condition of the bank. In the event, RBS's due diligence was more extensive than he made it sound and than was later claimed. Goodwin sent almost a hundred people to Amsterdam under the command of Mark Fisher, where the team established twelve 'workstreams' and undertook analysis running to more than a hundred pages as to how the integration would work. The concentration, as in so many of Goodwin's previous takeovers, was on cost savings and 'synergies' of applying the RBS model, as on every takeover since the days of Project Columbus and then NatWest. There was an examination and assessment of ABN Amro's balance sheet, although it concluded that the bank's clients were of 'high quality' and its assumptions about potential losses 'appear adequate'.

They had found 'no showstoppers', Goodwin reported back

to the chairman's committee, an off-shoot of the board, on 3 May. The momentum was definitely building. Scotland's new First Minister, Alex Salmond, even offered his support. Just days after taking office in May 2007, he wrote privately to Goodwin.[7] 'Dear Fred, I wanted you to know that I am watching events on the ABN front closely. It is in Scottish interests for RBS to be successful, and I would like to offer any assistance my office can provide. Good luck with the bid.' Salmond was an ex-RBS staffer and a good friend of George Mathewson, who advised him on the Scottish economy. Coincidentally, the hedge fund that Mathewson chaired – Tosca – had been a prime mover in calling for the sale of ABN Amro. With a flourish, Salmond signed his letter: 'Yours for Scotland, Alex.'

A legal fight rumbled on with unsuccessful attempts to block the sale of LaSalle to Bank of America. This might have been the moment for Goodwin to withdraw. That was certainly what some on the management team presumed would happen after LaSalle disappeared. Iain Allan was worried but he hoped that it would be off now. Dickinson remarked to Cameron that the deal must be dead, surely. His boss shook his head and said no, Goodwin was even more keen to do it. Cameron was asked to produce projections showing what marrying GBM with ABN Amro's investment banking activities might mean. Armed with the numbers from Cameron, Goodwin explained to the board that actually the likely loss of LaSalle was no impediment. The calculations still showed that it was worth doing, because the merger of the ABN Amro investment bank with GBM would give RBS global scale. The board was minded to push on and agreed to proceed when it was discussed at the annual strategy session, held at Gogarburn, on 20 June. Each and every one of them went along with it: Tom McKillop, Fred Goodwin, Gordon Pell, Johnny Cameron, Guy Whittaker, Mark Fisher, Larry Fish, Peter Sutherland, Bob Scott, Colin Buchan, Jim Currie, Joe MacHale, Archie Hunter, Charles Koch, Janis Kong, Bill

Friedrich and Steve Robson. The chairman's committee then voted unanimously in favour of proceeding when it met on 15 July. On 20 July the consortium published its offer of 71.1bn euros. The decision was taken to pay mainly in cash, rather than offering ABN Amro shareholders RBS shares. That would mean depleting capital and running it low for a while – as they had when they took over NatWest, Goodwin reminded his colleagues. Thereafter the plan was to quickly rebuild capital. There was no shortage of liquidity, the money flowing around the world that banks could access overnight to keep business going. It was going to be easy to borrow any amount that was needed.

While Goodwin was focused on the biggest deal of his career, something had been going wrong inside RBS's investment bank since the turn of the year. Again they were just small tremors, just a flicker of the needle on the dial in one corner of an enormous business that otherwise seemed to be heading for record profits. The downturn in American housing was starting to have an impact. The market in collateralised debt obligations (CDOs) that Levine's team in Greenwich had plunged into so enthusiastically from the middle of 2006, to deliver the growth that Goodwin and the RBS board sought, had started to turn bad.

In early 2007, Levine told Cameron that he was worried by the outlook and was looking to 'de-risk' in certain areas. That meant cutting back on dealings with companies that were up to their necks in lending to millions of Americans buying houses they could not really afford. But there was also the question of the CDOs, which Rick Caplan had been hired to help scale up from the summer of 2006. Caplan and Fred Matera's team, overseen by Bob McGinnis, had been assembling these CDOs and billions of dollars of 'super-senior' exposure (supposedly better than AAA) was piling up on the RBS balance sheet. Levine was convinced that it would provide a flow of new revenue that would boost profits, and bonuses, as head office in London wanted. Matera and McGinnis had been concerned, but decided to get on with doing it if that is what was required. 'If they wanted super-seniors, then you know, fuck it, whatever, they're going to get super-seniors,' says a member of the CDO team.

As far as Goodwin was concerned, the first minor manifestation of problems appeared in January 2007. Right from the start of the new year Cameron's revenue numbers on one of the 'structured credit' initiatives, which had been agreed the previous summer, were off target, as the CDO business stuttered. Goodwin focused on the shortfall. The primary responsibility of executives was to deliver on the numbers that they had signed up to, which all went towards fulfilling his annual plan in any given year. Yet the misfiring in the engine room of GBM seemed to be related to income of only £15m a month, almost nothing in the context of a bank heading for £10bn profits. GBM's monthly budget was in the region of $1bn a month. It was a niggling worry to Cameron and Brian Crowe, which was discussed most mornings in GBM, although the only pressure Cameron was put under at this stage in Goodwin's management meetings was about hitting budget. The RBS chief executive said to the chair of GBM: 'You got your income projections wrong. Why aren't you getting the growth you promised me?' He didn't then go to Cameron or Crowe and ask what the underlying problem might be with the markets or whether there was a serious issue. It seemed to Cameron, in the light of everything else that was going on in RBS right then, that it was a problem no bigger than a small cloud in a wide open sky.

In February 2007, HSBC suddenly announced it was making provisions for losses of more than $10bn related to the American mortgage market.[8] Demand for housing in the United States was collapsing, defaults were rising as sub-prime borrowers struggled to pay and foreclosures were up more than 30 per cent and rising on the previous year. Companies with optimistic names such as New Century Financial Corporation, which had done so much of the basic sub-prime lending in the boom, were starting to go bust. Greenspan had been increasing interest rates gradually since 2004, in an effort to dampen the explosion in lending.

Goodwin was still unfamiliar in any detail with the products involved, say colleagues. Since 2006 he had relied on the line that RBS 'does not do sub-prime', a position he amended subtly until by early 2007 he claimed they did not deal 'directly' in sub-prime, meaning they did not create sub-prime mortgages. Cameron also did not have as clear an understanding as he gained a few months later. 'We make the sausages but we don't keep any of the sausages,' is how he would explain it when asked in early 2007 by Goodwin and others about the CDOs the bank had churned out. As it turned out, Jay Levine's team had kept rather a lot of 'the sausages'. RBS moved to assure investors that it was not heavily exposed. All major banks were being asked these questions as analysts began to ponder how much they would have to write down if the situation deteriorated. On 1 March Cameron told analysts: 'We have around $4bn [£2.5bn] of collateralised lending and $2bn of warehouse. The amount of sub-prime, sub-investment grade exposure we have across both the warehouses and collateralised lending and residual interests, whichever way you look at it, is really very, very, very small. A minuscule amount of that. A minimal amount of those totals.' That was true, in the sense that the super-senior RBS CDOs were highly rated. But were the ratings reliable? What would happen if investors, unable to get coherent answers from any bank on what this complex stuff was really worth, fled from banks that were exposed?

Shortly after Cameron gave his assurances, Goodwin did express some concerns about what was going on at Greenwich, following an intervention from a surprising source. He had finally moved against Larry Fish, bumping him upstairs in March 2007 into a non-role as chairman of RBS Americas. A new CEO of Citizens, Ellen Alemany, joined from Citigroup. Fish acted appalled, although the suspicion was that his theatrical display on being told the news obscured the fact that he realised he had been given an elegant and well-paid route to retirement. 'Is this how I am to be treated after fifteen years and after everything I have done for this bank?' The answer was yes.

Fish used his new RBS Americas chairman position to straight away start pointing out problems. He said to Goodwin that he was worried about Greenwich: 'Fred, there's a lot of guys making a lot of money there. Jay's making a lot of money. They are making a lot of money for Johnny, Brian and Leith too.' Fish had made serious money himself, but compared with Jay Levine and the astronomical standards of the hedge funders of Connecticut he was an underpaid American retail banker. That spring Goodwin flew to see Jay Levine in Greenwich. A very awkward meeting ensued, in which the bonhomie of previous visits was replaced by clinical cross-examination. He was there, it was clear, to 'kick the tyres' and it was apparent that Goodwin was annoyed at the way Greenwich seemed to have too much freedom. He did not, however, probe deeply on the specifics of CDOs or the markets; his concerns seemed more procedural. Cameron was not present, and if Fish hoped that Goodwin would confront Cameron back in London then he was wrong. It seemed again to Fish and the Americans that Fred had a problem bossing Johnny, or directly telling him what to do.

The underlying picture across large parts of the banking system was even worse than it appeared on the surface. The vast financial machine that had been constructed by banks, piling layer upon layer of innovation and complexity, was malfunctioning. All manner of strange creations had come into being at the behest of US and European investment banks. There were synthetic CDOs, and CDOs squared, and CDOs stuffed full of unsellable bits of other CDOs, and CDO computerised 'robots' that filled up virtual warehouses with mortgages and bonds stamped by the ratings agencies.[9] The ratings agencies – Moody's, Standard & Poor's and Fitch – had been happy, for a chunky fee, to endorse many of these innovative CDO products with AAA ratings. The theory had been that because of the cleverness of the mathematical theories underpinning the process, the power of the computers used, the sophistication of the risk models employed and the assurances of bankers and policymakers, it would all dilute risk and help to create stability. The accountants could point to the endorsement of the ratings agencies when they signed off on banks holding so much of this stuff on their books. It had been deemed close to impossible imagining it blowing up in any serious way. Indeed the models used tended not to allow for this possibility.

As well as CDOs there was the multi-trillion-dollar market for credit default swaps (CDSs), traded to try to offload risk. The American investor Warren Buffett famously called the CDS a 'weapon of financial destruction'. Buffett was not wrong. Some investment banks had created sets of CDOs to sell to other banks and investors, and then taken out credit default swaps, effectively gambling against their own clients who had been daft enough to buy their products. In the name of innovation, a sinister alternative financial universe had been created, in which customer care and ethics had been swapped for pure greed and downright treachery.

The root of the problem was that those sub-prime mortgages now going wrong were the raw meat that had been fed into the CDO mincer. If the underlying mortgages were falling in value, how long would it be before the CDOs themselves lost value? Not long. The major US banks started looking at marking them down. At Greenwich, in an atmosphere of rising concern, there was considerable discussion about this from the early spring onwards. What should the 'super-senior' slices of CDOs that RBS had kept on its books be valued at? In theory they were the safest slices of the CDO, but who knew what was safe now? Bruce Jin, the head of Risk Management at Greenwich, approached Bob McGinnis and said he was very concerned about the amount of super-seniors on the bank's balance sheet. But this was exactly what had been envisaged when Levine hired Caplan and made him joint head of the CDO team, McGinnis explained. Fred Matera, Caplan's co-head of the CDO unit, had been examining the data and concluded that they would have to be 'marked down'. They were now valued at par – 100 cents in the dollar – and any reduction would mean taking a hit. Even marking down the value from 100 to 98 would mean a write-down, a real loss, of $100m on $5bn of CDOs. Caplan was reluctant, and called some contacts in other banks such as Citigroup, who said that there was no need to do it. McGinnis's argument was that there was a good reason why some other banks were reluctant to advocate mark-downs. Their CDO teams were holding even bigger amounts of similar material and wanted to avoid giant losses, particularly when it would hit bonuses for that year. Anyway, some other banks had been marking down already, heavily. McGinnis broke the news to Levine in April, which caused the colour to drain from the Greenwich boss's face. He would have to call London and explain what had happened. It was the first of several such calls.

In London, Cameron was getting to grips with understanding more about what the problem might be. On 14 May he sent an email to Crowe asking why the daily profit and loss numbers were deteriorating: 'How much leakage of sub-prime into CDO business?' Crowe responded: 'CDO is all sub-prime.' That month Cameron went to see Goodwin in his office, asked him how much he understood about CDOs and then did the chief executive a drawing on a sheet of A4. It demonstrated how a CDO was structured, with all of the different descending tranches with their various ratings, and super-senior at the top that was still stuffed with sub-prime. That was super-seniors of the kind RBS now had on its balance sheet. Goodwin simply didn't react. It was another example of what even his friends acknowledge. In areas where he is not comfortable he does not want to admit ignorance. Goodwin also knew that Iain Allan, sidelined on ABN Amro, was intuitively concerned about CDOs. He had tried to explain the potential seriousness of the situation to the chief executive and others, and had mentioned the possible risks in GBM.

Cameron, Crowe and Levine now considered hedging their exposure, by using the ABX sub-prime index that had been established the previous year. It enabled all banks and hedge funds to place bets that would pay out if the decline continued. Those who calculated that the US housing market was about to implode had been staking billions on such bets for months. Yet every time it was looked at in RBS, it became steadily more expensive to do. Some $250m of protection was taken out in July, although it was concluded that the market would recover so it was not worth going further. The discussions continued over what exactly the CDOs on the books of RBS were worth. That summer, Riccardo Rebonato, one of Cameron and Crowe's risk experts in London, arrived in Greenwich for a look. He told McGinnis that he wanted to make sure that everyone was comfortable with the 'marks'. At that point the super-seniors had been marked down to 88–90. Wouldn't a number like 65 perhaps be more appropriate? Fine, if that's what you want, said McGinnis, who had concluded the CDO game was up and that the argument about what they were worth was increasingly ridiculous and theoretical. Crowe was so concerned about developments in Greenwich that he suddenly dropped in and stayed for almost four weeks in July and August. While he was there, Caplan and McGinnis warned him it would be insane to buy ABN Amro in the circumstances. Crowe set up in the meeting room that had once been Ben Carpenter's office; Carpenter had stood down as joint CEO leaving Levine in sole charge. He interviewed many senior staff in an effort to establish what had been going on. By the time he went back to London he had concluded that Levine would have to go.

The disaster in the upper echelons of Greenwich was approaching its denouement. Having hired Caplan, colleagues noticed that Levine could now hardly stand to look at him or be in the same room. Another of the initiatives – the 'total return swap business' – that Caplan had advocated when he was hired was in trouble. Essentially it was a fancy name for lending money to hedge funds, which used it to gamble. Why has it become so big? Levine asked colleagues who thought that had been what he wanted. But it was Caplan's CDO problem that exercised him most. 'That guy, I can't believe it,' he told colleagues. 'Those fucking super-seniors.' McGinnis and Matera started work on laying off two thirds of the CDO team, while Caplan left in the middle of August, convinced that RBS was a shambolic operation out of control.

As the CDO machine at Greenwich was disintegrating, Goodwin was fixated on getting ABN Amro. At the regulator, where John Tiner had departed as CEO, they seemed very relaxed. If anything, the team from RBS felt that the FSA was going out of its way to be obliging: 'The priority seemed to be that they wanted a level playing field so that we would get a fair crack at it in competition with Barclays,' says an adviser to Goodwin. The regulator could have blocked a deal if it judged there was a risk to consumers, if RBS was running its capital too low in order to afford the takeover. Yet no consideration was given to intervening between the regulator being notified on 17 April that RBS was preparing a bid and the consortium publishing its offer on 20 July. More generally, Hector Sants, the new CEO, was clear that the FSA's monitoring of British banks had been deficient. He was beginning an overhaul in an attempt to break down the wall between the teams monitoring retail banks and investment banks, and to refocus the FSA. In chaotic circumstances it was about to be revealed just how unprepared they were for a market meltdown.

On 9 August 2007, as RBS raced to buy ABN Amro and the CDO business melted down, the 'credit crunch' began properly.

That day Robert Peston, on his BBC blog, diagnosed the decision of the French bank BNP Paribas to suspend three of its investment funds as a pivotal moment.[10] The funds contained sub-prime material that it was impossible to value, meaning it was impossible to sell. It was junk. A freeze began in the funding markets, with lenders uncertain whom to trust. Who held this rubbish and in what quantities? It was suddenly, frighteningly, unclear. In such circumstances those banks such as RBS needing to fund themselves with a lot of borrowing were going to find the cost going up. By mid-September the credit crunch spread to the British high street and there were queues outside branches of Northern Rock, as an old-fashioned bank run got under way. The Northern Rock business model had been built on lending large multiples of salary to Britons who wanted to buy a house, on the expectation that it could borrow this on the international wholesale money markets, markets that were now freezing. An ill-prepared FSA, Bank of England and Treasury were desperately trying to work out how to keep Northern Rock going, before moving later to full nationalisation at huge cost to the taxpayer.

In August and September there was considerable concern inside RBS over market turbulence, although it didn't yet turn into panic. At the end of August McKillop convened a meeting at Gogarburn, with Cameron dialling in from holiday. What was the exposure from this CDO-related activity, McKillop asked. It amounted, it was decided, to about £200m to £400m. The conclusion was that this was containable in the context of such huge revenues and profits. Perhaps in such fluid circumstances it was time to stop and rethink on ABN Amro. McKillop said to Goodwin that he was getting nervous and they discussed attempting to lower the price, or even finding an excuse to call a halt. The City lawyers Linklaters was commissioned to give an opinion, and concluded that there was no legal justification for withdrawing. 'It would have meant massive litigation so at the time, on the facts available, it just wasn't a serious option,' says one of Goodwin's team. That was to prove

an extremely expensive miscalculation. The FSA did briefly consider having a rethink, with Hector Sants and Callum McCarthy
concluding that they did not have sufficient grounds to intervene.
RBS was a big bank, and surely it knew what it was doing?
Incredibly, Sants then overlooked the rules on capital. He allowed
Goodwin and RBS to dip below 4 per cent, below the minimum
regulatory requirement on capital, to do the ABN Amro deal. The
last line of defence had crumbled.

By now it was obvious to the members of the management
team that the gradual lead-up to the deal had just been corporate
gamesmanship by Goodwin. All along he had desperately
wanted to get ABN Amro, to avoid being beaten by Barclays and
to make RBS a truly global company. There was also the question
of potential loss of face. Goodwin was chairing the consortium
and backing off, saying that he was standing aside for John
Varley, would risk humiliation in front of his peers and the
media. There were more whispers of nervousness in the management team, although they never got above a whisper. Alan
Dickinson, running the UK corporate bank, wondered what they
really knew about Dutch banks. At an executive meeting in this
period when Goodwin went round the table, seeking views, several of those present asked what was actually in ABN Amro, and
what the quality of its assets might be. Ominously, Crowe said:
'We just don't know.' Goodwin simply moved on to the next
person. 'You've got to stop him, Johnny,' Dickinson said to
Cameron afterwards. The chairman of GBM said he didn't think
Goodwin wanted to hear it. The RBS chief executive had anyway
decided that the numbers from Cameron's investment banking
arm were providing the reason for doing the deal. Expanding
the part of the operation which included GBM – and Greenwich
and all those 'super-senior' CDOs sitting there on the balance
sheet – ended up being the rationale. It was an enormous bet
on the kind of banking that was about to help trigger the blow-
up of the rest of the bank and then the British economy. Goodwin

wasn't alone, however. The bet was taken up willingly by the over-whelming majority of the shareholders of RBS – led by the large companies and pension funds that were the owners of the bank. When they voted on the ABN Amro deal it was a resounding yes, with 94.5 per cent of those shareholders eligible to vote backing the bid. Standard Life, Barclays, M&G Investment Management, Aviva Investors, Fidelity Investments, Franklyn Resources Incorporated, Bailie Gifford and Company, Insight Investment Management and Goldman Sachs International, all voted for it.

That autumn Goodwin was a chief executive with an extraordinary amount going on. In addition to the takeover, there was another serious distraction. He was leading a double life. In the greatest secrecy he had begun an affair with one of his colleagues. The complex at Gogarburn had hotel facilities for the business school and several colleagues noted that Goodwin and his mistress started spending more and more time together, after she hung around him at company events. That autumn he got himself a personal mobile phone, distinct from the RBS company mobile he had always relied on, and there was more whispering that he seemed preoccupied, although most of his senior RBS executives say they were unaware until after the bank had collapsed. Joyce Goodwin did not know, yet. Her husband was juggling a disintegrating personal life and difficulties at GBM, just as he moved to close the ABN Amro deal. On 17 September the Dutch Central Bank and the country's Ministry of Finance said that they had no objections. The consortium had won and on 5 October Barclays admitted defeat. RBS and its partners completed the acquisition less than a fortnight later. The timing could not have been worse. And then several of Goodwin's executives noticed that ABN Amro had a corporate slogan that sounded eerily familiar. RBS promised to 'Make it Happen.' The end of the Dutch Bank's TV adverts declared ABN Amro's mission in similar terms. The slogan was 'Making More Possible'. The takeover was certainly about to make more possible, in the wrong way.

13

Bank Run

'We've rerun all the models and it could even be as bad as £4bn.'

Fred Goodwin to Tom McKillop, March 2008

On 17 October 2007 the private jet carrying Fred Goodwin touched down in Amsterdam and a car sped the RBS chief executive towards the headquarters of ABN Amro. That day the consortium led by Goodwin was completing its takeover of the Dutch bank and he was due to make a presentation to staff. Goodwin was keen to impress. To avoid looking overly ostentatious he asked to be let out of his Mercedes further down the road, so that he could be pictured arriving on foot at the front door of his new purchase. In the ensuing conversations with wary senior Dutch bankers Goodwin was well behaved, going out of his way to try to woo his new employees.

Back in London that evening the tenor at dinner was downbeat. Matthew Greenburgh was hosting at Merrill Lynch, the investment bank that had advised RBS. Greenburgh's bonus that year, for his role on ABN Amro and other deals unrelated to RBS, would be in the region of £10m. Joining Goodwin at the long table for dinner were Mark Fisher, his sidekick and integration expert, John Hourican from Cameron's GBM team, strategy director Iain Allan (who had been sceptical about the deal after LaSalle disappeared), other members of the Merrill Lynch team and RBS's lawyers. It was all very different from the event held when the Royal Bank of Scotland conquered NatWest in 2000. Then, Goodwin, Mathewson, Greenburgh, assorted investment bankers and senior executives from RBS had gathered for dinner outside Edinburgh, toasting their triumph with Château Latour (1970) raided from the English bank's cellars. At the dinner to mark the ABN Amro deal, the wine was much more modest. The outlook hardly called for the finest Bordeaux.

It was obvious to some of those at dinner that RBS had completed the purchase of ABN Amro at an extremely difficult moment. Now they had to get to work unpicking Goodwin's latest acquisition. Mark Fisher was moved to ABN Amro, to begin dispersing the various components to Santander and Fortis, while the work of integrating the parts RBS had bought got under way. Brian Crowe – who had been ill, and who had had to take time off work – crossed over the street in Bishopsgate, to take charge of the ABN Amro investment banking arm.

It took Crowe away from Cameron's GBM, and Leith Robertson, who did not have Crowe's experience of markets, stepped up. Hourican went to ABN Amro as finance director. Again Mark Fisher was put in charge of integration, and given forty-five days by Goodwin to implement a plan in the same way they had always done since taking over NatWest. It rapidly became clear that this time it was different. Not only did Fisher find the Dutch regulator tricky to deal with, but the Dutch bankers also did not think much of being bought by foreigners. Added to this RBS had limited experience of Asia, although it now found itself with larger teams there and clients to figure out.

Cameron, Crowe and their colleagues realised suddenly that the doubling of the balance sheet thanks to the ABN Amro takeover was a massive problem. Little consideration had been given to this by Goodwin when the bid was being prepared. Indeed, throughout the boom years, massive expansion of the balance sheet was seen mainly as an inevitable consequence or by-product of the push for growth. At the end of 2004 it stood at £588bn. Before the chase for ABN Amro, at the beginning of 2007, it topped £870bn. Now, less than a year later, it had more than doubled. It was a staggering £1.9 trillion. To put that in context, this was a number bigger by at least £400bn than the entire output of the UK economy. RBS's share of the ABN Amro purchase price, once it had been handed the proceeds that the Dutch bank had secured for selling LaSalle earlier in the year, was only 14bn euros, a lot less than RBS had paid for NatWest years previously. Unfortunately, the price obscured a horrible truth. What they had purchased was a third of the company but it came with 70 per cent of the ABN Amro balance sheet.[1] The parts that Goodwin had agreed to buy were the riskiest, on the investment and corporate banking side, involving a huge amount of assets – loans, trading exposures, securities, CDOs. Just at the point when analysts and investors were worrying about who had hidden liabilities or books full of potentially toxic material, RBS had made itself the biggest bank in the world by balance sheet. Goodwin's wish to be bigger than the American giant J. P. Morgan had come true, at precisely the wrong moment.

What was all this stuff exactly? When Crowe's team got to work that autumn they discovered that the Dutch bank contained a lot of junk, as the investment banker John Cryan from UBS had attempted to warn Goodwin. Hourican plunged into the finances and discovered that the valuations that ABN Amro had put on many of the assets they held were at best optimistic. RBS was exposed on its own CDOs, and the leveraged finance deals that had been done by GBM. Now, it had just taken on more of the same material that was difficult to value with any precision. The vast balance sheet and RBS's activities also had to be funded, to keep the money flowing through it and on to customers. Like other banks RBS relied, to varying degrees, on the wholesale international money markets. It meant taking out a combination of longer-term loans and engaging in short-term borrowing from other banks that would extend overnight credit to each other. In the boom era of easy money it had become standard industry procedure, although as recently as the year 2000, RBS had had zero, net, reliance on wholesale funding.[2] With a balance sheet so vast RBS now needed to do rather a lot of it, tapping funds overnight or for a period of just a few weeks. Making the situation even more precarious, to the chagrin of Brian Crowe and Hourican, Goodwin had opted to fund the majority of the ABN purchase price with short-term debt that needed to be rolled over, or re-financed, in a few months' time. During the bid it had been presumed by RBS that this would be straightforward. Growth in the wider economy seemed strong, despite concerns about sub-prime property, and the markets flowed with a seemingly endless and steady stream of cheap money. Now it was starting to dry up. By November, the members of the bank's Group Assets and Liabilities Committee were growing concerned at what was happening to liquidity and Guy Whittaker, the finance director, established a subcommittee to deal with the subject. Goodwin demanded that it report to the board and concerned senior executives. 'Until then liquidity had been almost a joke when it was mentioned. Liquidity? Oh yeah, there's so much money out there,' says a board member. It was now deadly serious.

Did they have enough capital? To facilitate the ABN Amro deal, RBS had run it low. Goodwin had long argued for 'efficient capital' as the RBS way. In 2006 he noted: 'We don't like carrying more capital than we need to.'[3] This had started to concern the regulator, which had concluded only at the ABN Amro takeover that it might be a problem, although it had not attempted to block the deal. McKillop was invited to the FSA for a discreet chat and it was a little embarrassing. The officials were concerned that the RBS chairman seemed not to have a full grasp of the numbers on capital. 'Give me a bit more warning next time and I'll prepare properly,' an exasperated McKillop said. Goodwin was also called in. He told Hector Sants it was a question of liquidity, rather than capital. But the two are connected, as a senior Royal Bank staffer points out: 'It was obvious we had a problem accessing liquidity because the market feared we did not have sufficient capital.'

To do the ABN Amro deal, core tier 1 capital had been run below 4 per cent. In December 2007 the FSA quietly put RBS on its watch-list. The high hopes the board had placed in Guy Whittaker, the finance director who had worked so closely with Goodwin on ABN Amro, were now fading. His exasperated colleagues found he appeared to be struggling to understand or explain the concepts involved. They noted that he did not seem particularly reassuring or robust in a crisis. And he certainly could not stand up to the chief executive. He had meekly sanctioned Goodwin's plan to rebuild the capital after the ABN Amro deal, as the planned extra profits flowed from the integration.

To the astonishment of Goodwin, and adding to the pervading sense that he had just made a horrible mistake, Santander cleverly sold on one of its parts of ABN Amro. Here was a superb piece of business by Emilio Botín, friend of George Mathewson and Goodwin, and boss of Banco Santander. 'Emilio played Fred brilliantly,' says a member of Goodwin's executive team. 'He put his arm round Fred's shoulder and told him he was a great CEO and must lead the consortium, and all the while he was picking his pocket.' RBS was lumbered with the garbage, while Botín sold Antonveneta, an Italian bank owned by ABN Amro, for 9bn euros on 8 November.[4] It had been valued at 6.6bn euros when the consortium closed the deal in October. That meant he had made a profit of 2.4bn euros in three weeks. In Amsterdam, Mark Fisher was astonished when he heard.

The board, in the words of one member, was 'starting to get educated', a little belatedly. McKillop had supported the ABN Amro deal and now he was appalled by what he heard. The balance sheet was exploding and RBS discovered it had 'double exposures' all over the place. Goodwin attempted to maintain his cool, although he became steadily more anxious and tense in his dealings with the chairman. McKillop started to think he might need to find a new chief executive.

As Goodwin concentrated on ABN Amro, Greenwich was continuing to unravel. The argument raging at Steamboat Road about what the super-senior tranches of CDOs should be priced at was becoming more fraught. A worried Bruce Jin, head of Risk Management, hired Victor Hong as managing director for the department at the end of September. Hong came from J. P. Morgan, where he had been vocal in insisting that the firm should not get into the kind of 'super-senior' risks that RBS had, even though the money looked easy. It looked easy because this stuff was highly risky to the point of being toxic, he told his colleagues. The mark-downs that RBS had done on the CDOs struck Hong as wholly inadequate when he arrived. At the end of August they were recorded as still being worth 90 cents in the dollar. To be credible the marks needed to be much, much lower, Hong argued.

In October, when the ratings agency Moody's started downgrading the CDOs it had previously stamped AAA, some banks were hoping they were worth in the region of 80 cents. They were actually trading in some cases at between 20 and 50 cents, the *Economist* reported.[5] The argument made against tougher action was that it was hard to say accurately, and that some of the RBS CDOs were supposedly of a higher quality than those being marked down by other banks. Hong's attempts to meet with the auditor Deloitte, to raise his concerns, were blocked. By 8 November, after only six weeks in post, Victor Hong had seen enough of Greenwich. He then did something extraordinary, something that very few people in the entire RBS story did. He resigned on a point of principle. His terse resignation letter went to Chris Kyle, the finance director of GBM back in London, and was forwarded to Cameron. Hong wrote: 'My expected oversight and sign-off responsibilities for monthly price verification would be intolerable, based upon persistent discrepancies between trader marks and analytical fair market values.'

Bob McGinnis had already left on 9 October, the day the Dow Jones index on Wall Street hit an all-time high, often a sign of looming trouble and the imminent bursting of a bubble.[6] Jay Levine would leave at the end of the year and Symon Drake-Brockman, a protégé of Brian Crowe's, was flown in from London tasked with trying to assert control and 'de-risk' where he could. Drake-Brockman knew Greenwich, as part of his team in GBM was based there, but he needed help. He later re-hired McGinnis as a consultant, to help him try to deal with the mess. While some of Greenwich was still a good business, trading in US government debt for example, the move into being more aggressive on CDOs had been a disaster. It had coincided with something changing in Greenwich in 2006, noted several members of the team. Greenwich the town had become even more ostentatious as the rewards grew in hedge funds and banks, with proximity to ever-larger amounts of wealth fuelling greed. At the RBS office in Steamboat Road, traders and staff had argued with each other even more than usual about how much their colleagues were making in bonuses. An extreme hunger for risk-taking, profit and massive 'compensation' had blown a hole in RBS. The question was how big a hole. Drake-Brockman could not believe what he found when he pitched up at Greenwich to take over from the departed Levine. The back-biting, bitchiness and fighting over money was out of control. He summoned together senior staff and made a speech. He told the bankers and traders: 'All I've heard in recent years is that this is the very best place to be in RBS, that Greenwich is the jewel in the crown. Well, I don't think I've run into a more whiny, sappy group of individuals. You should be embarrassed. I'm embarrassed for you. Things are going to change.'

Yet it was already too late, as head of strategy Iain Allan realised. Back in Gogarburn he had become steadily more anxious as it became clear that RBS had a large number of CDOs. Allan, an actuary by training and visiting professor at Cass Business School, started to think that RBS and other banks might go bust. He was worried about the severity of the risks inherent in CDOs. The chief executive still did not seem to understand the scale of it. He took comfort from the AAA ratings. On 6 December, RBS announced write-downs for 2007 of £1.2bn, with exposure to CDOs making up the bulk of it. In the eyes of some observers, these declarations were still at the optimistic end of the spectrum. On financial blogs this was zeroed in on immediately: 'RBS seem to have rose tinted glasses when it comes to marking their own CDOs – there will be further write downs to come in due course,' commented one contributor.[7]

One member of the RBS board was extremely agitated. Steve Robson, the former Treasury mandarin who had had some doubts about the ABN Amro deal and had not spoken out clearly, was more troubled about shortcomings in the risk management processes and apparent flaws in GBM. RBS needed help, Robson concluded. He checked with Tom McKillop and then called Bill Winters, who ran J. P. Morgan's operations in London. Could they talk? Robson was now gravely concerned about the reckless way the bank had been run under Goodwin. The precise nature of his interest was unclear to Winters, however. Winters wondered whether Robson was scouting for a new chief executive, or a new head of GBM, or just looking for potential advice on what to do. Robson wanted Winters to speak to McKillop and then maybe Goodwin. When McKillop rang

Winters he explained the plan would be for him to take over from Johnny Cameron and then, almost certainly, succeed Goodwin. Winters explained he needed some proper guarantees, and not just on the health of RBS. He also had a lot at stake, with a career's worth of accumulated stock as bonuses that he had built up at J. P. Morgan. That would need to be bought out if McKillop was serious. It could be as much as $30m. They agreed to keep in touch.

As Christmas approached, those at the top of government were wondering about the true state of the British banking industry. The Chancellor was already in the middle of dealing with the collapse of Northern Rock, which had starkly revealed the inadequacies of the tripartite system of regulation the moment there was a bank-run. The set-up created confused lines of command in a crisis, between the FSA, the Bank of England and the Treasury. And there was no proper resolution mechanism for safely winding up a bank that had run out of money. Now, there were signs of stress in the bigger banks.

At short notice, a worried Goodwin asked to see Alistair Darling on a Saturday morning in December 2007. The RBS chief executive turned up on the doorstep in Edinburgh's Merchiston clutching a gift-wrapped panettone. It sat on the shelf in the Darlings' kitchen for several weeks, a reminder of Goodwin's gloom-laden visit. The RBS chief executive was uptight and agitated. The liquidity problem was making life very difficult, he explained to Darling, and the Governor of the Bank of England had to do something or little Northern Rock would be the least of their problems. But Mervyn King would not listen, said Goodwin. Darling knew this to be true, as he had had similar conversations with King since the beginning of the credit crunch. King's view was that the banks had got themselves into this mess and that it would introduce 'moral hazard' and 'rewards for failure' if the taxpayer was to start bailing them out. It was a fine academic theory, Darling felt, but not much use if the banking system ran out of money in the middle of a panic and then crashed the economy.

Darling was also curious to know why Goodwin had gone ahead and paid so much for ABN Amro, when the signs were that it was overvalued at the top of the market. The global transaction service was worth acquiring, his guest explained. 'If you ever want to transfer several million pounds across the world in two seconds, now we can do that,' said Goodwin. Great. In the happy and unlikely event of me needing to transfer several million pounds, I now know where to go, thought Darling. After Goodwin's visit, Darling quietly ordered his Treasury officials to start thinking about the threat posed by the biggest banks. There existed the tripartite committee, chaired by a Treasury official with representatives of the FSA and the Bank of England, which was supposed to act as an early warning system in the event of a crisis. Mervyn King's staff had belatedly done some war-gaming. But it was all rather theoretical, slow-moving and ill-focused. Darling discovered to his horror that no one seemed able to provide him with a simple explanation of the condition of each of the major banks. Not the Treasury, the FSA, the Bank of England and most troublingly, not even the banks themselves.

After Christmas the situation deteriorated as more bad news about ABN Amro's exposure was uncovered by Crowe and Hourican and reported to Cameron. In public Cameron did his best to sound optimistic and project a sense of confidence. He declared in an interview: 'I've been quite clear that I want RBS's culture to prevail ... our concepts of accountability and our focus on getting the job done. I see the RBS culture like a virus and I want to make sure it gets into the veins of ABN Amro.'[8] If anything, it was the other way round. RBS, already weakened, was getting a dose from ABN Amro. The basic work of integration rattled along as it usually did when RBS did an acquisition, with departments merged and targets met. Yet that was almost irrelevant when it was now a daily event for Cameron to have to report grim discoveries to an increasingly testy Goodwin. Like RBS, ABN Amro had plenty of exposure to CDOs, and to monoline insurers, the companies with which banks took out insurance on bonds they issued. The monoline insurers had been going bust, cracking under the weight of the credit crisis; the insurance contracts that many banks had were useless.

To Cameron's horror, another problem manifested itself. Little thought had been given during the bid to what would happen to the deposit base when the two banks were fused together. His team discovered that being an even bigger bank had drawbacks. Says a senior RBS banker: 'If a company had £100m deposited with us, and £100m with ABN Amro, we just presumed that they would have £200m of deposits with us after the takeover. That's not how it worked. The corporate customer did not want to have too much money in one place. We were now one bank. So they said no, look, we're going to have £120m with you and then take the other £80m and put it over here with someone else. We were getting more and more of this.'

In January the board began to discuss taking emergency action. What might they be able to sell quickly, to strengthen their position? Direct Line, the insurance business, was considered, although selling anything in these market conditions for more than a knock-down price would be difficult. In the midst of this, RBS had to produce its annual results in February 2008. There were more discussions about how much should be accounted for in terms of potential losses from CDOs.[9] The matter was debated in meetings of Archie Hunter's audit committee. The auditor, Deloitte, said that actually it might be prudent to mark down another £200m to £400m, given the uncertainty on valuing CDOs. Joe MacHale, a member of the audit committee, argued that it was immaterial in the light of the size of the balance sheet and the profits they were going to announce.

On 24 February RBS did declare a record profit, one last time.

Before tax it was £10.3bn. Yet Goodwin's swagger was gone. At the results presentation there were searching questions from analysts representing other banks and investors about CDOs and the state of the balance sheet. What was the true capital position? The exchanges were uncomfortable with Goodwin and McKillop pressed for answers. Goodwin struck his colleagues as being particularly nervous. Guy Whittaker, also looking suddenly way out of his depth, tried to deal with persistent demands that they say, now, precisely what the tier 1 capital number really was because it was difficult to tell with all of ABN Amro loaded on the balance sheet. Analyst Simon Samuels asked: 'Guy, what is the core equity tier 1 ratio on a look through basis, so excluding the pieces of ABN that you don't own. Are you saying it's a number that you know and you don't want to share with us or it's not knowable?'

Whittaker's response was shaky. 'Um ... it's a number, you can work it out. It's not a number that we can ever realise because we will never get to that point where we can split it up to do that. Erm ... it does begin with a four ... I think that would be as much as we would like to say at this point.'

It does begin with a four. Samuels had another go. 'I am sorry, we can work out or you can work out? Can you just tell us what the number is then?' McKillop stepped in: 'It's not a meaningful number in terms of how we operate ... right now.' The line in public was that they did not need to raise more capital from shareholders, which means offering existing shareholders the chance to buy new shares at a discount. Such an exercise is known as a 'rights issue'. The Royal Bank might use the proceeds to strengthen its capital position. But Goodwin claimed that RBS did not need to do it. There were, he stressed, 'no plans for inorganic capital raisings or anything of the sort'.

Within weeks he was forced to rethink, as it became evident that he would have to try to reassure the markets to withstand the escalating crisis. On 14 March, the Wall Street investment bank Bear Stearns had to be saved by the American authorities. It was sold to J. P. Morgan, with a loan facilitated by the Federal Reserve. In the aftermath, with the markets chaotic, other British banks came under pressure too. Four days after Bear Stearns the share price of HBOS fell 17 per cent. RBS found that liquidity became even more problematic. Cameron was looking at the CDO index, which kept a running score of what they were worth, and he told Goodwin it was a horror show.

It was obvious to some RBS staff that the senior management had landed them in the soup. After a dinner hosted by the bank in Edinburgh, a drunken RBS investment banker approached Goodwin as he was having a drink with Cameron, Whittaker, Mark Fisher and several others.[10] The banker told Goodwin that he would be 'fucked' if the ABN Amro deal didn't work out and that then he would have to resign. A furious Goodwin hit back. 'This was a deal that justified itself on the basis of GBM. It was done for you guys, by you guys, and you keep fucking it up. Get back to that money-making machine of yours and don't come moaning to me asking me to raise new capital.'

Actually, raising new capital was exactly what Goodwin was going to have to do. On the evening of Friday 28 March, he rang McKillop at home in Chelsea to explain how big the losses might be on the investment banking side. 'Tom, the markets are terrible. We've rerun all the models and it could even be as bad as £4bn.' McKillop could not believe it had gone so bad so quickly. 'I think you should get advisers in over the weekend and start working up a rights issue.' Goodwin agreed. Whittaker also called McKillop that evening and received a similar message.

Cameron's team was asked to prepare a full assessment of what they thought the losses in GBM might amount to, although it was never made clear whether they meant for half a year or the entire year. They came up with the figure of £5.94bn, which was based on where they thought they stood at that point plus some extra allowing for a slight further deterioration in the market in the months ahead. The CDO mark-downs might get worse. The rights issue should be almost £6bn and a bit more as a 'cushion'. Goodwin took the £5.94bn figure and began discussing with the board and the FSA exactly how big the extra 'cushion' should be. 'We took the view that if we're going to do one, we needed to do the biggest one we can possibly manage,' says a board member. The idea was to 'kitchen sink' it, or raise more money from investors than the management thought they strictly needed, to err on the side of caution. Such sentiments might have been a good idea several years previously. The regulator was also applying considerable pressure. On Wednesday 9 April, Goodwin was summoned to see Hector Sants, CEO of the FSA, at his office at Canary Wharf. The position on capital was very tight, Goodwin admitted, and at this rate RBS was likely to be in breach of its guidelines. Sants, fearing that Goodwin seemed reluctant and would avoid a rights issue if at all possible, demanded that RBS give him a written commitment that they were pursuing one. They were.

These are the events on which focus the claims of investors aiming to sue RBS and its directors. In early 2013 one group issued a claim for £3bn in compensation, alleging that the rights issue prospectus published subsequently misled investors and that Goodwin, McKillop, Cameron and others, hid the fact that its capital position was worse than it appeared. This is disputed by RBS, which says that the final figure was based on the best possible assessment of the facts available at the time. Matthew Greenburgh and Merrill Lynch had been called in to help by Goodwin, along with Goldman Sachs and UBS. The three banks acted as underwriters. Says one of Goodwin's team: 'They sent in their experts who knew what they were doing, and that was everyone's best guess of a plausible bad-case scenario.'

On the evening of Sunday 20 April, McKillop convened a conference call involving the full board. They signed off on a rights issue that would be a then incredible-sounding £12bn.

Each board member was asked if they were comfortable with the figure and there was no dissent. It was a shocking, shaming reverse for a bank which just seven months previously had chaired the consortium undertaking the biggest takeover in the history of European banking. Now, on Tuesday 22 April, RBS announced the biggest rights issue in British corporate history. Only weeks after declaring record results, and saying publicly that there were no plans to try to raise any more capital from shareholders, the RBS leadership was asking for £12bn from investors. Ironically, on the day of McKillop and Goodwin's announcement Fitch downgraded RBS and Moody's put it on negative watch. Here were two of the ratings agencies, which had rubber-stamped so many of those products such as CDOs, for a fee, now downgrading a bank that had placed faith in the AAA ratings of the agencies.

In the days after the announcement of the rights issue there was incredulity on the part of the senior executives that Goodwin was not fired on the spot for this. The board discussed the possibility of a swift change at the top but it was decided that Goodwin should stay, at least for six months, to somehow clear up the mess. Says one of McKillop's colleagues: 'It was Tom's third chance to get rid of Fred cleanly and he didn't. Just as he didn't when he arrived and then when Fred suggested ABN Amro.' Goodwin had led the Royal Bank to this but incredibly he was still in post. So deficient had been the succession planning over many years stretching back to Mathewson's time that there was no one immediately to hand from the existing senior management team who could step up in a crisis even to be a stand-in CEO. McKillop went back to Bill Winters, and took Goodwin to his meeting with the American. It was humiliating for Goodwin, and very difficult.

Goodwin told Winters that they would work as partners, and he would probably be gone by the end of the year. Winters liked McKillop but did not like what he heard about RBS. He asked for a list of assurances on the bank's risk profile. In essence, what did they really have on their books? He wanted a full read-out on liquidity. It occurred to Winters that it wasn't that they had this information and were reluctant to divulge it to him, but that they didn't have it. A few days later Peter Sutherland also asked to see Winters, and made it clear that Winters should forget any ideas of a guaranteed elevation to the post of RBS chief executive if he took over at GBM and replaced Johnny Cameron. They were very happy with Fred, he was told. This seemed weird to Winters. You are the guys in trouble coming to me. Didn't Sutherland want Goodwin out? Why would Winters give up a career at J. P. Morgan to run something like GBM reporting to Fred Goodwin? What was this really about? He wondered whether RBS were serious operators or not.

Iain Allan had certainly had enough, and he was signed off sick in May. The strategy director had been sidelined by Goodwin since he had made it clear that he did not like the ABN deal. He had one last conversation with Johnny Cameron about CDOs, the CDOs that Allan had tried to persuade Cameron and Goodwin were extremely dangerous. 'Iain, you were right,' the GBM chairman told him. It was not much of a consolation.

At the June strategy session held for the board and senior management, McKillop went round the table asking for views on their plight. Alan Dickinson, who now ran the UK bank and had been asked to take on retail as well as corporate banking, said he had never seen anything like current market conditions in all his decades as a banker. He had already told his team that spring he was 'calling the recession' and that the UK was headed for a serious downturn the following year. Soon this would filter into 'the real economy', where RBS like other banks had made a lot of loans in the boom years. Gordon Pell concurred. Larry Fish said the liquidity situation was desperate, much worse than anything he had encountered in his long career.

Goodwin had never been particularly good at receiving bad news, and now there was hardly ever any other kind. In June when Johnny Cameron was being driven to watch the racing at Ascot he received a phone call from Whittaker, the finance director. He and Goodwin had seen Cameron's forecast for the year ahead and thought it was unnecessarily negative. Whittaker tried to talk Cameron round for forty-five minutes. The GBM chairman insisted: 'Things are going bad again, they're going to get worse.' Eventually Goodwin took the phone from Whittaker and a shouting match ensued. How could Cameron say he might have to mark this stuff, the CDOs for example, down even further when it had already been marked down? Goodwin did not want to have to take Cameron's forecasts to the board. Cameron argued that it didn't feel good out there and there would be more write-downs. In the end, Goodwin prevailed and the forecasts were nudged upwards.

After the announcement of the rights issue there was a brief rallying round. The prospectus was certainly enough to convince a lot of investors and RBS staff to subscribe to the rights issue. Former chairman George Mathewson thought the new shares were a bargain. They were being offered at 200p, when existing shares had closed at 363p on Monday 21 April, the day before the rights issue was announced. It was not only a matter of pride, in sticking by the bank he loved at a difficult moment. Mathewson was convinced that the City and those smart-alec traders he could not stand were wrong. Once again they were underestimating the Royal Bank, as they had done so often in the past. The market would come to its senses, once the excitement had died down about sub-prime mortgages. The Royal Bank was solid. Soon those new shares bought at 200p would be worth a lot more than that, he was sure, so Mathewson resolved to buy as many as he could. The former chief executive and chairman put up his own money, borrowed some more, and loaded up with several million pounds' worth.

Early that summer it seemed for a few weeks as though the rights issue had done the trick. All £12bn of shares had been taken up by the time the rights issue closed. The febrile condition of the markets calmed and it was a little easier to get access to funding. They had, Matthew Greenburgh pointed out to Goodwin, replenished an amount equivalent to what they had paid for ABN Amro. But it quickly became apparent it was merely a brief respite, with ABN Amro itself a major complicating factor. Says one of the management team: 'There were still twice the number of problems but the same number of us, and we were trying to run two banks under two different regulators, yet pretend they were one bank. It was horrendously complicated and time-consuming, dashing to and from Amsterdam. The people there, they were bolshie and didn't want to do as they were told, and had a long-standing way of doing things differently. At a time when all banks needed their management highly focused on the task in hand, managing their positions, we were trying to integrate a bank.' On 1 July, for the first time, the share price closed at 199p, below what Mathewson and all those other investors had paid when they signed up to be part of the rights issue.

Cameron, whose marriage was disintegrating messily, and Crowe, whose health was poor, were working long hours with their teams, trying to keep the bank going as the liquidity situation worsened. Traders in GBM were reassigned and told that the priority was to find wherever they could deposits from corporate customers who wanted to lodge money in RBS accounts. A desperate scramble for survival got under way. They were now leaking money. From the start of August 2008 to the first week of October, RBS lost £10.4bn in corporate deposits and £8.7bn in retail.

When Lehman Brothers went bankrupt on 15 September it induced a fresh wave of global panic and collapse. AIG (the American insurer), the Icelandic banks, Washington Mutual in the United States and Bradford & Bingley in the UK went bust or had to be rescued. Fortis, which just a year before had been one of the 'three amigos' in the consortium that won ABN Amro, was humiliatingly nationalised by the Belgian government. It was also the end for HBOS. Inside it was the Royal Bank's old rival Bank of Scotland, founded in 1695. Its reckless lending on commercial property and severe funding problems meant that the government was happy to encourage a takeover by Lloyds, which had until that moment taken a more cautious approach as others expanded at high speed. Within weeks it was to prove an expensive decision by the directors of Lloyds. Gordon Brown was accused of fixing the deal after he and Victor Blank were photographed deep in conversation at a drinks party.[11]

The meltdown of the banking system in Ireland – where growth possibilities had recently been declared limitless by the head of Ulster Bank – compounded matters for RBS. The announcement that the Irish government would guarantee deposits in all the country's banks created a stampede away from Ulster Bank. It did most of its business in the Republic but was not covered by the guarantee as a UK-owned institution, so in just four days it lost £732m in deposits.

On 24 September the board met at Gogarburn, to have its first attempt at working out what had gone so wrong. The head of internal audit had prepared a discussion document, which contained criticism of Goodwin's management style. Cameron and Goodwin also produced a paper and slideshow presentation, with the chief executive standing steadfastly by the GBM chairman. The pair posed a series of questions and went through CDOs, monoline insurance and leveraged finance. There was criticism of Larry Fish. It was suggested that Citizens had swapped some of its safe investments, which it used to make money from its excess of savings deposits, for a parcel of riskier sub-prime mortgage bonds. Several members of the board were angry and convinced that Fish had not given them the true position. Goodwin put on a good show, emphasising that all in all he had a great team who really could not have made any other set of decisions when faced with the situation facing them at the time. It was listened to fairly respectfully by the board. Stephen Hester, who had just joined as a non-executive as a potential successor to Goodwin, was there and asked a lot of questions.

In the days after the Gogarburn board meeting there was no time for further reflection, with the crisis approaching its peak. Brian Crowe had been withdrawn from his ABN role by Goodwin and put in charge of the rescue effort, working with John Cummins, the bank's treasurer. Crowe tried wherever possible to look for ways to scale back the balance sheet and rein in activity, although it was past the point where it could make much of a difference. Increasingly they were relying on overnight funding, as it was impossible to get anything else. There was some money being accessed from the Bank of England, but as yet nothing like enough. The 'wholesale' funding gap, money RBS needed to find every few days, was now £100bn. This was unsustainable, with vulnerable banks being picked off as those in the markets assessed which institution would be the next to fall. Hedge funds sensed an opportunity. It emerged in mid-September that John Paulson, the American billionaire, had made $3.7bn in 2007 betting that the sub-prime mortgage market would collapse. Now his team had placed bets against RBS, 'shorting' it on the expectation that it was about to go bust. On 26 September, a Friday, the RBS share price closed above 200p for the last time.

In the management team tempers were completely shredded, as the shortage of sleep and excess of stress strained relationships. The desperate ideas being generated in meetings by his frazzled colleagues struck the quiet Brian Crowe as financially illiterate and completely detached from the reality of what was happening in the markets. One of Crowe's friends said he was angry with himself as much as Goodwin, that the answers had been inside his head all along, on CDOs and not doing ABN Amro, and he had been all but mute when it mattered. 'Brian had seen it coming, kept it to himself and never spoke up properly to Johnny or Fred, and this is where it had got us.' At one such meeting near the end, when Goodwin offered his view, Crowe snapped: 'Learn something about banking, Fred.' It was a bit late for that.

By the afternoon of Sunday 5 October, when Goodwin flew into London it was evident that this was going to be a decisive week. Monday the 6th was spent on the twelfth floor of 280 Bishopsgate. He was 'firefighting', chairing meetings about the desperate funding situation, and he reviewed the paper that had been prepared for him to present at the next morning's Merrill Lynch Banking and Insurance conference being held at the Landmark hotel. The Chancellor announced to MPs that the government was ready to stand behind the UK banking system, although he could offer few details. Goodwin left his office late and headed to spend the night at the Ritz hotel.

14

Boom Goes Bust

'We must, in an uncertain and unstable world, be the rock of stability on which the British people can depend.'

Gordon Brown, 13 October 2008

The twelfth floor of 280 Bishopsgate had a quite bizarre atmosphere on the morning of Wednesday 8 October. Exhaustion and months of battling to keep the bank afloat seemed to have detached several of the inmates from reality. After a night spent at the Treasury on Whitehall, Fred Goodwin and Guy Whittaker prepared for the detailed bailout negotiations to come in the days ahead. But Goodwin was particularly exercised about his own position. He hit the roof when he picked up a copy of the *Daily Telegraph* that morning. Jeff Randall revealed in a story published on the front page that Goodwin and McKillop were out.[1] Echoing his abortive attempt to sue the *Sunday Times* several years previously, Goodwin demanded a retraction and apology from Randall. The onslaught was so fierce and the denial from Goodwin so vehement that the journalist prepared to hand in his resignation. But his source was spot on.

Of course Fred Goodwin was for the chop, even though he didn't yet know he was no longer meaningfully in charge. Both Brown and Darling had already told ministers and officials that his removal was a condition of the bailout. This had also been communicated discreetly to Steve Robson who sat on the board. Shredding Fred was a non-negotiable demand.

RBS board members were also now in an awkward position. They had signed off on Goodwin's expansion, they had acquiesced when it came to the ABN Amro takeover and they were active participants in the UK's biggest corporate smash of all time, but the law stated that they were still on the board of an independent company. Their duty was to act as directors and not take orders from ministers. Did that mean anything any longer in an era of governments taking over failed banks?

The broad outline of the rescue, when it was announced at breakfast time on 8 October, produced for a few hours a surreal kind of calm after the madness of the preceding day, with its talks between bankers and Treasury officials long into the night. At a press conference at Number 10 Gordon Brown and Alistair Darling emerged blinking into the light of the TV cameras to announce that RBS was going to have billions of pounds of capital injected by the government, on the behalf of taxpayers. The exact details would be worked out at the weekend. HBOS, folded into Lloyds, would also need a large chunk of the £50bn shock and awe recapitalisation. Another £250bn of loan guarantees was made available for the banks, and another £100bn of short-term funding to replace the wholesale funding, or liquidity, that had dried up. The enormity of it was mind-blowing. 'The City of London has never seen anything like it in its long and illustrious history,' said the BBC's business editor Robert Peston.[2] 'The state will own a very substantial proportion of our biggest and proudest banks. What a sorry end to Britain's longest ever period of unbroken economic growth.'

In Scotland, home of RBS, there was astonishment, shame

and some anger. The First Minister, Alex Salmond – author of that warm note of encouragement to Fred Goodwin ahead of the calamitous ABN Amro deal – had attempted to criticise the London-based 'spivs and speculators' who had supposedly engineered a bank run on two such fine Scottish institutions. This line of attack now looked silly. Hedge funds might have exacerbated the situation at the death, but they were not the root cause of what had gone wrong in Scotland's banks. It became apparent that the real 'spivs and speculators' were actually some of those working 'inside' the offices of RBS and HBOS.

The *Scotsman* newspaper declared it was 'the end of the road'.[3] A bank with a proud history – with roots in the Edinburgh of the Scottish Enlightenment – was reduced to this. Alan Cochrane, writing from Edinburgh in the *Daily Telegraph*, noted: 'There was a time in the not too distant past when the words "bank" and "Scotland" conjured up an image of dour respectability, certainly, but also of financial caution and of the utmost probity.'[4] The Scots had taken such pride in that image. Now, he added: 'It is as if the old maid on the corner has been exposed as a harlot.'

It was the British taxpayer that was about to get royally screwed. Not that that was the intention of anyone preparing to finalise the bailout. Alistair Darling and his officials were not relishing putting so much money into the banks. They were aiming to prevent the financial system freezing, to keep the country's cash machines dispensing ten-pound notes and, they believed, to avoid civil unrest. Yet by any measure a bailout running to tens of billions was a colossal indication of failure, an indictment of the reckless policies pursued during the boom years. The system of regulation had failed utterly to check the banks. The Bank of England had allowed a credit bubble to be inflated. And the government had assured the country that it was all built on solid ground, so it was permissible for consumers to carry on spending ever more borrowed cheap money. Gordon Brown stressed publicly that he was appalled by what had gone on at RBS. Privately he said he felt betrayed (a big theme with Brown when things went wrong) and he could not believe that Goodwin had failed to warn him of impending disaster. As though the chief executive of a bank was going to lean across the dining table at Chequers and say 'Gordon, I think we might go bust.' Goodwin understood enough about his position as CEO of a bank to keep talking it up until the very end.

On Thursday the 9th the FSA invited itself to Bishopsgate and summoned the RBS board and executives. The RBS team was thinking in terms of needing £10bn from the taxpayer, when the Treasury ministers and officials and now the FSA were convinced it would be at least double that and probably much more besides. Thomas Huertas of the FSA told them it would be more like £20bn. There were incredulous exclamations. Goodwin indicated that he now agreed with the FSA and said he thought it was probably just about all over. Afterwards McKillop called Bill Winters at J. P. Morgan one last time. Would he perhaps consider again coming on board? They talked about how it might work. Winter's fears six months before about risk-management had been vindicated. And the question of RBS buying out his J. P. Morgan shares was even more problematic now, considering that the government was about to be a big shareholder in the Royal Bank. For all his talents, it was not hard to envisage hiring Winters being a public relations disaster. When the board met on Friday the 10th it was agreed that Goodwin would go and Stephen Hester would be his successor. The Treasury had decided the same.

Darling was due to be out of the country that Friday, in Washington for a meeting of G7 finance ministers and the annual meeting of the International Monetary Fund. There was international interest in what the British had done – or rather had not done yet but had announced they would. Tom Scholar, the Treasury official working closely with Shriti Vadera on the recapitalisation plan for RBS and HBOS, went out ahead of Darling on Wednesday. The Chancellor followed with his private secretary,

Dan Rosenfield, and media adviser Catherine MacLeod. The flight, and autumn sunshine of Washington, offered respite for a team that had been living on their nerves for weeks. Between meetings, with other finance ministers such as US Treasury Secretary Hank Paulson, there was time for a late lunch on the terrace of the British Embassy in Washington. It was only interrupted by Yvette Cooper calling from the Treasury in London to say that she was so exasperated she had locked Shriti Vadera out of a meeting.

Scholar had already headed back to London to join his colleague John Kingman for the talks that weekend to finalise the bailout. Scholar landed back in Whitehall at lunchtime on Saturday, entering the Treasury building now swarming with investment bankers and lawyers. Matthew Greenburgh, friend of Goodwin and key player on the NatWest and ABN Amro deals, was there. He was not advising RBS this time, however. It was Lloyds who had hired him to help steer it through the bailout it needed as the new owner of HBOS. Bill Winters's team was involved too, as J. P. Morgan had been hired by the government to work on its behalf. Bankers crowded the corridors and filled the various meeting rooms. It was like an awayday, a festival for London-based senior investment bankers. They had helped fuel the boom. And here they were picking up lucrative work in the bust.

The pivotal meetings were with RBS. McKillop, Goodwin, Whittaker and Bob Scott, the senior non-executive director, all turned up sporting their RBS ties, embossed with the bank's logo, and were soon lined up waiting to hear the terms. The taxpayer would put in £20bn, and the bank would effectively be a ward of state with roughly 60 per cent of the shares in the hands of the government. They had no choice about anything, it was made clear. This was not so much a negotiation, more of a 'drive-by' shooting, Goodwin said. It was later interpreted as an angry comment, although the Treasury team thought it was intended as a wry attempt at black humour. Goodwin seemed more reconciled to what was happening than McKillop. Fred was cool as a cucumber, as far as the Treasury officials were concerned. 'Goodwin was the least emotional of all the bankers,' says someone who was there that day. 'I think he had realised the game was up. Whereas McKillop looked as though he had not realised what it meant for McKillop. The speed with which these guys were going from being the pinnacle of the Scottish establishment to pariahs was remarkable.'

It fell to Paul Myners, Lord Myners, the newly appointed Treasury minister who had lost his place on the NatWest board when Goodwin masterminded the takeover in 2000, to deal with Goodwin's departure. 'Myners was rather revelling in it under-standably,' says a colleague. He asked to see McKillop and Bob Scott once Goodwin and Whittaker had left to head back to Bishopsgate. Goodwin would have to go, he explained. Yes, said McKillop, the board had decided that was the way to proceed. Excellent, and would McKillop go? The RBS chairman indicated that he would not. Myners suggested a compromise after Bob Scott said that the board would resign en masse if the chairman was removed by the government. Would McKillop stay on for a few months, until the next AGM, to hand over to a new chairman? Yes, said McKillop. The government did not want Fred getting a bonus either, said Myners. There was no danger of that, McKillop said. 'The issue won't be his bonus, his contractual arrangements will give him a big pension,' said Scott. Goodwin's successor, Stephen Hester, was also in the building by this point, with efforts made to keep him apart from Goodwin to avoid any embarrassment. Entreaties were made to his employer, British Land, to let him start early. His employer agreed that as it was a national emergency he could begin some initial RBS work first thing on Monday. Hester saw Gordon Brown in Number 10 and was hired as chief executive.

On the Saturday evening, McKillop convened the RBS board. Johnny Cameron was in south London, after a day spent pacing the floor of the office in Bishopsgate along with other colleagues who wanted to be around but were suddenly no longer in the loop. There was no theatrical resignation speech. Goodwin simply explained that it was done, that the government would probably own more than half of the Royal Bank. It was the sheer speed of the collapse, and the way liquidity dried up, that so astonished McKillop. He still could not quite believe it. Several members of the board were discontented with the way the government was handling it, and resigning en masse was discussed, although it was difficult to see in what conceivable way this group could feel aggrieved after everything that had happened. It was decided to wait and see. Soon all but three – Archie Hunter, Colin Buchan and Joe MacHale – would be removed.

On Sunday morning Darling's team was confident they had the bailout set up and could start to think about how to handle the announcement. Investment bankers turning up at the Treasury late that morning observed an exhausted Lord Myners sitting in the courtyard garden in the middle of the building smoking a cigar, his feet up, reading the Sunday papers. The bankers whispered that Myners was reading a profile of himself. The approach adopted for the bailout was that designed by Shriti Vadera and Scholar, on the advice of various City lawyers and investment bankers. They had started discussing it back in the summer, hoping that it would not have to happen. Mervyn King's preference had been for full nationalisation, with RBS split into a good bank and a bad bank containing its toxic assets. This had been done in countries such as Sweden, which had suffered earlier banking collapses. Earlier in the year King had done some work on the idea, although his relationships with Darling and Brown were so poor by that point that he could not build support for an alternative to the proposals that Vadera and Scholar were devising.[5] The politicians doubted King's judgement too much. That weekend there was some discussion among Nick Macpherson, Kingman, Scholar and other officials about the merits of simply opting for the possibly cleaner option of full nationalisation. Why leave the shareholders with anything? The politicians decided that they did not want full control, and would rather it was run at arm's length. In October 2008 Mervyn King filed in neatly behind the Darling plan when the crisis hit. The government would inject the capital directly, owning shares in several of the banks but not taking all-out state control.

On the Sunday afternoon and evening control was slipping away from Goodwin. Neil Roden, the HR director who had worked closely with Goodwin at Clydesdale Bank, and then RBS, now had to 'exit' his boss in extraordinary circumstances. McKillop had summoned Roden from Scotland after the board confirmed the decision. On the Sunday Goodwin turned up at 280 Bishopsgate to arrange his departure. It was a laborious process, involving going through documents and arranging a so-called 'compromise agreement', which allowed him to stay on working in Edinburgh for a few weeks. Goodwin drafted in an Edinburgh law firm, Maclay Murray & Spens, to represent his interests. That evening the outgoing chief executive talked to Lord Myners by telephone about his departure. By this point those in the Treasury were absolutely astonished at how much attention the RBS executives were giving the issue when the banking system was in the middle of a meltdown. The board had delegated the question of Goodwin's departure to McKillop and Bob Scott and the decision was taken to treat Goodwin 'in the normal way', by which it meant he was being regarded as 'a good leaver'. This had the effect of doubling his pension pot. Bob Scott had asked Neil Roden to have the pension numbers totted up and thought Goodwin had a pot of £15m or maybe a good bit more. Scott maintains that he told Myners this when the pair spoke that Sunday evening, but Myners denies it. In his defence Myners and his colleagues were battling to deal with a collapse of the financial system and operating at high speed. Myners did emphasise that the government did not want RBS to breach any contractual requirements as it had no desire to end up in court. At 1.30 a.m. on 13 October it was all settled anyway, when in a conference call the board, in the form of the chairman's committee, agreed the deal that would give Goodwin an annual pension of £703,000. By 3 a.m. he had put his signature to the various documents required. The veneer finally cracked at several points and Goodwin became very emotional about leaving the bank he had built and brought to this point. Visibly upset, at 3.30a.m. he was deprived of his pass for the building and signed out of 280 Bishopsgate for the last time.

He wasn't the only one upset. The taxpayer was about to make an eye-watering commitment. On Monday 13 October, Brown and Darling hosted another Downing Street press conference at which the precise terms were laid out. The state was putting £20bn into RBS, and would own 63 per cent of it, and £17bn into Lloyds and HBOS, meaning the taxpayer held 41 per cent of the newly merged entity. Brown, in the sonorous tones which had on so many occasions hailed the British economic miracle of low interest rates, a surging City and constant growth, emphasised that this mattered to every family and business in the country. 'The action we are taking is extraordinary ... We must, in an uncertain and unstable world, be the rock of stability on which the British people can depend.'

Boom and bust had not been ended after all. The world had become, as history suggests it can quite suddenly, 'uncertain and unstable'. Just at the point when this became apparent, in a febrile atmosphere, Brown seemed for a while to have been reborn, to the astonishment of his enemies and joy of his supporters. Hailed by leaders in other countries, the self-proclaimed supposed 'saviour' of the world and proud engineer of massive bailouts was recast briefly as the man who knew what to do in a crisis. Knowing what to do seemed to involve taking hundreds of billions of pounds of other people's money and spending it. After more than a decade in government spending money, this was an activity at which Brown was always going to excel.

In the event, the UK government also had to come back with many more taxpayer billions for the Royal Bank later. 'It quickly became clear that the recap hadn't worked,' says an official. Several more attempts were required to begin stabilising the stricken bank, once it became apparent how big the losses run up by Goodwin would be. In February the government was compelled by market pressure to organise a second bailout, with another £19bn of capital. In the end the taxpayer ploughed in a total of £45.2bn and owned 82 per cent of RBS. An asset protection scheme was also required, which allowed banks to insure their bad loans, thus reducing their risk of losses and reassuring them sufficiently so that they might begin giving new loans to businesses that needed it. RBS placed £325bn of bad loans in the scheme.

With the banking system broken, a downturn in the real economy was never going to be far behind. A deep recession began. The economies of America and the leading Western countries slumped. In the UK the boom years had been built on a great deal of private-sector debt. There had been an explosion in what many Britons were allowed and prepared to borrow, on the back of assurances that this was a new paradigm. On the eve of the financial crisis, in June 2008, total UK personal debt was £1.4 trillion.[6] That meant it had doubled in under a decade. The average Briton owed £3256 on credit cards and 33 per cent of mortgages taken out were interest only. McKinsey produced a report that labelled the UK, along with Japan, one of the most indebted countries on earth by the time of the crisis in 2008. Add together government, household and corporate borrowing and the UK had a debt to GDP ratio of 469 per cent, much higher than America on 300 per cent. Even stripping out the foreign debt of the UK banks from that figure, the UK was still borrowed – at 380 per cent – up to its eyeballs.[7]

That lending undertaken by RBS and the other banks in the UK and Ireland had not been done in isolation. On the other end of those loans were real people, customers who would now struggle to pay, as trade contracted, order books closed, companies struggled and consumers took fright. There were dire implications for government and the public finances, as well as the banks. The sizeable increases in public spending instigated by Blair and Brown had been predicated on the notion of a benign outlook stretching out far into the horizon. As the economy shrank, there was a dramatic fall in tax revenues. The deficit, the gap between income and government outgoings, shot up, as happens in a recession, although this was a very deep recession. The deficit was £69bn in 2008, £156bn in 2009 and £142bn in 2010. That was money added to the vast stock of national debt. In 2012, after the coalition government made great play of trying to make economies, the national debt sailed above £1 trillion heading for £1.5 trillion.

Early in 2009 RBS had its own enormous deficit to worry about. Goodwin's replacement Stephen Hester readied himself to unveil RBS's annual results that February and when they came they were horrific. In 2008 the Royal Bank had lost £24.1bn, the biggest corporate loss in British history. Once the numbers had been sifted it was not all down to what had happened at GBM in London, or in Jay Levine's operation in Greenwich. The investment bank accounted for £8.6bn of losses, 28 per cent of the total. A third of the overall losses were in old-fashioned poor lending on commercial property. The exposure to the property mania in Ireland was particularly disastrous. Between 2008 and 2010 Ulster Bank, in theory just one small corner of the RBS empire, accounted for £4.4bn of losses, with much more to follow. The commitment to flat-out growth in Alan Dickinson's corporate bank, and Cormac McCarthy's Ulster Bank, had turned out to be extremely costly.

Where the problems with CDOs and investment banking had done most damage was in the long bank run on RBS during 2008. Investors did not know then about the later losses in Ireland or elsewhere, which only showed up when the recession began. In the crucial period, when panicked investors and analysts wondered who held what relating to sub-prime mortgages, it looked as though Goodwin and his team could not say or did not know. And it had been largely in order to grow GBM that Goodwin had done the cursed deal in the Netherlands. The rapid expansion of the investment bank fuelled the corporate confidence that led Goodwin and his colleagues to buy ABN Amro and double the balance sheet at just the wrong moment.

The losses – whether they had come from fancy trading or duff basic lending – made the demands by the new RBS management that it should carry on dispersing bonuses seem almost unfathomable to many watching Britons. Not only were bankers avoiding prosecution, they were demanding money on top of their pay packets, having been saved and subsidised by the taxpayer. In attempting to explain that in order to make money to pay back the taxpayers it was necessary to hire the best, Hester was making a case unlikely to cut through. Not when living standards were falling for millions of people. Equally, it was not an easy argument to make when the banking scandals kept on coming in the years after 2008. There was Libor manipulation, centring on traders attempting to fix the London 'inter-bank' lending rate, the figure used by global banks to make their calculations when they were lending to each other. The chicanery had been going on among small groups of traders at the largest banks for years. The traders sent juvenile emails and messages boasting of how easy it was to manipulate a benchmark that was supposed to underscore the City of London's position as a leading financial centre. RBS paid £390m in fines to various regulators, Barclays £290m and the Swiss bank UBS £940m.

It was decreed that RBS needed to offer a sacrifice to public opinion. When the investigation into Libor concluded, the government privately demanded the head of a senior RBS figure.

John Hourican, who ran the successor to Johnny Cameron's GBM, was like Hester ignorant of the traders' rate fixing but fearing a public backlash the government wanted someone at or near the top to go. Under pressure, with the Treasury demanding it, he agreed to resign. In the event there was little public anger, perhaps only weariness. Once again a group of well-paid traders had been found to be at it. Only someone who has been living in solitary confinement since 2008 could possibly be shocked. Hourican, once deemed a possible successor to Hester, was removed, in the end probably needlessly.

Libor was not a one-off though. The revelations about the conduct of the banks came in waves. There was the scandal of interest rates swaps, in which businesses were sold products that they very often did not need or understand.[8] Customers were encouraged, sometimes compelled if they wanted a loan, to take out cover that would protect them in the event of interest rates rising. The reverse happened. Rates, after the crisis, plummeted. The investment bank trader culture, of hedging, and swaps, with devices invented that ended up fleecing customers who thought they could trust their bank, had infected ordinary lending to businesses. Billions more were set aside by the banks to compensate customers when the racket was exposed. Equally, payment protection insurance (PPI) was from the late 1990s another egregious example of the way in which banking changed in the long boom years, as bank executives sought new ways in which to drive growth and their own 'compensation', which is what the rest of us call 'pay'. Retail banking may have been run relatively conservatively by Gordon Pell and others at RBS, contributing a few billion to the losses after 2008 and nothing out of line with what personal lending usually loses in a recession for any bank. But at RBS and other financial institutions a sales culture took hold, in which staff were given aggressive targets and taught to sell hard to customers. Many customers who ticked the box for PPI were clearly operating under the mistaken assumption that their banks, while being very far from perfect, broadly had their interests at heart.

Some of those who designed Project Columbus for the ambitious George Mathewson in the early 1990s reflect on such scandals now and see that the reforms they helped unleash at RBS unwittingly helped create the disaster. Many of the bank's lower-paid staff were recast as salespeople and assigned goals and revenue targets by management which seem to have blinded those involved to the reality of what was being foisted on the customer.

Of course, the overwhelming majority of the staff of the Royal Bank, earning modest salaries, did nothing wrong. Indeed, many had lost out themselves. If they had taken shares in the rights issue, at the offer price of 200p, after October 2008 they had lost 90 per cent of their investment. As recently as April 2007, on the eve of the ABN Amro bid, the bank's shares had been worth more than 600p. The collapse represented a terrible, calamitous destruction of wealth. Hundreds of thousands of retirement nest eggs had vanished. In the weeks after the collapse Alan Dickinson and several of his colleagues toured the branches and call centres, offering bewildered and mutinous staff a chance to take it out on someone from the management. One RBS cashier, close to retirement, explained quietly to Dickinson that year after year over the decades she had invested in RBS stock every time it was offered to her. Not long ago her carefully husbanded investment had been worth almost £250,000, and now a mere fraction of that was left. She had trusted those at the top and believed unfailingly in the reputation of the bank for which she worked. Of course, the impact was felt well beyond the staff, by many more small investors gulled by the bank's proud Edinburgh history and more recent success into believing that it could never fail.

Fred Goodwin got much of the blame. He was even named as the 'world's worst banker' by *Newsweek* magazine: 'He aced every requirement for a hubristic CEO.'[9] In February 2009, three months after he left RBS, inevitably there began the war over his pension. The revelation that RBS had agreed to pay him £703,000 a year scandalised opinion. The mood was for the architects of the banking disaster to be jailed, not for them to enjoy retirement on a pension twenty-seven times the average wage. In an effort to defuse the row, discreet diplomatic entreaties were made, involving the then Chancellor, the new chairman of RBS, Sir Philip Hampton, and several Treasury officials. If he would cut his pension in half that would go some way to assuaging the widespread anger. Edinburgh is a small city, Darling reminded Goodwin. People could be cruel. He had a family to think of. Better surely to make the gesture of conceding and hope to convince the public that it was an act of penitence. And look, £350,000 was still a lot of money.

Goodwin was, as he had often been in the past, stubborn in a negotiation. One of the reasons he was determined to hold on to the pension pot in its entirety was that it also contained his contributions from the Clydesdale Bank and before that Touche Ross and Deloitte, accounting for more than fifteen years of his career. That quirk can be traced back to the unusual way he was hired by George Mathewson in 1998. When Goodwin arrived he had been given vague assurances that he could transfer over all of his pension, and be treated as though he had actually been at the Royal Bank since the age of twenty. 'It was a shocking thing to have done in corporate governance terms,' says an RBS executive. 'It was a case of, aye that'll be fine, we'll sort that out later.' In 1998, Miller Mclean, the company secretary, was given the job of resolving it, which took years and ended with Goodwin getting a contract that gave him an advantageous pension arrangement. In October 2008 he had only agreed to go in the manner he did – without any kind of pay-off – on the understanding that his £16.9m pension pot was intact. He was very clear he would go quietly if he kept it. Yes, Darling told him, but that ignored how angry taxpayers now were. McKillop and Myners also clashed over differing accounts of that meeting in October 2008 in the Treasury. Had the government been properly informed? McKillop insisted it had been made clear that Goodwin had a big pension. In June, after months of pressure, Goodwin accepted a cut. He had resisted, sustained another drawn-out hit to his reputation and then conceded.

For the sake of their two children, Fred and Joyce Goodwin tried living abroad, sheltering in the South of France and Switzerland with various friends. They found it hard to settle and Goodwin told friends in Britain he was determined not to be forced out of his own country, Scotland.

Soon after they returned the marriage collapsed. Joyce Goodwin had not known about the affair with a member of staff at RBS. When her husband took out a super-injunction to ban the press revealing details of how he had breached the bank's code of practice and spent several years conducting an affair with a member of his own staff, Joyce could not avoid learning the truth. There exists an extraordinary situation in which, as the result of the judgment by Justice Tugendhat on 9 June 2011, Goodwin's now former mistress cannot be identified, seemingly for life, to protect her privacy. It is as though the affair – which it is not denied happened at the height of the period in which Goodwin was making catastrophic mistakes – is deemed to be the financial crisis equivalent of Bletchley Park, the secret installation in World War Two that was not allowed to be mentioned for decades after the end of hostilities. This is bizarre. Should the justice system really shield the public from the truth? In the summer of 2011 Goodwin moved out, back into the old family home in the Grange, Edinburgh. His wife remained in another house they had bought in Edinburgh because it came with large gardens and high security. The family had faced attacks after the financial crisis and the police had to be called in when their house and a car was vandalised. A group calling itself 'Bank Bosses are Criminals' claimed responsibility. The perpetrators were applying a very broad definition by using the word crime. Incredibly, almost everything that caused the financial crisis was entirely legal.

If Goodwin could not be jailed there must be another means available of settling the score. And then, in early 2012, it was suddenly remembered that he had a knighthood. A campaign began to remove it, with questions asked in the House of Commons and ministers in the coalition government busily stirring the pot. A body hitherto hardly ever heard of, the Honours Scrutiny Committee, was charged with looking into it. Perhaps only in Britain could this happen, as all the while the former chairman of the doomed HBOS, Lord Stevenson, continued to sit on another such government honours committee handing out gongs to those from the arts and media. (He stood down later.) The Queen and Prince Charles were concerned about the implications of the Goodwin case and sympathetic to him, it was said. He had been a good custodian of their charities and served quietly after his departure from RBS. Nonetheless, the pressure was too great and the committee announced that Sir Fred Goodwin would revert to plain old Mr Goodwin. And so too by extension Lady Goodwin would once again be Mrs Goodwin. Alistair Darling spoke up and condemned the removal of the knighthood. Writing in *The Times*, he declared: 'There is something tawdry about the government directing its fire at Fred Goodwin alone; if it's right to annul his knighthood, what about the honours of others who were involved in RBS and HBOS?' There was more than one man to blame for the financial crisis.

15

Fallout

'The big lesson is that the unthinkable can happen if you let it'

Sir Philip Hampton, chairman of RBS (2013)

We were in Fred Goodwin's old office at 280 Bishopsgate. The furniture and colour scheme were chosen by the former chief executive, but Ross McEwan preferred not to talk about the past or the man who built RBS and presided over its collapse. Instead, the new chief executive, who in October 2013 took over from Goodwin's successor Stephen Hester, wanted to talk about the future.

'I've never met Fred, I'm here to deal with what we have as a bank today, to create a really good bank out of it. And I think we can ... That's the thing that drives me every morning to get out of bed and come and work here.'

McEwan, a switched-on New Zealander with an easy charm, is much more comfortable and impressive off camera than some of his early media performances suggested. But if initially he struggled a little in public it is hardly surprising, considering the scale of what he faced in his first few months in charge. It is traditional for any new chief executive to 'kitchen sink it', meaning to get bad news out of the way early in their reign so that what comes later is seen as an improvement. However, the torrent of bad publicity for RBS in the final months of 2013 went well beyond that.

Within weeks of McEwan taking over, the bank was hit by more fallout from old disasters. The rackety IT systems broke down again, on several occasions leaving furious customers unable to access their accounts. The decision in 2000, hailed by some of Fred Goodwin's colleagues as a masterstroke during the NatWest integration, to keep bolting everything onto the smaller Royal Bank platform turns out to have not been so smart. McEwan said that RBS is spending hundreds of millions attempting to fix it.

Then in November 2013 an adviser to the Business Secretary Vince Cable also produced a report alleging that a restructuring division of RBS had deliberately put customers out of business so it could hoover up their assets at knockdown prices. That report – by entrepreneur Lawrence Tomlinson – was a curiously one-sided document. It may well turn out that there are cases where RBS staff broke the rules. In shrinking the balance sheet so aggressively, some of its bankers certainly seem to have treated certain business customers in a cavalier and very cruel fashion. Yet Tomlinson's report did not mention that he was himself an aggrieved RBS customer. The Treasury was furious with Cable and civil servants distanced themselves from the exercise. But in a climate in which banks are still detested, guilt was taken as read and it was all presented as yet another unmitigated RBS-related disaster.

The legal case of the Shareholder Action Group also got underway in court in London late in 2013. And then the bank's finance director, Nathan Bostock, resigned after only ten weeks in post. This was not the fresh start that the government had hoped to bequeath to McEwan, who was appointed very much as the Treasury's man. The Chancellor wanted to clear the way by announcing that RBS would be split into a good and a bad bank, although it is hard to escape the conclusion that this amounted to little more than rebranding the existing non-core division established under Hester, to make it look as though the government was taking radical action.

McEwan did not see it like that. And he praised his predecessor effusively, crediting Hester with restoring RBS to a 'safe and sound' position, with tier one capital of more than 9% and high levels of liquidity. Having joined under Hester in 2012 to head up the retail banking operation, he said he wanted the focus of the entire bank to be on customers.

'How do we turn it into a good bank again from a customer perspective? We've got really good people who despite what has happened to the organisation over the last five or six years actually love this place, and love it on behalf of their customers. My job is to make sure that our staff and our customers get really good technology platforms and processes that work well for them, to make it easy to do banking again.'

The difficulty may turn out to be that he is being asked to achieve several potentially contradictory goals. The government wants RBS to shrink, concentrating on the UK and selling off its American operation. Indeed, it appointed McEwan to deliver a safer and more traditional bank with a much-reduced markets business. 'Let's stick to the knitting, which is very strong in the UK,' he said. 'That doesn't mean we won't have an international network but let's make sure it works for the UK and our shareholders at the same time.' At the same time the regulator, the PRA, is asking all banks to carry even more capital. 'That's a good thing long term for the UK banking sector,' said McEwan. 'We don't want to go through what we've been through in the last five or six years ever again.'

But can the bank make itself even safer, hold more capital

and then produce big enough profits to attract investors? McEwan said it could: 'Banks should be able to return greater than their cost of capital if people run good banks that look after customers' needs.' The end result, after the 2015 general election, may well be that the smaller RBS turns out not to be worth anything like the £45.2bn the government paid for it. Several weeks after I interviewed McEwan, bank insiders told me that when it is eventually reprivatised in tranches the taxpayer should expect a shortfall of as much as £10bn.

And then there is the continuing legacy of past bad behaviour. McEwan acknowledged that until 2016 at the earliest RBS – and other parts of the banking industry – will continue to have to deal with historic issues stemming from the boom years and the crisis, by compensating customers, paying fines and responding to investigations in areas such as foreign exchange dealing. 'To be quite honest, as you dig deeper and deeper into banking businesses there will be other conduct issues that come out.'

What went so badly wrong in the culture of banks? McEwan was refreshingly blunt. He said it was down to 'a single focus on profitability ... an ever increasing desire to improve profit results year on year to give back to shareholders.' For all that, his realism was tinged with optimism: 'I don't look back beyond the last couple of years. We are where we are. We have what we have. And we need to start using some of the great assets we have here to do a lot better.'

None of this is Stephen Hester's problem any more. Having stayed to help hand over to McEwan, he disappeared in October 2013 for a long rest, almost five years to the day since RBS under Goodwin almost went bust. Hester's desire was just to 'hang', to take a break before considering his next job and working out what really matters in life. In February 2014 he announced that he had accepted an offer to take over as CEO of troubled insurer RSA. But before he left I interviewed him about his removal.

Wasn't he angry? He said not, and he seemed pleased to be

leaving. 'I never take things personally anyway. Business is business. Politics is politics. People make decisions, they're entitled to. I've made decisions my whole life about people who've worked for me. So I never have any personal resentments about these things.'

He defended his record: 'I feel lucky that the great majority of what we set out to do we did successfully. I was only one of 100,000 people. That will always be seen as a really big set of business and societal accomplishments by the people at RBS . . . I'm proud of what we have all accomplished.'

But why was he dispensed with? A disagreement over the question of whether or not RBS is really fixed was at the root of his removal. In essence, the argument raging in the early summer of 2013 rested on a dispute about whether enough had been achieved. While Hester's supporters, and the government as well, gave him credit for ably defusing the biggest time-bomb in British banking history and in difficult circumstances cutting that astounding balance sheet more than in half, there was a fight on what to do next with RBS. Worse, there were those inside government and in the City who said that the clean-up was not as comprehensive as it should have been and that the RBS balance sheet was still full of horrors needing to be owned up to.

Hester denied it vehemently, saying there were 'no secrets or mysteries' about the state of RBS and that he got it into a sound condition, where it was capable of being privatised: 'The facts show that RBS has recovered ahead of all the plans that have been in place for five years.' But by mid-2013 the government was of the view that more radical surgery was needed and that Hester was not the man to do it. Hence his departure.

So, did the Chancellor George Osborne lean across the table, point at Stephen Hester and, Alan Sugar style, snarl 'Yer fired'? No. His termination was the product of months of Whitehall scheming and internal Royal Bank wrangling. Just before

Christmas 2012, the fear inside the Treasury was that RBS might be turning into a 'zombie' bank, the name given to enormous institutions that stagger along laden with toxic assets, dragging down the economy in the process. The Chancellor wanted to begin privatising RBS in time for the 2015 election, but wanted to be as sure as possible that there were not nasty surprises lurking in its loan book. A central concern was what would happen if privatisation went ahead and there was then a serious external shock, such as a resumption of the crisis in the Eurozone or a blow-up in the Chinese economy. The Treasury estimated that there being £60bn of potentially questionable assets in RBS would mean that they would only need to be 10% worse than claimed for it to punch a £6bn hole in the bank. At the time, the Treasury's nightmare scenario involved launching a privatisation only for ministers to have to launch another state rescue later.

Against this backdrop, the line that had been pushed since before the crisis by Sir Mervyn (now Lord) King at the Bank of England, that RBS should be split into a so-called good bank to be privatised and separate state-owned bad bank, containing the toxic material, started to get a fresh hearing in the Treasury in late 2012. The Chancellor was not sure, and in public seemed to have set his face against it. But behind the scenes it was being discussed as part of a debate about what on earth to do with RBS. The BoE and the regulator had also started pushing its idea that the banks in general still have insufficient capital and are not ready for the next crisis.[1] In this context there was also a split about what shape and size RBS should be. Hester was firmly of the view that it should continue as a large universal bank, with an investment bank and international operations. The government view by early 2013 was that it should be ultra-safe, like Lloyds concentrating only on the UK, with much less investment banking and fewer foreign entanglements. Hester disagreed, pointing out that operations such as Citizens were potentially going to be very profitable again if the US economy recovers strongly. If the Treasury could not get Hester to change his mind about the way ahead, it would make a change at the top of RBS.

Hester's difficult relationship with Osborne – which was polite on a one-to-one basis – complicated matters. Osborne is obsessively political, and the Treasury struggled to cope with the notion that the RBS CEO preferred not to play the Whitehall game. After the government announced in late 2011 that it would implement the Vickers proposals to force banks to ring-fence, meaning separate retail and investment banking, there was astonishment in the Treasury that Hester would not endorse the policy. Hester's refreshing view was that, as he did not agree with it, he was not going to pretend.

Pay was another long-running source of tension. Hester's supporters in the City say that in his years at RBS he earned much less than he would have as chief executive of another firm (which is certainly true). Critics respond that bankers after the crisis still had a completely warped idea of what constitutes low pay. The argument about Hester's 'compensation' became a fixed item on the media calendar and in 2012 he was furious when Treasury pressure meant he had to waive a £963,000 bonus following an outcry.[2]

By early 2013, Hester was seen rather unfairly by the politicians, and by the regulators working for the new head of the Prudential Regulation Authority, Andrew Bailey, as a problem that needed dealing with. In March 2013, Hester's advisers at RBS told him that support for him from the politicians and the regulators was weakening, and that he should start to think about what he might do next. Simultaneously, Sir Philip Hampton, the Chairman of RBS, was coming to the view that it was time to find a new CEO who might have a less problematic relationship with the government. By the spring of 2013, there was a meeting of minds with the Treasury and those running

UKFI, the body that oversees the taxpayers' 82% share of RBS, supposedly at arm's length from the government. The relationship between Hester and Hampton was never good and, while it always remained professional, insiders say that a testiness in their dealings eventually tipped over into outright conflict. Hester is driven, used to getting what he wants and impatient when he does not get it, whereas Hampton saw it as his job as chairman to act as a brake, stress-testing assumptions and asking awkward questions. Hadn't part of the historic problem at RBS been that strong chief executives faced insufficient challenge from the chairman and board?

Ahead of Hampton and the Treasury hiring a new CEO, there remained the question of the RBS board, which in theory and law had responsibility for any decision. Here it got messy. It was communicated to the board that the government would be supportive if its members decided to find a new chief executive. At the board meeting ahead of the RBS AGM in May, there were the first formal discussions and there was division. Several members of the board were unhappy and there was a groundswell of opinion in favour of Hester staying at least until March 2014, which would have been the fifth anniversary of the launch of his five-year reconstruction plan. If Hester wanted to fight to stay on, they would back him. 'We didn't want him to go, the Chairman and the government did,' says an insider. The board took legal advice about the government's position. Hampton explained that while the board members should decide, they really had to take very seriously what was wanted by ministers, who represent the taxpayer. And the government was clear that it backed a change.

Hester brought matters to a head in May 2013. Dialling in by phone to a board meeting, he said that he would only stay if he had full support, meaning the unequivocal support of them all. There was an awkward silence on the line when he had finished speaking. Afterwards Hampton let him know that as he could not count on full support it had been decided that it would be best to arrange for his employment to be terminated by mutual consent. In addition, the Treasury was keen to save at least two million pounds by having him leave now. If Hester had stayed until 2014 he would probably have got a bonus in the interim, triggering a much higher pay-off in line with the terms of his contract.

When I asked how he thought he would be viewed by history, Hester shrugged. 'Individuals are never really as important as they're made out to be. Whether in good times or bad times. I've said to you before, I don't think Fred Goodwin was as bad as he's subsequently made out to be, and he wasn't as good as he was made out to be at the peak of his reputation. And the same will be true of me. I think life will go on remarkably quickly. Pages get turned. That's just how the world works.'

Indeed, when I interviewed Hester on an earlier occasion in 2012 his view of Goodwin was surprisingly generous, considering the state of the inheritance he bequeathed in the autumn of 2008. 'I liked Fred. I thought he was a talented man. I thought he came across as much more humble in person than his external reputation. I don't have anything against him personally. That doesn't mean to say he didn't make some significant business mistakes – that's another issue.'

Quite. Hester's diagnosis of what went so spectacularly wrong at RBS in the boom years after the NatWest takeover is damning. 'We financed ourselves in an unstable way, we were too leveraged, the strategy wasn't clearly focused on the things we were actually going to be good at, risk controls were poor, management process was a bit dysfunctional, and we were driven too much by profit expansion without thinking about the inputs.'

The pace of expansion, particularly at GBM, bordered on the insane, surely? The investment banking profits in the boom years seemed so vast and the growth so rapid that it encouraged

Goodwin to keep pushing the entire bank, and never to ask what might go wrong if the market went into reverse. It was to grow that part of the business that he pressed on with ABN Amro.

'The investment bank underlying was a good business, with good people doing good things that customers really want,' said Hester. 'But it had been allowed to grow at a pace and a scale that was much too fast and became dangerous.'

Instead it was mainly bad basic banking that did the damage, he believed. 'We will have lost [from the crisis] more money on regular lending than we will have ever lost in the investment bank. Our worst loss is our real estate lending in the British Isles, Ireland being the worst, UK being the second worst. So again it was convenient to media and politicians to say this is all about evil investment bankers doing complicated things that we didn't understand, but I don't think it's at all to do with that. This is about a world economy that revved itself too much and about some asset bubbles that policymakers allowed to develop and banks financed, the worst of which was in real estate, and it's no coincidence that the countries that suffered the most economically and the banks that suffered the most are ones that were in countries that were allowed to have big real estate booms – Ireland, Spain, United States, Britain.'

It was an old-fashioned mania then, in which once again people forgot that bust quite often follows boom?

Hester nodded: 'Somehow, every single generation, people forget and there's another real estate boom.'

At the other end of the corridor on the twelfth floor of 280 Bishopsgate sat Sir Philip Hampton. The RBS chairman occupies the large corner office that used to belong to Sir Tom McKillop, with views stretching out over north London and beyond. Hampton is a City veteran, an accountant who switched to investment banking with Lazard and then chaired the supermarket Sainsbury's. He made a stand when he was finance director at Lloyds Bank, opting to leave because he did not think the assumptions being made about growth were sensible. It is not easy or cost-free to resign from a job on a point of principle when corporate culture tends to require that all employees sing the company song. But a few more senior resignations in RBS in the run-up to disaster might have alerted the board, or helped to prompt the kind of constructive opposition that was so badly needed ahead of the ABN Amro deal. He believes that the disaster at RBS in 2008 demonstrates why powerful chief executives need checks and balances. 'Lots of people thought Fred Goodwin wasn't much constrained by the board or regulators. It's very difficult for anyone, over time, to make the right judgements if they are not much challenged.'

Why does Hampton think the smash happened? 'To me the big lesson is that the unthinkable can happen if you let it. Just because UK banks hadn't gone bust since Victorian times didn't mean they couldn't. Wholesale borrowing by UK banks was almost zero, net, in 2002. By 2008 it was £760bn. RBS had around £300bn. With hindsight it was a ludicrous borrowing binge. RBS borrowed far too much, and lent the money very unwisely.'

A lot of people have suffered unfairly as a result, he acknowledged. 'The people who have most right to be angry at the bank's financial collapse are people who did nothing wrong and lost their jobs, or in the case of many small shareholders, much of their life savings. Big financial failures can have massive collateral damage, which is why we need a strong banking system and effective regulation.' A total of 41,000 of the bank's employees, in the UK and abroad, have been laid off since 2008. It has not been easy for many of those who kept their jobs either. The vast majority of the bank's staff are not traders, or leverage finance merchants, they are people working hard in branches, call centres and back offices for modest remuneration.

Perhaps it will come as some consolation to former staff that Goodwin lost at least £7m. That includes his losses on the shares which he held on to until the crash and the loss of the pay-off he was legally entitled to demand but gave up. George Mathewson was also hit, to the tune of more than £5m it is suggested. His losses from buying millions of pounds worth of shares in the rights issue were big enough to make his financial position so precarious that after 2008 he almost went under, say friends. With the aid of various directorships, he rebuilt his finances.

In 2012 I went to see Mathewson in his office at Stagecoach, the transport company, on the outskirts of Perth, Scotland. Stagecoach was the creation of his friend Sir Brian Souter, who built it from a one-bus company into a transport giant. It is a product of the entrepreneurial impulse that Mathewson was trying to foster when he ran the Scottish Development Agency in the 1980s.

Until May 2013, Mathewson was chairman. In keeping with Souter's cost-conscious approach to business, the international head-quarters of Stagecoach is in a drab, unprepossessing, identikit 1980s building that could have been used to film *The Office*.

Pacing up and down as he talked, Mathewson was still a ball of energy, darting off at tangents, jumping between subjects and firing off pithy observations. It was that style – open to ideas, restless, enthusiastic – that those who worked on Project Columbus found so attractive in the early 1990s when they were remodelling the Royal Bank. It changed their world, as one of them put it. Mathewson might have been sober-suited but he wasn't a boring banker; he was an entrepreneurial engineer determined to build something that might demonstrate to his small country that it could achieve great things again. Then what he built collapsed. Ever since his approach has been very different to the one adopted by Goodwin, who has said almost nothing and become the Greta Garbo of corporate calamity. Mathewson has continued to speak publicly, offering his views on banking and the economy. One critic says this is shrewd. The man who built the modern RBS, who created its culture, and then groomed Fred Goodwin, is there right in front of us 'hiding in full view'.

Who did Mathewson blame? 'I know all the people involved in this, and I think the blame for this thing is very widespread. I think that I tend to reserve my ire for those who participated in this because of their trying to line their own pockets, as opposed to people who made genuine mistakes of judgement or have been caught out by events ... I think I could blame the government, I could blame the Governor of the Bank of England ... But I kind of think it doesn't help everybody to go about blaming people and particularly not blaming individuals. I think the Fred Goodwin thing has been ridiculous. Why should he have all the blame, as a lightning rod for everybody else?'

Was Mathewson bitter that the bank he built ended up in the condition it did? 'Bitterness is a waste of energy. I feel sad, actually, particularly for the staff who lost all that money throughout Scotland, shareholders, and various places. I feel very sad for them. I felt sad for myself at the time, but I can't honestly say I felt bitter because I don't think anybody, apart from one or two, were doing anything other than what they felt was right. I don't think Fred Goodwin did anything other than what he felt was right.'

Really? Everyone involved apart from one or two just did what they felt was right and that's how it goes, to the tune of £45bn plus of taxpayers' money? That's incredibly convenient for all those who let hubris blind them to the risks they were taking with other people's money. But many of his old team are still very loyal to Mathewson. 'When you see him he hasn't changed, he's still wee George,' said one of them enthusiastically. He still keeps in touch with Fred, although very few of his former colleagues have seen Goodwin since. Mathewson has plenty to keep him busy, anyway. He is a friend and economic adviser to Alex Salmond. After RBS, Mathewson's next project is helping the campaign to make Scotland independent.

Of the others, Johnny Cameron has had the most attention. He tells friends he deeply regrets that when Goodwin asked him to produce the numbers to justify the ABN Amro deal he did it and was too much the soldier swept up in the momentum, complying with Goodwin's request rather than being a general, leading. He will regret it until his dying day. Now he does some part-time work at Gleacher Shacklock, a boutique investment bank, and sits on the board of a charity working on the rehabilitation of offenders. He did not lose a fortune when RBS went down, as he had been 'light' on the bank's shares, and did not take up any shares in the rights issue. Incredibly, he is the only RBS senior figure who has faced any formal professional sanction (other than the stripping of Goodwin's knighthood). This is an odd aspect of the aftermath, no matter what one thinks of bankers in general or Cameron in particular. True, in an epic disaster it can sometimes be the way that culpability settles on one or two individuals as others slink away hoping never to be mentioned again. Cameron made some misjudgements, which are detailed in this book. Yet it makes no sense that he alone should have been singled out for investigation by the FSA when others intimately involved have quietly continued their careers. In his case it was down to a confluence of circumstances. The chairman of GBM had received assurances on his departure that he would be allowed to work again. He was offered a City post just when the row over Goodwin's pension flared up, whereupon the FSA announced it was going to investigate him.[3] The results of the investigation – along with the regulator's report into itself – were turned into an FSA document titled 'The failure of the Royal Bank of Scotland'. Many leading players in the drama were never interviewed by the regulator and, while it contains interesting information, it is not a full account of the rise and fall of RBS. In a very British way, there ended up being no proper wide-ranging committee of inquiry into the UK's biggest ever banking disaster, or biggest ever so far.

The FSA itself did not survive the crisis. Conceived as a model of regulation fit for the twenty-first century, it actually lasted less than two decades. Its former responsibilities have been divided, with the establishment of a new Financial Conduct Authority. The Prudential Regulation Authority, under the Bank of England, is now responsible for the stability of the financial system. Its first boss is Andrew Bailey, the Bank of England official who helped Vadera and Scholar design the rescue in October 2008 while flushing the banking system with emergency liquidity. The death of the FSA means that somehow Mervyn King ended up being the governor who had presided over a massive extension of the Bank of England's powers by the time he stood down, despite it having made errors on a grand historical scale on his watch.[4]

Brian Crowe gave up Mammon for God. After leaving RBS he was ordained as a vicar and preaches in the Parish of Crosthwaite and Lyth, near Kendal in Cumbria. Leith Robertson, his dealmaking deputy in GBM, is still in business. He is an adviser to a corporate finance company in the City and chairs 1st Credit, a debt-collection company. Sir Tom McKillop, the former chairman, issued an apology at the special meeting held for shareholders in November 2008 to approve the bailout. The meeting took place in the hall of the General Assembly of the Church of Scotland in Edinburgh, an appropriate place for sins to be acknowledged. He and Goodwin walked past the waiting photographers, through the courtyard featuring a large statue of John Knox, the austere founder of the Scottish Presbyterian movement. From the stage McKillop told the audience: 'Both personally and in the office I hold, I am profoundly sorry about the position that we have reached ... The buck stops with me as chairman and with the leadership of the Group. Accountability has been allocated and fully accepted. I am also acutely aware – every day – of the fact that thousands of our employees, past and present, have believed so much in their company that they gave more than their labour to it. They bought shares ... They were proud of what RBS had achieved and were delighted to be associated with it. The anxiety they now feel is of great concern to the board, the executive and to me ... And I am also sorry if any of our customers have suffered anxiety as a result of the situation.' McKillop joined the board of two pharmaceutical companies. He tells friends that if he could turn back the clock he would have stuck with his first instincts when George Mathewson rang him in 2005 to ask him if he would chair RBS. He should never have said yes.

Larry Fish is semi-retired and launched the Fish Family Foundation, which funds programmes educating immigrants and 'green-card' holders on how to become full American citizens. His pension pot, the equivalent of almost £20m, was bigger than Fred Goodwin's. Alan Dickinson joined the board of Nationwide, and Carpetright. Gordon Pell, one of the original promoters of payment protection insurance, retired after a stint as deputy chairman of Coutts. Pell donated his earnings at Coutts to charity, it is said. Benny Higgins, who ran retail, was frozen out by Goodwin and left HBOS when he declined to do the aggressive lending required. He went on to run Tesco Bank. Cameron McPhail, who headed up Project Columbus, left RBS early in the Goodwin era and is now based in Jersey, from where he runs several businesses. Iain Allan, the RBS head of strategy sidelined by Goodwin when he raised concerns about ABN Amro, CDOs and the investment bank, has continued as a visiting professor at Cass Business School after an extended period of illness. Howard Moody, public relations man to Mathewson and Goodwin, left before the crash and works as a freelance consultant. Guy Whittaker lives in London and at the time of writing does not have a job. His predecessor Fred Watt qualifies as one of the luckiest men in the country by virtue of being the finance director who decided to leave RBS in 2006. Matthew Greenburgh, Goodwin's favourite investment banker, retired from Bank of America Merrill Lynch in 2010, aged forty-nine.

Plenty of those on the board that voted for the ABN Amro deal continued life in the City. Peter Sutherland remained chairman of Goldman Sachs International, based in London, although he stood down as chairman of BP in late 2009, before the Gulf of Mexico oil spill. He is a regular attendee at Davos and the Bilderberg Group, beloved of conspiracy theorists who suspect it of plotting to take over the world on behalf of a global corporate-political nexus. Steve Robson was badly shaken by the RBS experience, say friends. He remained on the board of the Financial Reporting Council, the body that sets the professional standards and codes for accountants, actuaries and investment firms. In May 2013 he resigned as a director of Glencore-Xstrata, the commodities and mining group.

The Australian Bob Scott, who was the senior non-executive director and chair of the remuneration committee that approved all the pay packages, stepped down from Yell after pressure from shareholders.[5] Apparently the RBS connection did annoy investors who had lost money. Janis Kong, who used to run Heathrow Airport, went on the board of Kingfisher, the owner of B&Q. Archie Hunter is retired, as is Bill Friedrich, the American lawyer. Another American non-executive, Charles 'Bud' Koch, the former boss of Charter One, stepped back from finance.

Colin Buchan stood down from the RBS board in 2011. Investment banker Joe MacHale left the RBS board in May 2013, the last of the group who were there in 2008.

John Connolly, the former boss of Deloitte, RBS's auditor, stepped down and became chairman of G4S just in time for the security group's difficulties over its failure to hire sufficient numbers of staff to fulfil its contracts for the London Olympics.

Victor Hong, the risk manager man who actually resigned from Greenwich on a point of principle, disputing the marking of CDOs, is now a consultant on risk management and regulation.

Jay Levine became an investor in a firm headed by his former colleague, Ben Carpenter, which they hoped would become 'the new Greenwich', although it was a struggle to get such ventures off the ground after the financial crisis. Levine runs Springleaf Financial, a consumer lender that was badly hit by its earlier exposure to sub-prime mortgage loans. He and his wife Tammy have three houses in Greenwich and a family foundation that has sponsored cutting-edge research on economics. The Levine Family Fund sponsored a conference on 'Neuroeconomics and Endocrinological Economics' at his alma mater University of California, Davis.[6] According to the conference organisers: 'Neuroeconomics has emerged as a new field in recent years, as both economists and neuroscientists have used brain scanning technology such as functional magnetic resonance imaging to investigate how people make decisions.' Rick Caplan set up an advisory firm on mortgage securitisation. Fred Matera works for Redwood Trust, a California-based firm that deals in mortgage-backed securities. Bruce Jin, once the head of risk at Greenwich, now works in a senior position for Nomura in New York. Bob McGinnis has retired from the business and spends winters in Florida.

And then there is Fred Goodwin. His attempts to forge a career after RBS have not yet come to much. A position as an adviser to RMJM, the Edinburgh-based international architecture practice, did not work out, although the firm was facing financial difficulties before he arrived. The affair that broke his marriage also ended, with his girlfriend moving to Germany, leaving him home alone in Edinburgh, where he stays to be near his two children. His time is spent repairing vintage cars.

Some friends have stuck with him, such as Sir Angus Grossart, the financier who was on the board at the Royal Bank until 2005, and Jackie Stewart, the former racing driver who was prepared to speak up for him at the height of the furore.

Sometimes Goodwin will escape abroad for a few days when

he receives an invitation to shoot or to play golf. Every time he goes to catch a plane at Edinburgh Airport, the journey from his house takes him along the old Glasgow Road. On the left, as he approaches the airport turn-off, is Gogarburn, the giant complex he planned and completed as the global headquarters for a great international bank. Like all who drive that way out of the Scottish capital, on the journey he is compelled to pass underneath the high arch of a bridge built to specifications he approved. In the middle of the arch hangs a decoration no passing motorist can avoid seeing. Finished in a dark metallic grey, hung between the suspension wires, it is 1.95 metres high, 1.95 metres wide and 200cm deep. It is a giant RBS logo.

Afterword

There were plenty of opportunities to stop Fred Goodwin. And yet hardly anyone at RBS really tried. Why? Money had quite a lot to do with it, with many of those involved making so much of it. A member of Goodwin's staff, a woman who observed his senior executives carefully, put it brilliantly. 'Grown men saying they were too scared of Fred to give him bad news? Isn't that a bit pathetic? Was their reluctance to say anything related to the fact that they were trousering millions of pounds?'

Compensation, no let's be old-fashioned and call it pay, was so high at senior levels across the banking industry that those in receipt of the largesse had little incentive to cause trouble. The 'bollockings' and occasional indignities at RBS were worth tolerating. If you could just close your eyes, after grumbling a little to colleagues and working long hours, then you would get to the end of the year, when another enormous bonus would land in your account. It wasn't greed alone, of course. Others were motivated by the desire to build empires.

Those responsible include arrogant chief executives, weak management, boards that did not do their job, incompetent auditors, supine large shareholders, negligent regulators and a catastrophic Chancellor who fell for the epoch defining delusion that the ship he was steering was unsinkable. But beyond the blame game lies an awkward question that will not go away, even years after the crisis. If Britain's banks became so big and dangerous that when several of them blew up they blew up the economy, are we comfortable that the sector is still so enormous?

As research for the Bank of England shows,[1] in 1960 the UK clearing banks were tiny. They had balance sheets that totalled a mere £8bn combined, which was just 32 per cent of GDP. Soon more Britons wanted to open accounts and the banks expanded to cope with the demand of a surging consumer society. In 1970 bank balance sheets were £20bn, or 38 per cent of GDP. In 1980 the figures were £128bn and 55 per cent and in 1990 £428bn and 75 per cent. By then banks were becoming big players in the mortgage and credit card markets and soon they broke the 100 per cent barrier, with some pushing on into investment banking-style activities too and expanding aggressively with international operations. By 2000 the borrowing and lending binge was getting into full swing and the clearing banks were increasing their leverage until they had balance sheets of £1.4 trillion, 143 per cent of UK GDP. From there it rocketed. In 2010, shortly after the financial crisis, the figure stood at an astonishing £6.24 trillion. That was 450 per cent of GDP. The figure was more like 500 per cent if other UK banks and savings institutions, not only the clearing banks, were included. Think about that for a second, and look at the extraordinary graphic at the end of this chapter which the Bank of England's economists produced to illustrate those figures. Over fifty years bank balance sheets grew until they were five times the size of the UK economy, which is one of the world's largest economies.

As they grew much bigger there were fewer clearing banks. A wave of mergers and takeovers swept the industry. In 1960 there were sixteen such institutions, yet by 2010, after decades of consolidation, there were just five much bigger groups: RBS,

Lloyds, Barclays, HSBC and NAB (effectively meaning Clydesdale Bank, owned by National Australia Bank). RBS itself had swallowed eight of the sixteen that existed in 1960. And this smaller group of big banks were much, much larger relative to the rest of the economy.

Some small economies such as Iceland and Ireland tried a similar experiment, loading excessive weight and responsibility on their banks. Switzerland has long been an economy built on international finance. French banks also grew fast in the boom years. But of the major economies it was the UK that really loaded up most noticeably. The American experience was quite different, despite the subsequent sub-prime problem. US companies tend to take a different attitude to borrowing, leaning more on shareholders for resources. Certainly the US banking system grew in the decade before the crisis but it had been consistently below 100 per cent of GDP since 1960. By October 2008, Britain had undertaken an extraordinary experiment in financialisation and concentration of control.

When it was happening the growth was hailed widely as evidence of the UK's supreme success as a financial centre, although little attention was paid to the size of balance sheets or the implications in the event of a major economic reverse. It was all deemed to be a tremendous innovation – until the banking system blew up. Whereas previously the failure of a major bank would have been a serious but manageable event for the authorities, now the biggest banks were operating on such an incredible scale that if one fell over it threatened the rest of the banking system and the entire economy.

Who decided this experiment was a good idea? The Left blames what happened on the deregulation of the 1980s and on reckless bank CEOs such as Fred Goodwin, which is the 'they started it' defence. The Right blames the badly designed regulation of the post-1997 period and the addiction to private sector and then public debt. To borrow a phrase sometimes used in the

City, both sides are 'talking their own book', that is talking up their own position and refusing to acknowledge that the crisis presents a challenge to their worldview.

While it is true that the chronic difficulties the banks helped create in 2007 to 2008 led to the economy freezing up, from which flowed large annual deficits and a ballooning total national debt, it is not credible for members of the Labour government of that period to present themselves as innocents knocked off their feet by global forces. When the times were good Labour leaders feted the banks and knighted those who ran them. Indeed, they enjoyed spending the tax revenues which came from financial services and even publicly attributed the nation's success in large part to their own policies. Gordon Brown claimed to have ended boom and bust. Of course the British banking boom was also facilitated by the international authorities devising rules that made it easier for banks to expand their activities globally, increase leverage and grow profits. But the fuel – the petrol poured on the fire by policymakers that made it all possible – was excessive cheap money.

The Conservatives, and Thatcherites, can hardly escape responsibility either. Tory politicians tend to blame the disaster almost entirely on Tony Blair and Gordon Brown's Labour government, saying that it was spending too much and not regulating the banks properly. For public consumption some add in a little light 'banker-bashing' in case the outraged taxpayer – who pays the ultimate bill for the economy blowing up – suspects they are too close to rich men in the City.

It is easy to elide over the decisions contributing to disaster. The rise of British banks such as RBS, and their emergence as cross-border entities that were so big they could do such damage when they got into trouble, did not begin when Gordon Brown became Chancellor. Of course the process accelerated rapidly while he was in office, and he enjoyed the reflected glory that came from the City and the banks being such strong players in the global markets. Nevertheless, the roots of the so-called financialisation of the economy, meaning that banks and financial institutions became such a large part of our national life that their needs gradually became paramount, run deeper than that.

Undoubtedly the UK banking system had needed to change. The 1960s model of banking was too small and underpowered to cope with the demands of a flexible modern economy. Banks and building societies often behaved loftily towards potential borrowers or depositors, as though the customer was lucky to be allowed through the door. But what then happened went beyond modernisation and an attempt to become more responsive to demand. British banking became three things.

First, on the retail side banks turned themselves into selling machines with targets for growth. Traditionally banks were viewed as custodians of customer deposits, now some of them were remodelled as financial supermarkets who sold what they could get away with whether the customer needed it or not. The payment protection insurance racket across the industry is a prime example. Weren't banks just like any other retailer? As if to prove the point, at the height of the boom HBOS hired a Harvard Business School-trained supermarket executive, Andy Hornby from Asda, to succeed James Crosby as chief executive. It later turned out that banks really are not like supermarkets. They are the conduit for much of the money supply and it is highly problematic when they go bust, particularly if their balance sheet is the size of the country's economy.

Secondly, the investment banking and to a lesser extent the corporate banking side became an industry with an exotic sheen, where pay and bonuses attracted the brightest who might previously have gone into industry or the professions. Undoubtedly that sprang from the reforms of the 1980s. The instinct that propelled the overhaul of the City was certainly sound in one sense. Contrary to what is sometimes believed in Britain, those reforms did not invent the internationalisation of modern finance, they were partly a response to what was already happening here and elsewhere. Aided by the rapid spread of computerisation and financial innovation, finance was becoming steadily more global. In the Victorian era, London had been the trading capital of the world in terms of real goods as well as finance. If there was a sufficiently radical restructuring of the City in the 1980s, and foreign money and institutions were allowed to flow in and British money to flow out to seek better returns, the Thatcherites hoped London might once again build on its advantage and become the undisputed leader, at least in financial services. While it is true that the 'Big Bang' legislation of the 1980s did not directly deal with banking it did enable foreign investment banks to buy City firms and create London-based modern institutions which banks such as RBS rushed to emulate. Big Bang reinvigorated the trading culture and helped create a mania for expansion, scale and takeover. Can anyone credibly argue that those obsessions didn't seep into mainstream banking and even into those institutions that did not have investment banking arms?

Thirdly, there emerged the idea of the large British bank as an enormous corporation, or mega-bank with a vast headquarters and a dominant personality as CEO. Fred Goodwin wanted RBS to transcend old-fashioned humdrum notions of banking by joining the ranks of transcontinental, globalised big business.

Being too big was not just a problem at RBS, as became clear after the financial crisis. It was revealed that subsidiaries of HSBC, a giant institution that had twice tried to buy the Royal Bank of Scotland and is registered in London but trades mainly outside the UK, had been caught being used by money-launderers and drug dealers while Lord Green was chief executive and chairman. Green, who subsequently became a government minister, knew nothing of this. He is an ordained Church of England vicar and a fine and upstanding individual. He is even the author of a volume entitled: *Serving God? Serving Mammon?* When the scandal broke, his friend Lord Butler, the former cabinet secretary and a member of the HSBC board for a decade, robustly defended Green in the House of Lords. Perhaps unwittingly, Butler made the case for smaller and more manageable institutions: 'While it may be the case that the chairman and chief executive officer of a major international company is accountable for everything that happens in that company, there is no possible way in which the chairman and chief executive can be responsible for everything that happens in a worldwide group of the size of HSBC.'[2]

Quite. But if a bank with the potential to blow up the economy is so large and complex that even its supporters admit people of ability and impeccable moral authority cannot control what it does, then what is the point of it existing in such a form? Should we simply shrug, and say this is just the way of the global economy, get used to it and be ready to stump up for more bailouts in an emergency?

Any argument that not all the big banks screwed up is of limited comfort. Of the UK's big four, two (RBS and Lloyds) ended up being partially owned by the taxpayer. A third, Barclays, had the luckiest of escapes, coming within a whisker of taking over the toxin-riddled ABN Amro. It subsequently had to seek a recapitalisation from the Gulf. Then the fourth, HSBC, had those money-laundering difficulties. Registered outside the UK, some of those who navigated the sub-prime mortgage crisis most deftly, and were smug as a result, later hit trouble. In 2012 the ultra-safe J. P. Morgan was temporarily beached by the 'London Whale'. Its trading vehicle based in London ran up losses of $6.2bn that stunned those in charge in New York. J. P. Morgan's celebrated risk-control processes had simply failed.

The scale and potential ungovernability of the biggest banks does not mean that small is always beautiful. Some of the banks and building societies that had to be rescued during the crisis were relatively small, and narrowly focused on particular types of lending, with no investment banking activities. However, the critical difference is that when they went bang the bailouts they demanded were nothing like the £45.2bn shareholding the tax-payer took in the enormous RBS. When a big enough bank explodes, it can help blow up the economy.

Do we want extremely big banks, if they can do this much damage? The argument from the largest banks is, unsurprisingly, that we do need them because their size creates efficiencies of scale.[3] Being so big means they can pool services and back-room facilities to create better products and more profit for shareholders. This was the Fred Goodwin model. Since the financial crisis that notion has been challenged, most notably in the UK by Andrew Haldane of the Bank of England. It is a well-established theory that some banks were so systematically important that when the crisis came they were 'too big to fail'. Government felt it had no choice other than to rescue them. Haldane refers in addition to them being 'too big to be efficient' in the first place. Academics have explored the 'implicit subsidy' of 'too big to fail' banks, which suggests that they obtain lower funding costs from the markets because it is factored in that we, the taxpayer, will not let them go bust if it comes to it.[4] So their apparent efficiencies of scale may well depend on us being there to foot the bill and bail them out.[5]

As Professor John Kay has pointed out, this is not a sustain-able set-up in a democracy: 'When the next crisis hits, and it will, that frustrated public is likely to turn, not just on politicians who have been negligently lavish with public funds, or on bankers, but on the market system. What is at stake now may not just be the future of finance, but the future of capitalism.'[6]

If they are too big to fail and too big to be efficient, then ulti-mately the mega-banks are too big to be useful. So far the UK government has been resistant to radical ideas of ordering the break-up of the banks, although it wants to encourage new entrants to the banking market and has done a little, not much, to encourage that. It has moved, on the recommendation of the Vickers Commission, to force banks to create a 'ring-fence' between investment banking and plain old retail banking. In the case of RBS, if such restrictions had been in place Johnny Cameron in GBM would have been ring-fenced in a separate part of the company from Gordon Pell at retail, with distinct pots of capital and so on, so one could not leech from the other. Would that really have prevented Fred Goodwin from growing RBS at too fast a rate? I doubt it. The new capital rules, which force banks to keep much more than they did before the crisis, are likely in time to make more of a difference. There is also talk of the new ring-fence being 'electrified', although everything I have learned about senior bankers during the research for this book tells me that even if it had 50,000 volts coursing through it they would find a way to tunnel under or vault over the fence.

The UK banks are still enormous, with balance sheets that have come down although they continue to dwarf GDP. As of the end of 2012 the combined figure was £5.9 trillion, or 383 per cent of GDP. This worries policymakers. In front of the Parliamentary Commission on Banking Standards, Mervyn King mused on this topic as he prepared to leave office in 2013. Just think of the trouble that might have been averted in Britain if he had focused on such themes at the start of his tenure in 2003.

Yet that was simply not the mood of the time. The intellectual climate was such that there was an over-reliance on the application of new economic theories, mathematical modelling and the growing 'tyranny of data'. The 'efficient market hypothesis', developed in the 1970s, dominated thinking on financial markets for most of the next four decades.[7] It held that markets are rational and that prices simply reflect all the information available to investors. What a nice idea, if you presume that everyone has access to and takes time to read the same material. You also need to exclude awkward human concepts such as greed, fear, confusion, stupidity and a weakness for manias.

In the same period hedge funds were developed, often at the instigation of academics, to exploit theories about probability and establish how 'data-mining' and computer power might help when it came to understanding the market and spotting opportunities. Why trust the gut instinct of an excitable old-fashioned trader, when a calm appreciation of trends and potential outcomes could deliver much better returns? This smart insight made a small number of people extremely rich. In turn, ambitious banks hired 'quants', or 'quantitative analysts', to help them use similar techniques in the creation of new products. Hence the collateralised debt obligation (CDO) and other innovations. The ratings agencies would, for a fee, even stamp such products AAA and accountants would give their sign-off. On top of the assumption that the new thinking made the world safer, because it had originated from such clever people, were gradually built risk-management systems, and bank-regulation and accountancy standards that accepted as a given the viability of the underlying theories. Banks such as RBS were actually rather late arrivals on the scene, and pretty hick in their understanding of what was really happening. Goodwin plainly did not give it much thought, or if he did he never mentioned it to his closest colleagues. But the emphasis throughout was on the production and measurement of data, data and more data. If the numbers added up in a neat line for the auditors and fitted with the theoretical models designed by those outside the bank, and the ratings agencies had done their AAA thing, then it must be OK, surely? One can see why this would make sense to Fred Goodwin, an accountant. It simply seemed that finance was getting simultaneously safer, bigger and more profitable as a result of innovation.

Data and modelling are useful in all manner of human activities, such as measuring performance in business, health, education or sport. The potential danger comes in elevating it to such an extent that insufficient room is left for the application of common sense. Data can point the way, but if we let it tell us what to think and feel we are in trouble.

Inevitably, in finance, it turned out that the quants and analysts had made some simple and very expensive mistakes with their numbers. The models used by many of the banks were only as good as the underlying assumptions that they had been built on. If you constructed your model based on data from the last fifty years, assuming that a US housing crash on the scale of the Great Depression was highly unlikely because it was a long time ago, and we've moved on a lot since then, then you had a problem when the eventual crash was bigger than allowed for by the models.

Suddenly, when circumstances changed, old-fashioned human doubt was reintroduced. Theoretically risk had been diluted, with different types of it mixed together into the giant alphabet soup of the CDO, all several steps removed from the original sub-prime mortgage being taken out by people who could not afford it. Yet the underlying models were wrong. American house prices could fall further than was thought. Trust vanished. It became hard to tell what anything was worth. Cue a panic. Disaster.

Having been such an enormous success in high finance, these ideas are obviously next being applied to politics. The victory of Barack Obama in the 2012 US election was attributed in some quarters to his campaign's mastery of vast amounts of data and 'micro-targeting' of voters. Forget ideas, or ethics, or arguments. Look at the numbers. 'The Victory Lab' by Sasha Issenberg talked of a new 'data-driven order'. It attracted the attention of party strategists in Britain. Says the promo for Issenberg's book: 'Armed with research from behavioural psychology, data-mining, and randomized experiments that treat voters as unwitting guinea pigs, the smartest campaigns now believe they know who you will vote for even before you do.'

This is sounding familiar. Data-mining, probability, quant theory. It is what the hedge-fund industry and other financial innovations were built on. The 'micro-targeting' done by Team Obama enabled the harvesting of many tiny groups of voters that together added up to victory. The politician's equivalent of profit is votes. Similarly, hedge-funders worked out that if they could harvest small individual profits but do it so many times on an epic scale, playing with huge sums of money, then that would add up to victory, or a very large profit.

We are entering a world of 'big data'. Global companies such as Google, which are very friendly with big governments, collect vast amounts of information about us and design algorithmic models which we are told can work out what we want to buy or eat before we know we want it. Many of us enjoy some of the benefits, even if it is remarkable how trusting we are. Google and Apple are not philanthropic endeavours, they are giant businesses that want our money and maybe more, eventually. We once unquestioningly enjoyed the benefits of big finance and easy money provided with the approval of policymakers on the basis that we were now safer and smarter. Or we enjoyed it until it blew up the economy and ushered in years of recession and flatlining growth.

This is not a Luddite appeal for the rejection of technology or a call for a return to an imaginary pastoral idyll. It is a plea for scepticism and the human scale. To say that there is little that can be done to deal with the dangers of monopolistic internet companies or oligopolistic big banks that cannot be controlled even by those paid to be in charge, is a counsel of despair. As if twenty-first-century 'bigness' is simply the equivalent of the weather and we are powerless to do anything but accept it and stump up for the repairs after the next storm. The American President Theodore Roosevelt was particularly interested in similar themes. More than a century ago he was 'trust-busting', using the law to prosecute and break up exploitative and giant business monopolies such as that owned by John Pierpont 'J. P.' Morgan, to empower consumers and citizens. Not everything Teddy Roosevelt did worked, and his critics say he vested too much power in government instead. But he was attempting to deal creatively and intelligently with a question that faces us again. Do we exist to serve banks and companies? No. They should exist to serve us.

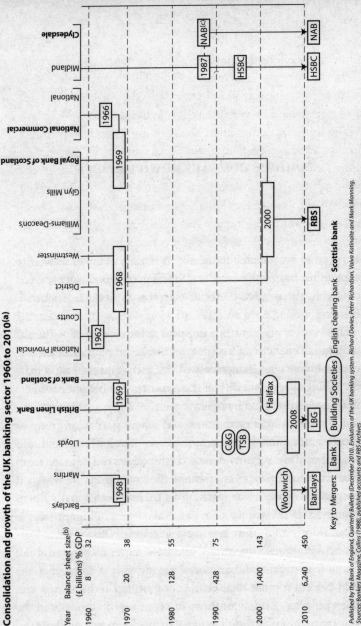

Consolidation and growth of the UK banking sector 1960 to 2010(a)

Published by the Bank of England, Quarterly Bulletin (December 2010). Evolution of the UK banking system. Richard Davies, Peter Richardson, Vaiva Katinaite and Mark Manning.
Sources: Bankers Magazine, Collins (1988), published accounts and RBS Archives

(a) The figure shows bank mergers involving the 16 London and Scottish clearing banks present in 1960, together with their acquisitions of building societies and demutualised building societies.
(b) The balance sheets of institutions are included from the point of merging or acquisition.
(c) Clydesdale was owned by Midland Bank until 1987 when it was sold to National Australia Bank.

Sources and Acknowledgements

Early on in my research for *Making It Happen* a banker seeking to explain his trade asked me how well I understood collateralised debt obligations (CDOs). About as well as most political journalists, I responded. I am not a financial journalist by trade, meaning that most of my career has been spent in the vicinity of politicians rather than financiers. Of course, writing about politics for a living means I have witnessed plenty of chicanery and confusion masquerading as certainty. But for sheer chutzpah, what some bankers managed to do, aided by policymakers, really scoops the pot.

I wanted to understand how and why a particular group of those senior bankers, those at the Royal Bank of Scotland, did what they did, and to understand why others did not stop them and in some cases even created the conditions in which it became possible. I was learning as I went, occasionally open-mouthed at the vanity of what otherwise intelligent people would do if a lot of money were available. Others made mistakes, with honest intentions, and now regret that they did not do more to prevent the disaster. But gradually it dawned on me that behind a great deal of the complicated terminology and theorising quite a few of those in positions of authority in the run-up to the crisis didn't, when it came down to it, understand all that much either. They had at best a partial understanding of the businesses that had made them so much money.

Fred Goodwin did not understand what CDOs were until the bank he ran had quite a few of them and the financial system was about to catch fire. One of his colleagues even did a drawing for him explaining how it worked, and got no reaction. Others also explained it, although by the time the implications penetrated it was much too late.

I set about interviewing as many former RBS bankers as I could, with executives and board members opening their diaries, notebooks and papers. Almost all the interviews, with more than one hundred individuals, were conducted off the record. The aim was to get candour and frankness from as many leading players and witnesses as possible. Many who spoke to me at length wanted to be able to deny to their colleagues – other board members, or fellow executives, or their new employers – that they had spoken. Some are still worried about potential court cases.

This is not a book about the banking bailout, but for several key chapters I did need to understand the events before, during and after the RBS rescue. The argument will rage for decades about whether the giant bailout should have been implemented differently or not done at all. I am generally a banking bailout sceptic, but I can see that those attempting to deal with the disaster did not have the luxury of being armchair critics and were doing their best in appalling circumstances. They were operating during a civil emergency and were working for only a small fraction of what the bankers they were dealing with got paid.

In the final chapter Ross McEwan, Stephen Hester and Sir Philip Hampton are interviewed on the record. In addition, in that final chapter I have quoted George Mathewson on the record. The former chief executive and chairman is such a central figure in the rise and fall of RBS. From 1987 to 2005, for eighteen years, he was either the driving force in the company or its father figure. I wanted him to explain what he thought it was all about. The man he hired and groomed as his successor, Fred Goodwin, spoke to me neither on nor off the record. All bids to interview him, with approaches made through friends, were rebuffed or ignored. Still employed within RBS are several people who have been extremely generous with their time and recollections. I won't name them and they know who they are. It would have been impossible to cover so much ground, and get access to so many key witnesses, without their assistance.

I have attempted at every stage to write a book that explains high finance, the extraordinary story of RBS and the blow-up of the UK economy, in terms that are, I hope, as straightforward as possible. If there are any mistakes either in terminology or understanding the errors are mine alone and I apologise.

A long list of people deserve thanks. Ken Mooney, a former investment banker studying at Cass Business School, crunched the numbers expertly and analysed the data on RBS's share price. Ruth Reed and her team at the Royal Bank of Scotland archive were wonderfully efficient and a source of great assistance. Richard Davies, formerly of the Bank of England and now at the *Economist*, and Belinda Turner of the Bank of England, pointed me to fascinating research on the UK banking system and questions such as banks being 'too big to fail'. Richard produced, in British terms, the single most revealing graphic of the entire financial crisis period which is reproduced in the Afterword with the kind permission of the Bank of England.

Ian MacGregor, the editor of the *Sunday Telegraph*, and colleagues Damian Thompson, Andrew Brown, Tom Chivers and Luke McGee all showed considerable patience when I needed time away from writing for them to work on the book.

Professor John Kay has thought deeply and written insightfully about the themes explored in the Afterword. He was kind enough to spend time talking with me early on in my research, firing my enthusiasm and suggesting interesting lines of enquiry. Harry Wilson, the banking editor of the *Daily Telegraph*, who has broken so many stories in his field, offered wise advice.

Ferdinand Mount provided encouragement and pointed me in the direction of the collapse of the Ayr Bank and Adam Smith's observations on that early Scottish banking disaster. David Broadhead and his staff at The Travellers Club were wonderfully accomodating and helpful throughout.

I want to single out friends and colleagues who provided invaluable guidance and support. Gerald Warner read the manuscript, made canny observations and provided a much-needed boost at several points of low ebb throughout a long project. Bruce Anderson proofed the manuscript and suggested improvements. Patience Wheatcroft was, as ever, a huge source of inspiration and encouragement. Ian Stewart, editor of my old paper in Edinburgh, the *Scotsman*, cleared the way for me to access the archives and Craig Nelson tracked down the pieces I needed. That proper banker of the Swiss school, Henry Angest, of Arbuthnot Banking Group, was a great host at various points and he is an incisive thinker on the City, international finance and human nature.

Simon Nixon, a friend and former colleague from my spell at the *Wall Street Journal* in London, brought his enormous expertise to bear, challenging my assumptions and arguments with marvellous clarity of thought. Similarly, Peter Thal Larsen, Ben Wright, William Wright, Iain Dey, George Trefgarne and Martin Vander Weyer each provided hugely valuable insights into banking, the culture of the City and RBS. Steadfast friends – Andrew Neil, Jonny Patrick, Anna Holland, Jenny Hjul, Andrew Wilson, Kirsty Milne, Con Coughlin, Ben Wallace, Alison Gray, Tim Montgomerie, Fraser Nelson, Michael Donn, Adam Bruce, Johnnie McKie, Michael Paterson, George Bridges and Gillian Bowditch – encouraged me to press on when my spirits flagged. The same is true, as ever, of Jack and Margaret Martin and Jim and Pamela McJannet. Both Alan Cochrane and Chris Deerin were selflessly prepared to listen to me ruminate at length about this book, sometimes over a glass of wine. They brought their brilliant journalistic instincts to bear. And without the meticulous research of that unbeatable wine critic and dear friend Will Lyons, I would never have known how much a bottle of Château Latour 1970 cost in 2000 prices. It was the wine drunk at the private dinner held to celebrate the Royal Bank takeover of NatWest.

My agent, the fantastic Peter Robinson, never flagged in his faith that this was a book that needed writing. Martin Bryant edited and improved the manuscript with great care and precision. Mike Jones and the team at Simon & Schuster were superb, expertly steering this, my first book, from conception to completion.

The biggest debt of gratitude I owe is to my wife Fiona and son William, who both tolerated my lengthy fixation on the Royal Bank of Scotland and all matters related to the financial crisis. Throughout they provided love, support and laughter. If William becomes an investment banker when he grows up then he cannot say, when he has read this book, that I failed to warn him.

Notes

Chapter 1

1 Banks ask Chancellor for capital, Peston's Picks, 7 a.m., 7 October 2008.
2 *Hansard*, 6 October 2008, statement on the financial markets. Darling's exchanges with George Osborne, then the shadow chancellor, were particularly fraught that day. Osborne offered temporary Tory support for efforts to rescue the banking system. But Darling's team felt that Osborne had gone public with demands for the recapitalisation of the banks that weekend when the Tories had been told in confidence that the government was considering such a move.
3 Unlike in the case of Northern Rock there were no queues. The run on RBS – the withdrawal of deposits – was more gradual, taking many months and involving large corporate customers removing large amounts. At no point was there a shortage of cash in the retail branches.
4 FSA report, *The failure of the Royal Bank of Scotland* (2012), paragraph 458.
5 Hornby had arrived at HBOS from Asda following a spell at the Boston Consulting Group. After the financial crisis he became chief executive of Alliance Boots, and then in 2011 Gala Coral, the bookmaker, bingo and casino operator.
6 There remains a certain amount of bitterness about the curry. Several senior officials were not invited to partake.

Chapter 2

1 The best account of the Company of Scotland and the Darien disaster is Douglas Watt's. He mined the Company's records and Scotland's national archives. Instead of the traditional concentration on alleged English perfidy, he offers a devastating assessment of the miscalculations made by William Paterson and his colleagues. *The Price of Scotland* (2007).
2 'Historic new records shed new light on Scotland's Darien disaster', *Caledonian Mercury*, July 2011.

3 William Ferguson, *The Oxford Companion to Scottish History* (2001), p.162.

4 Equivalent Company, company of debenture holders, 1721–1851, RBS Heritage.

5 In the mid-1920s Neil Munro, the celebrated Scottish writer, most famous for the Para Handy stories, was commissioned by the Governor and directors to write *The History of the Royal Bank of Scotland 1727–1927* to mark the bank's bicentenary. It contains an entertaining account of the earliest days of RBS.

6 In *Edinburgh in the '45: Bonnie Prince Charlie at Holyrood House* (1995), John Sibbald Gibson brings to life the occupation of the Scottish capital by the Jacobites. Gibson came from Paisley, served with No. 1 Commando in the Second World War and then combined a career as a civil servant in the Scottish Office with his work as a historian.

7 John Campbell's diary was published, with an introduction, by the Royal Bank in 1995.

8 On the birth of the modern insurance industry and the actuarial profession, see Niall Ferguson's *The Ascent of Money* in 2008, pp.191–200.

9 The Country Bankers Act of 1826 allowed for joint stock banks in England as long as they were outside London. The success of the system in Scotland was cited as a reason for reform.

10 Neale, James, Fordyce and Downe was a London-based finance house that had indulged a taste for wild speculation and shorting stock. There was a panic, a shortage of liquidity, and many private bankers both north and south of the border went bust. The disaster is charted on pp.124–34 of S. G. Checkland's *Scottish Banking: A History, 1695–1973*.

11 Neil Munro's *The History of the Royal Bank of Scotland 1727–1927* contains a list of those present at the bicentenary dinner at the North British Hotel and a full transcript of the various speeches made.

Chapter 3

1 Tom Devine in *The Scottish Nation: 1700–2000* (2000) sets industrial decline in political context. As Scotland's old industries started to come under global pressure, the Tories and Unionists were increasingly seen as unsympathetic. In 1967 the Scottish National Party's Winnie Ewing won the Hamilton by-election and after that pressure grew for 'home rule' or devolution.

2 In the late 1970s and early 1980s it was taken for granted by those seeking to take over a bank that it was necessary to gain informal approval from the Governor of the Bank of England.

3 *Report on proposed merger between the Royal Bank of Scotland and the Hong Kong and Shanghai Banking Corporation and Standard Chartered Bank, the Monopolies and Mergers Commission*, HMSO, 1982.

4 See David Kynaston, *City of London: The History, 1815–2000* (2011).

5 Direct Line was the brainchild of Peter Wood.

6 'The rise and fall of the RBS American Dream', Kenny Kemp in the *Sunday Herald*, 6 February 2011.
7 George Younger left no memoirs, although David Torrance's biography *George Younger: A Life Well Lived*, published in 2008, is excellent. Younger did write an account of Thatcher's fall for *Scotland on Sunday* in 1993.

Chapter 4

1 'Modest venture which grew to span the world', *Herald*, 21 November 1991.
2 The Clark family fortune – as in Tory politician Alan Clark and Kenneth Clark of *Civilisation* fame – originated with the family's now long-gone textile business in Paisley. The other major textile concern in the town was J & P Coats.
3 When Goodwin was at RBS and the *Sunday Times* published a piece which revealed the incident and his father's role he made no complaint and did not even mention it when discussing the article with colleagues.
4 *Scottish Banking: A History, 1695–1973*, S. G. Checkland (1975), pp. 335–57.
5 Cole-Hamilton went on to be chosen as the captain of the Royal & Ancient, at the home of golf in St Andrews, for 2004–2005. By coincidence, after the financial crisis, Goodwin had to withdraw his application to join the R&A.
6 Later Cicutto did go on to run NAB, but he resigned in 2004 after a difficult period for the group.
7 For a considerable time after the film was released in May 1995 Scottish politicians of all parties competed to exploit the patriotic *Braveheart* effect. The film was credited with a surge of interest in Scottish history.
8 Goodwin's former colleagues are divided on whether he was ever serious about making the move to Australia, or whether he did it hoping it would give him bargaining power.

Chapter 5

1 Scottish Housing Market Review, Scottish Executive, 2007.
2 The building work at Harvey Nicks caused some disruption, particularly when the developers were accused by Fred Goodwin's staff of getting dust on his car.
3 *Independent*, 8 May 1997.
4 'Halifax trumps Royal Bank', *Independent*, 10 March 1998. The defeat by Halifax was embarrassing, although Mathewson felt it had provided the opportunity for his team to gain experience ahead of future potential takeovers.
5 Statement by NatWest board, issued on 24 September 1999.
6 'The bidding for NatWest', *Economist*, 30 September 1999.

7 'Wanless's £3m pay-off', *Herald*, 4 May 2000.

8 Royal Bank of Scotland press release, Friday 26 November 1999.

9 'National Westminster attacks offer from rival Royal Bank of Scotland', *Wall Street Journal*, 21 December 1999.

10 'Value of Royal Bank bid falls', *Guardian*, 1 December 1999.

11 From then on Goodwin used the Savoy as his London base, except when the hotel was being renovated and he moved to a suite at the Ritz.

12 The Lex column did back the Bank of Scotland bid in the next morning's *Financial Times*.

13 'The Giant Killer', *Sunday Herald*, 13 February 2000.

14 'A victory for skill and financial enterprise', *Scotsman*, 11 February 2000.

Chapter 6

1 In 1994, for their father's 80th birthday, the Brown brothers had a selection of their father's sermons published as a book by Gordon Brown's friend Bill Campbell, the owner of Mainstream publishing in Edinburgh: *A Time to Serve: A Collection of Sunday Sermons*.

2 In a piece for the *Daily Mail* in 2006, Tom Brown (no relation but a close friend of Gordon Brown's) explained how his father's teaching had shaped the aspiring politician's philosophy: 'In the Name of the Father: the Gospel of Gordon', 26 October 2006.

3 Brown's efforts to rebrand Smith reached a climax when he was Chancellor. See his involvement in the Enlightenment Lectures at Edinburgh University in 2002 – 'Can both the Left and Right claim Adam Smith?' He also wrote the foreword to *Adam Smith: Radical and Egalitarian* by Iain McLean (2006).

4 See *DC Confidential*, by Sir Christopher Meyer, for an account of those first visits.

5 'Learning from Clinton, stealing from Thatcher', John Rentoul in the *Independent*, 18 January 1995.

6 *Gordon Brown: The First Year in Power*, Hugh Pym and Nick Kochan (1998).

7 *Servants of the People*, Andrew Rawnsley (2001).

8 *Gordon Brown*, Tom Bower (2004); and *Servants of the People*, Rawnsley.

9 *Hansard*, 20 May 1997. Clarke accused Brown of creating confusion and behaving like 'a Chancellor in a desperate hurry'.

10 The seven shadow chancellors were Ken Clarke (for little more than a month after the 1997 election), Peter Lilley, Francis Maude, Michael Portillo, Michael Howard, Oliver Letwin and George Osborne.

11 Growth figures, World Bank data set.

12 'Ex-Treasury chief Robson accused of "suppressing" Cruickshank', *Independent*, 23 February 2005.

13 Halifax house price index data.

14 'Big Bank shockwaves left us with today's big bust', *Observer*, 9 October 2011.

15 Greenspan was speaking at Lancaster House on 'World finance and risk management', on 25 September 2002.

Chapter 7

1 Younger was a popular figure across party political boundaries, and when he died aged seventy-one there were fulsome tributes from the party leaders. On behalf of RBS, Mathewson described him as 'a natural leader who inspired loyalty and warmth'.
2 'Showing his rival a clean pair of heels', *Sunday Herald*, 17 March 2002.
3 Computerworld Honors Program archives, interview with John White, 1 April 2008.
4 'Not your typical CEO', Larry Fish lecture at MIT, 19 October 2005.
5 RBS annual report.
6 *The Smartest Guys in the Room* (2004), by Bethany McLean and Peter Elkind, is the classic account of how they perpetrated the fraud.
7 'Dixon Motors falls to RBS', *Daily Telegraph*, 23 April 2002.
8 Lord Stevenson was also well connected in New Labour, as a friend of Peter Mandelson and Tony Blair. In 1990 he gave Mandelson a consultancy post at his market research firm.
9 RBS annual report.
10 'Brisk and brusque', *Forbes*, 6 January 2003.
11 The Harvard paper was jointly authored by Nitin Nohria, who in 2010 became dean of the faculty at Harvard Business School, and James Weber.

Chapter 8

1 'Fred's new Fawlty Towers', *Sunday Herald*, 15 October 2000.
2 Edinburgharchitecture.co.uk
3 'Nicklaus to appear on new fiver', *Daily Telegraph*, 12 July 2005.
4 Martin Sorrell interviewed in 'Building the Brand', 2007. (http://www.youtube.com/ watch?v=jHsEBtHnc7g).
5 'Royal Bank buys Churchill Insurance for £1.1bn', *Daily Telegraph*, 12 June 2003.
6 As in the UK the pace of consolidation and growth of the banking sector was aggressive in the Republic of Ireland. Low tax rates and low interest rates combined to create a banking boom.
7 'RBS "absolutely horrible" say Churchill staff', *Daily Telegraph*, 5 March 2004.
8 Goodwin owns a 1972 Triumph Stag.
9 'RBS dismisses fears it overpaid for Charter One', *Scotsman*, 10 May 2004. Despite the standard public denials, it rapidly became apparent to members of Goodwin's management team that the price had been too high.
10 'Revealed: RBS's secret jet', *Sunday Telegraph*, 4 April 2004. The paper's City

editor at the time was Robert Peston, and the reporter who broke the story was Edward Simpkins.

11 At the height of the financial crisis, anticipating embarrassment over Goodwin's knighthood, Treasury officials made discreet enquiries to establish who had nominated the chief executive of RBS.

12 Dewar's record on honours was controversial. He famously denied the actor Sean Connery a knighthood after becoming Scottish Secretary in 1997, on the grounds that the former James Bond was a supporter of the SNP. A media storm ensued, and in 1999 Connery was awarded a knighthood in the New Year's honours list.

13 'The full list: The Blairs' dinner guests', *Daily Mail*, 19 June 2005.

14 'Fred's Bridge Too Far', *Sunday Times*, 17 October 2004.

15 RBS, analysts call hosted by Fred Goodwin, 18 June 2005.

Chapter 9

1 The main theme of *Gladiator* plays over a film which charts a day in the life of RBS, and of the planet. It concludes with Scotland seen from outer space as the sun slips behind the earth. As the music surges, the following words appear on screen: 'Every day. Over 170,000 people. In more than 50 countries. With 1 commitment. Make It Happen.' It is difficult to avoid the conclusion that the message the viewer is supposed to take away is that RBS, and Scotland, is the centre of the universe.

2 As the then editor of *Scotland on Sunday* I was there.

3 The full text of the Queen's short speech is available at www.royal.gov.uk

4 The appointment of Sir Philip Hampton as chairman after the bailout of RBS represented a break with past form. For one thing he was English – before Mathewson the chairman and deputy chairman tended to be Scottish grandees and not career bankers.

5 The *Independent on Sunday* reported in November 2005 that he was considering leaving, after pressure from shareholders for increased returns or even a break-up of the group. Mathewson was quick to deny the reports.

6 'Guest list for the dinner in honor of Prince Charles and Camilla, Duchess of Cornwall', *New York Times*, 2 November 2005.

7 The Mathewson portrait never made it to Gogarburn, it stayed in St Andrew Square where RBS kept some buildings as meeting rooms. It was noticed after he had gone that someone had ordered that the RBS and NatWest logos in the portrait be painted over.

8 'Royal Bank of Scotland saviour takes his final curtain call', *Independent*, 29 April 2006.

9 The current Cameron of Lochiel is Donald, Johnny Cameron's elder brother.

10 'Heimlich Institute honors RBS for lifesaving ad', Heimlich Institute, 21 September 2004.

11 Sutherland visited the Kremlin as part of a delegation in 2003, although

BP's investment in Russia via TNK-BP later descended into an extremely bitter row with the Russian government.

Chapter 10

1 'Greenwich's outrageous fortune', *Vanity Fair*, July 2006.
2 Edward O. Thorp was one such pioneer in America, a Maths professor who perfected a gambling system and wrote the best-selling books *Beat the Dealer* and then *Beat the Stock Market*. In the early 1970s he applied his talents to creating a hedge fund, Princeton Newport Partners.
3 *When Genius Failed: The Rise and Fall of Long-term Capital Management*, Roger Lowenstein, 2000.
4 '$363m is average pay for top hedge fund managers', *USA Today*, 26 May 2005.
5 Kruger founded Five Mile Capital.
6 Angelo Mozilo built Countrywide, plunged deep into sub-prime and after the crisis was targeted by the US authorities. See 'Mozilo settles Countrywide fraud case for $65m', Reuters, 15 October 2010.
7 See *Fool's Gold: How Unrestrained Greed Corrupted a Dream, Shattered Global Markets and Unleashed a Catastrophe*, Gillian Tett, 2009.
8 The senior team at Greenwich were initially contemptuous of their new owners, just a small Scottish bank, say several of those there at the time.
9 'RBS revealed as key part of consortium behind Ferrovial's BAA bid', *Scotsman*, 6 March 2006.
10 A complaint of some senior RBS investment bankers was that it paid too little, because Goodwin was reluctant to sanction salaries of a similar size to those paid to Diamond and his colleagues at Barclays. Several members of the RBS board mentioned that this was a concern in terms of attracting talent.
11 It was only a small fish tank, the GBM chairman told friends, and he clashed with Mark Fisher on the subject when Fisher raised objections. Cameron felt he had earned the right to demand a fish tank without interference from colleagues.
12 Earlier in his career, in the early 1980s, Whittaker had spent a spell at RBS as a foreign exchange trader.

Chapter 11

1 Barclays was founded in 1690, by goldsmiths in London, although it did not become a joint stock bank on the model used by the Scottish banks until 1896. That year twenty small family-run, private banks came together with £26m of deposits under the Barclays banner. www.barclays.co.uk (history).
2 Lloyds was founded as a private bank in Birmingham by John Taylor and Samuel Lloyd in 1765.

3 'London increases its lead in foreign exchange trading as global turnover drops by 5%', TheCityUK, 30 July 2012.

4 British Bankers Association credit derivatives report 2006.

5 'Amounts outstanding of over the counter derivatives', Bank of International Settlements, quarterly review, March 2013.

6 'Evolution of the UK Banking System', by Richard Davies, Peter Richardson, Vaiva Katinaite and Mark Manning, Bank of England (2010).

7 There is an excellent account of the development of VaR and its role in the crisis of 2007–2008 in Nicholas Dunbar's *The Devil's Derivatives* (2011).

8 The Securities and Investments Board, overseeing the financial industry's regulators, was formed as a result of the Financial Services Act in 1986.

9 In Tiner's defence, a considerable amount of his attention was focused on the insurance industry. He led the Tiner review which introduced major changes to insurance regulation, credited with helping to ensure that the major insurers in the UK did not blow up in the financial crisis.

10 'Total Tax Contribution of UK Financial Services', PWC report for the City of London (Dec 2008), p. 5, figure 2.

11 Moore has gone on to be a campaigner for banking reform and his evidence given to the Treasury Select Committee and Parliamentary Commission on Banking Standards was key, as the *Guardian* noted. 'In praise of . . . Paul Moore', *Guardian*, 10 April 2013.

12 The FSA's own report on RBS contains a long section on the FSA's organisational and intellectual failings in the period before the start of the financial crisis.

13 The lengthy profile by Chris Giles of King – 'The court of King Mervyn' – is a superb dissection of the culture of the Bank of England under King. *Financial Times*, 5 May 2012.

14 'Uncertainty, policy and financial markets', speech by Sir John Gieve, 24 July 2007.

15 'Auditors: market concentration and their role', House of Lords Economic Affairs Committee report, March 2011.

16 National Audit Office meeting with the Chancellor, FSA report on RBS, p. 261.

17 'Deirdre Hutton, CAA chairman: profile', *Daily Telegraph*, 21 April 2010.

Chapter 12

1 'Liquid balance', *Financial Times*, 11 January 2005.

2 The Exchange Bank was established in Amsterdam in 1609, its rise fuelled by the wealth created by merchants and traders in a period when the city was arguably the centre of world trade.

3 ABN Amro was founded as the result of a merger in 1991, but can trace its roots back to 1824.

4 TCI letter to ABN Amro board, *Financial Times* Alphaville blog, 21 February 2007.

5 Andrea Orcel was another star Merrill Lynch investment banker. He stayed on when Merrill Lynch was taken over by Bank of America during the financial crisis, and only left in 2012 to run UBS's investment bank.

6 Some European banking consolidation, replicating what had happened on a national scale in countries such as the UK, was anticipated by the European Commission. Charlie McCreevy, the EU Commissioner for Internal Markets and Services between 2004 and 2010, oversaw reforms designed to help facilitate it.

7 'Revealed: Salmond's support for Goodwin over disastrous RBS deal', *Sunday Herald*, 10 August 2010.

8 In 2006 HSBC had expected to make provision for $8.8bn of bad mortgages; it then shocked the market by increasing that figure to $10.56bn. 'HSBC to Boost Loan-Loss Provisions on Bad Mortgages', Bloomberg, 8 February 2007.

9 Again, Nicholas Dunbar's book *The Devil's Derivatives* expertly chronicles the various mutations.

10 'US exports poison', Peston's Picks, 9 August 2007.

Chapter 13

1 FSA report on RBS.

2 Sir Philip Hampton, interview with author, see Afterword.

3 Fred Goodwin, annual results conference, 28 February 2006.

4 'Antonveneta sold to rival for €9bn', *Financial Times* Alphaville blog, 9 November 2007.

5 'Is Merrill the tip of the iceberg?', *Economist*, 28 October 2007.

6 The Dow Jones closed at 14,164.43 on 9 October 2007. It was more than five years before it closed above that level, in March 2013.

7 'Sighs all round as RBS details £1.5bn write-downs', *Financial Times* Alphaville, 6 December 2007.

8 Johnny Cameron interview, in *Financial News*, March 2008.

9 On 8 February 2008 Credit Suisse issued a report that questioned whether RBS had been realistic enough in its marks on CDOs. 'Certainly the 17% mark against the ABS CDO portfolio looks very low compared with the 58% average taken by Merrill Lynch, Citigroup, Morgan Stanley and UBS.' Credit Suisse, equity research, 1 February 2008.

10 The encounter was revealed by the *Daily Telegraph*, in its investigation by Harry Wilson, Philip Aldrick and Kamal Ahmed. 'RBS investigation: Chapter 3 – run up to the collapse', 11 December 2011.

11 This is firmly denied by those involved. Treasury sources point out that a deal had been in the offing well before the conversation between Brown and Blank over drinks, although Lloyds was certainly pressured into doing the deal in other respects.

Chapter 14

1 'Royal Bank of Scotland chiefs to be forced out under bailout deal', *Daily Telegraph*, 8 October 2008. Jeff Randall later received an apology from RBS.
2 'Humbling of our banks', Peston's Picks, 12 October 2007.
3 'End of the road', Bill Jamieson, *Scotsman*, 13 October 2008.
4 'Is Alex Salmond's "Arc of Prosperity" done for?', *Daily Telegraph*, 9 October 2008.
5 'The real story behind Sir Mervyn King and RBS', Ed Conway, economics editor of Sky News. www.edmundconway.com.
6 Credit Action, 1 August 2008.
7 'Debt and deleveraging: The global credit bubble and its economic consequences'. McKinsey, July 2011.
8 See the string of stories and revelations by Harry Wilson, banking editor of the *Daily Telegraph*.
9 'The world's worst banker', *Newsweek*, 1 December 2008.

Chapter 15

1 Basel III forces banks to hold considerably more capital than before the crisis, and in time it will introduce new rules on liquidity and leverage.
2 'RBS chief waives bonus over NatWest glitch', *Daily Telegraph*, 29 June 2012.
3 In early 2009 Cameron discussed joining Greenhills, the boutique investment bank.
4 King stepped down in June 2013, at the end of his term, and handed over to Mark Carney, the former Governor of the Bank of Canada.
5 'Scott steps down after scrutiny from shareholders', *Financial Times*, 21 May 2009.
6 Workshop on Neuroeconomics and Endocrinological Economics, University of California, 20–21 November 2009.

Afterword

1 'The evolution of the UK banking system', Bank of England (2010).
2 'Lords leader backs trade minister in HSBC money laundering scandal', Nicholas Watt, *Guardian*, 23 July 2012.
3 'Don't break up the Big Banks', Walter B. Harrison, former J. P. Morgan Chase chief executive, writing in the *New York Times*, August 2012. He wrote: 'Large global institutions have often proved more resilient than others because their diversified business model ensures that losses in one part of the enterprise can be cushioned by revenues in other parts.' This seems not to have been the case in the collapse of RBS.
4 'The Social Costs and Benefits of Too-Big-To-Fail Banks: A "Bounding"

Exercise', John H. Boyd and Amanda Heitz, University of Minnesota, February 2012.

5 'The implicit subsidy of banks', Joseph Noss and Rhiannon Sowerbutts, Financial Stability paper, 15 May 2012. Bank of England.

6 '"Too big to fail" is too dumb an idea to keep', John Kay, *Financial Times*, 27 October 2009.

7 The credit for the development of the efficient market hypothesis is often given to Professor Eugene Fama, of the University of Chicago Booth School of Business.

Index

Index

Index

Index

Index

Index

Index

Index